P9-AFV-217

DATE DUE

NO 1 4 '96			
DE 3 '96			
AG 8 4			
OC 16 98			
AP 6 04			
NO 2 05			

DEMCO 38-296

Learning Together and Alone

Learning Together and Alone

Cooperative, Competitive, and Individualistic Learning

FOURTH EDITION

David W. Johnson
University of Minnesota

Roger T. Johnson
University of Minnesota

ALLYN and BACON
Boston   London   Toronto   Sydney   Tokyo   Singapore

Riverside Community College
Library
4800 Magnolia Avenue
Riverside, California 92506

Editor-in-Chief, Education: Nancy Forsyth
Editorial Assistant: Christine Nelson
Composition Buyer: Linda Cox
Manufacturing Buyer: Louise Richardson
Cover Designer: Suzanne Harbison
Production Administrator: Deborah Brown
Editorial-Production Service: P. M. Gordon Associates

Copyright © 1994, 1991 by Allyn and Bacon
A Paramount Communications Company
160 Gould Street
Needham Heights, Massachusetts 02194

Copyright © 1987, 1975 by Prentice-Hall, Inc.
A Paramount Communications Company
Englewood Cliffs, New Jersey 07632

All rights reserved. No part of the material protected by this copyright
notice may be reproduced or utilized in any form or by any means,
electronic or mechanical, including photocopying, recording, or by any
information storage and retrieval system, without the written permission
of the copyright owner.

Library of Congress Cataloging-in-Publication Data

LB 1032 .J595 1994   )perative, competitive, and
                                         ohnson, Roger T. Johnson.—

JOHNSON, DAVID W., 1940
                                         es (p.   ) and index.
LEARNING TOGETHER AND ALONE
                                         ndividualized instruction.
                                                4. Lesson planning.

LB1032.J595 1994
371.1′02—dc20
                                                       93–23259
                                                          CIP

Printed in the United States of America
10 9 8 7 6 5 4 3 2 1   99 98 97 96 95 94

Contents

Preface

As you may have surmised, we are brothers, and as such we are very familiar with competition. As we were growing up, we raced to see who would get through a door first, measured to see who got more cake (or more of anything), and argued to see who would sit by the window in the car. One incident we both remember vividly is the corncob fight. For a few years while we were growing up in Indiana, we lived (and worked!) on our grandfather's farm. We regularly practiced our throwing accuracy with corncobs, and more than occasionally we practiced on each other. In one of these desperate battles, we had each gathered a large feed sack full of cobs and were flinging and dodging our way through the barn. When the older one of us gained the upper hand, as he usually did, the younger brother scampered up the ladder into the hayloft, taking a well-aimed cob in the seat of his pants. The hayloft advantage provided a problem for the older brother as he was nipped a couple of times without even coming close to his opponent. So taking his sack of corncobs between his teeth, he started up the ladder (the only way to the loft). As he got about halfway up, he realized he was getting pelted with more cobs than could be thrown at one time and looked up to see the younger brother standing at the top of the ladder shaking out his bag of corncobs and enjoying himself immensely. The tables turned, however, when the older brother reached the top of the ladder and the younger brother discovered he was out of ammunition. Then it was the younger brother's turn to be pelted as he crouched in the hay while the older brother let him have it—one by one. We still argue about who got the most out of the battle, the brother releasing the waterfall of cobs down the ladder or the brother delivering the one-by-one pelting in the hayloft.

We are sure that people who knew us then are surprised to see us cooperating on this book and in the related teacher workshops we conduct. It should be no surprise; the ideas presented here on how to recognize inappropriate competition and facilitate cooperation are important enough for even two brothers to cooperate. We are also accidentally, but admirably, suited to work together on this topic. David struggled through graduate school at Columbia University, gaining the skills of an academic social psychologist, while Roger, after teaching several years at the elementary school level, took the easy route through the University of California as a part-time staff member in teacher education. With the years of classroom teaching experience and the research and writing in social psychology represented by our combined backgrounds, and brought together at the University of Minnesota, we readily recognized the potential of this conceptual scheme—structuring learning in ways consistent with instructional aims.

We aren't against competition (although the literature and research on competition are damaging to its reputation). We are against *inappropriate* competition—and most of the competition in classrooms is inappropriate. We are for cooperation, not only because its sharing, helping, communicating, and mutual-concern aspects are consonant with our values but also because research supports its use in a large number of situations. All the research we have reviewed, the research we have conducted, and our own instincts indicate that cooperation is the appropriate goal structure for most instructional situations. It also seems to be the least talked about, if not the least used, goal structure in schools. Individualization is in some places touted as a replacement for competition in schools. The idea of students working on individually assigned tasks at their own pace instead of competing against each other is attractive to teachers, but the overuse of the individualistic goal structure is hard on teachers, requires a mountain of materials, and is described by many students as the "lonely" curriculum. The basic social competencies needed to interact effectively with other persons, furthermore, are completely ignored under an individualistic goal structure. We believe that all three goal structures—competitive, individualistic, and cooperative—should be used, and that students need to learn how to function in all three. Students should master the skills to compete with enjoyment, to work individually on a task until it's completed, and to cooperate effectively with others to solve problems. Perhaps just as important, students should know *when* to compete, *when* to work on their own, and *when* to cooperate. The greatest need in classrooms is the carefully planned cooperative goal structure, which becomes the framework within which competition and individualization take place. We cover a lot of pages on cooperation.

In our work with teachers in goal structuring workshops and in our own classes at the University of Minnesota, we have found a few obstacles that hinder implementation. First, teachers often do not realize the enormous potential that facilitating appropriate goal structures has for their classroom. The research is clear (see Chapter 2). Achievement will go up, attitudes will become more positive, and missing skills will be mastered when goal structures are used appropriately. After all, goal structures concentrate on what is the most powerful variable in the learning situation: the interaction patterns and interdependencies of the students as they work toward a goal. The second obstacle to recognizing the importance of using cooperative as well as competitive and individualized activities is the powerful mythology that surrounds competition. How many times have you heard a version of social Darwinism that suggests "it's a dog-eat-dog world" or "a survival-of-the-fittest society" or that "students need to learn how to compete so they can survive in the business world." Even the business world does not believe that the world is savagely competitive. As a social psychologist with management training, David could spend much of his time teaching people in business and industry how to reduce inappropriate competition and increase cooperation in their companies. Society cannot be described as competitive; it is by definition cooperative, a point that is examined in detail in Chapter 3. Within the cooperative framework of society, however, there *is* competition, sometimes too much.

Another obstacle we have observed is the "I'm-already-doing-that" feeling many teachers have when we describe cooperation. If you really are doing it as well as it can be done, much of this book will not be useful. Yet frequently we find that teachers who say (or think) they are using goal structures appropriately are surprised by certain aspects of each when these goal structures are carefully described from a social psychological point of view and when the steps for implementing and monitoring them are explained (see Chapters 3, 4, and 5). Finally, the educational history of many students and teachers is such that they find cooperating within the school rather strange and difficult. Our own students seem relieved when they find that they are not going to have to compete against each other, and a sigh of relief seems to go through the classroom when the cooperative approach is announced. Students, however, are usually somewhat reluctant at first to cooperate with each other and tend to work individualistically when they should be cooperating. It takes some relationship building and trust development before they are able to share ideas and help each other effectively to produce a true group effort. Your students may have some of the same attitudes (so may the teachers in your school), and, if they do, you may need to teach and encourage the skills needed to work together (see Chapter 8).

We wish we could be with you as you implement appropriate goal structures in your instructional program. We would like to help. For most of you, this book and the ideas shared here are the best we can do. We assume your classes will blossom as our own have and as those of teachers near us have. One thing is certain: for those of you who want to match the appropriate student interaction patterns with instructional goals and want to move to a predominantly cooperative classroom, the rationale for doing so is here, and you will be able to discuss goal structuring fluently with anyone. We hope that enough of the strategies have been given, but implementing ideas is your profession and if something is left out, we trust you to find and include it. Above all, enjoy the process. Practice your own skills as you encourage them in your students. You may even try a little cooperating with fellow teachers! In fact, we suggest that the best way to work with the ideas in this book is to approach the task cooperatively with a friend and fellow teacher with whom to share thoughts and successes. Enjoy yourself, persevere, and accept any resulting success with some modesty.

Thanks are due to many people for their help in writing this book and preparing the manuscript. Credit must be given to Edythe Johnson Holubec, our sister, who's always there to lend a hand cheerfully when it's needed; and Judy Bartlett, who is so often called on to assemble the whole from bits and pieces. We also owe much to many social psychologists who have conducted research and formulated theory in this area. We owe much to the teachers who have listened to our "bridge building" and given us help in "reconstructing" when we needed it. We owe much to our students, who have been patient with our enthusiasm and helpful in challenging and implementing our ideas. We owe much to our reviewers, Dawna Lisa Buchanan-Berrigan of Shawnee State University and Peter Yacyk and Walter J. Eliason of Rider College, for their help. Finally, we owe much to our wives and children for making our lives truly cooperative.

David W. Johnson
Roger T. Johnson

Learning Together and Alone

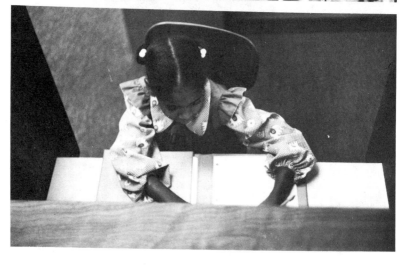

1

Cooperative, Competitive, and Individualistic Learning

STUDENT–STUDENT INTERACTION

On July 15, 1982, Donald Bennett, a Seattle businessman, was the first amputee ever to climb Mount Rainier (reported in Kouzes & Posner, 1987). He climbed 14,410 feet on one leg and two crutches. It took him five days. When asked to state the most important lesson he learned from doing so, without hesitation he said, "You can't do it alone."

Not all educators agree. In every classroom, no matter what the subject area, teachers may structure lessons so that students:

1. Engage in a win–lose struggle to see who is best (competitive; see Table 1.1).
2. Work independently on their own learning goals at their own pace and in their own space to achieve a preset criterion of excellence (individualistic).
3. Work cooperatively in small groups, ensuring that all members master the assigned material (cooperative).

Who's the best? When students are required to *compete* with each other for grades, they work against each other to achieve a goal that only one or a few students can attain, which requires them to work faster and more accurately than their peers. In competitive situations there is a negative interdependence among goal achievements: Students perceive that they can obtain their goals if and only if the other students in the class fail to obtain their goals (Deutsch, 1962; Johnson & Johnson, 1989a). Students are graded on a norm-referenced basis. They recognize

TABLE 1.1 Characteristics of Social Interdependence

CHARACTERISTIC	COOPERATIVE	COMPETITIVE	INDIVIDUALISTIC
Fate	Mutual	Opposite	Individual
Benefit	Mutual	Differential	Self
Time Perspective	Long-term	Short-term	Short-term
Identity	Shared	Relative	Individual
Causation	Mutual	Relative	Self
Rewards	Unlimited	Limited	Unlimited
Motivation	Intrinsic	Extrinsic	Extrinsic
Attribution	Effort	Ability	Ability
Celebrate	Own success and others' success	Own success and others' failure	Own success

their negatively linked fate (*The more you gain, the less for me; the more I gain, the less for you*), strive to be better than classmates (*I can defeat you*), work to deprive others (*My winning means you lose*), view rewards such as grades as limited (*Only a few of us will get "A's"*), celebrate classmates' failures (*Your failure makes it easier for me to win*), and believe that the more able and deserving individuals become "haves" and the less able and deserving individuals become the "have nots" (*Winners always win; losers always lose*). Unfortunately, most students perceive schools as predominantly competitive enterprises (Johnson & Johnson, 1983a). Students either work hard to do better than their classmates, or they take it easy because they do not believe they have a chance to win.

Can you do it on your own? When students are required to work *individualistically* on their own, they work by themselves to accomplish learning goals unrelated to those of the other students (Deutsch, 1962; Johnson & Johnson, 1989a). Individual goals are assigned; students' efforts are evaluated and rewarded on the basis of how their efforts compare to the preset criterion of excellence (i.e., on a criteria-referenced basis). Each student has his or her own set of materials, works at his or her own speed, doesn't disturb the other classmates, and seeks help or assistance only from the teacher. Whether an individual accomplishes his or her goal has no influence on whether other individuals achieve their goals. Students are expected and encouraged to focus on their own goals (*How well can I do?*), have a strict self-interest (*What's in it for me?*), see their success as dependent on only their own abilities (*If I am able, I will receive a high grade*), celebrate only their own success (*I did it!*), and ignore as irrelevant the success or failure of others (*Whether my classmates achieve or not does not affect me*).

Can you be part of a team? *Cooperation* is working together to accomplish shared goals. In cooperative learning situations there is a positive interdependence among students' goal attainments: Students perceive that they can reach their learning goals if and only if the other students in the learning group also reach

Recipe for a
Well-Structured Classroom

- 1 Heaping Cup of Cooperative Learning

- 2 Tablespoons of Competition

- 2 Tablespoons of Individualistic Learning

- Blend ingredients gently
  with thoughtfulness and care

- Amount of each ingredient
  may be altered to suit
  individual tastes

their goals (Deutsch, 1962; Johnson & Johnson, 1989a). Within cooperative efforts, individuals seek outcomes that are beneficial to themselves *and* beneficial to all other group members. The idea is simple. Class members are split into small groups (often heterogeneous) and instructed to (a) learn the assigned material, (b) make sure that the other members of the group also master the assignment, and (c) make sure that everyone in the class has learned the assigned material. Students discuss material with each other, explaining how to complete the work, listening to each other's explanations, encouraging each other to work hard, and providing academic help and assistance. When everyone in the group has mastered the material, they look for another group to help until everyone in the class understands how to complete the assignments. Individual performance is assessed regularly to ensure that all students are learning. A criteria-referenced evaluation system is used.

Cooperative efforts result in participants' recognizing that all group members share a common fate (*We all sink or swim together*), striving for mutual benefit so that all group members benefit from each other's efforts (*Your efforts benefit me and my efforts benefit you*), recognizing that one's performance is mutually caused by oneself and one's colleagues (*United we stand, divided we fall*), empowering each other (*Together we can achieve anything*), and feeling proud and jointly celebrating when a group member is recognized for achievement (*You got an A! That's terrific!*).

Teachers decide whether to structure students' learning goals to promote competitive, individualistic, or cooperative efforts. In every classroom, instructional activities are aimed at accomplishing goals and are conducted under a goal structure. A *learning goal* is a desired future state of demonstrating competence or mastery in the subject area being studied. The *goal structure* specifies the ways in which students will interact with each other and the teacher during the instructional session. Each goal structure has its place. An effective teacher will use all three appropriately. In the ideal classroom, all students learn how to work cooperatively as part of a team, compete for fun and enjoyment, and work autonomously on their own. Teachers decide which goal structure to implement within each lesson.

TABLE 1.2 Goal Structures

	APPROPRIATE COOPERATION	APPROPRIATE COMPETITION	APPROPRIATE INDIVIDUALIZATION
Interdependence	Positive	Negative	None
Type of Instructional Activity	Any instructional task. The more conceptual and complex the task, the greater the cooperation.	Skill practice, knowledge recall and review, assignment is clear with rules for competing specified.	Simple skill or knowledge acquisition; assignment is clear and behavior specified to avoid confusion and need for extra help.
Perception of Goal Importance	Goal is perceived to be important.	Goal is not perceived to be of large importance to the students, and they can accept either winning or losing.	Goal is perceived as important for each student; students see tasks as worthwhile and relevant, and each student expects eventually to achieve his or her goal.
Teacher–Student Interaction	Teacher monitors and intervenes in learning groups to teach collaborative skills.	Teacher is perceived to be the major source of assistance, feedback, reinforcement, and support. Teacher is available for questions and clarification of the rules; teacher referees disputes and judges correctness of answers, rewards the winners.	Teacher is perceived to be the major source of assistance, feedback, reinforcement, and support.
Teacher Statements	"David, can you explain the group's answer to #3?" "Be sure to ask me for help only when you've consulted all group members for help."	"Who has the most so far?" "What do you need to do to win next time?"	"Do not bother David while he is working." "Raise your hand if you need help." "Let me know when you are finished."
Student–Materials Interaction	Materials are arranged according to purpose of lesson.	Set of materials for each triad or for each student.	Complete set of materials and instructions for each student. Rules, procedures, answers are clear. Adequate space for each student.
Student–Student Interaction	Prolonged and intense interaction among students, helping and sharing, oral rehearsal of material being studied, peer tutoring, and general support and encouragement.	Observing other students in one's triad. Some talking among students. Students grouped in homogeneous triads to ensure equal chance of winning.	None; students work on their own with little or no interaction with classmates.

(continued)

TABLE 1.2 *(continued)*

	APPROPRIATE COOPERATION	APPROPRIATE COMPETITION	APPROPRIATE INDIVIDUALIZATION
Student Expectations	Group to be successful. All members to contribute to success. Positive interaction among group members. All members master the assigned material.	Review previously learned material. Have an equal chance of winning. Enjoy the activity, win or lose. Monitor the progress of competitors. Follow the rules. Be a good winner and loser.	Each student expects to be left alone by other students; to work at own pace; to take a major part of the responsibility for completing the task; to take a major part in evaluating own progress and quality of efforts toward learning.
Room Arrangement	Small groups.	Students placed in triads or small clusters.	Separate desks or carrels with as much space between students as can be provided.
Evaluation Procedures	Criterion-referenced.	Norm-referenced.	Criterion-referenced.

DECIDING ON A GOAL STRUCTURE

When individuals take action, there are three ways what they do may be related to the actions of others (see Table 1.2). One's actions may promote the success of others, obstruct the success of others, or not have any effect at all on the success or failure of others. Whenever people strive to achieve a goal, they may engage in cooperative, competitive, or individualistic efforts. Such social interdependence exists continually. It is one of the most fundamental and ubiquitous aspects of being human, and it affects all aspects of our lives including our productivity, quality of relationships, and psychological health. Nothing is more basic to humans than being "for," "against," or "indifferent to" other people. Whether it is quite personal or so impersonal that we are barely aware of it, we regularly underestimate the role that social interdependence plays in human life.

Knowing how and when to structure students' learning goals cooperatively, competitively, or individualistically is one of the most important aspects of teaching. The decision needs to be carefully made according to a set of criteria:

1. What are the objectives of the lesson and the instructional task aimed at achieving them?
2. How important is the learning goal to students and to the teacher?
3. What teacher–student interaction is needed? How much teacher assistance and guidance do students need to complete the task?
4. What student–materials interaction is needed? What materials and equipment are needed to conduct the lesson, and how available are they?

5. What student–student interaction is needed? How much peer assistance and guidance do students need to complete the task?
6. What are the role expectations for students during the lesson?
7. What type of evaluation system is needed for the lesson?

In order to decide which goal structure, or combination of goal structures, to use in a lesson, teachers must understand what cooperative, competitive, and individualistic efforts are, the conditions under which each is effective, and the teacher's role in using the goal structure. In this chapter each goal structure is defined and the ways they may be used in an integrated way are discussed. The research comparing the effectiveness of cooperative, competitive, and individualistic efforts is discussed in Chapter 2. Cooperative learning is discussed in depth in

Our horse, Maud, could give a fantastic ride! She did not like leaving the barn. The four oldest of us—Frank, Helen, Roger, and David—would have to drag her away from the barn, trying to get far enough for a long ride. Then we would all jump on her back and wait for the inevitable. First she would try to scrape us off on fences as we tried to ride her away from the barn. Once she got turned in the barn's direction, we got the ride of our lives. She would race full speed to the barn. (The younger author never seemed to remember to duck as Maud flew through the barn door.) The point is that Maud was not committed to leaving the barn, but she had a strong commitment to return to it. All teachers have seen the difference between students who are committed to learning goals and those who are not. If students are not committed to instructional goals, they are like Maud going away from the barn. If students are committed to instructional goals, they are like Maud returning to the barn. Take the advice of the younger author and duck at the barn door when you successfully "turn on" your students.

Using Goal Structures Appropriately

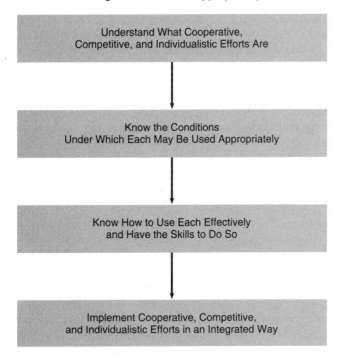

FIGURE 1.1   Using goal structures appropriately

Chapters 3, 4, and 5. Individualistic and competitive learning are discussed in depth in Chapters 6 and 7. Then several of the complexities of cooperative learning are dealt with in subsequent chapters.

UNDERSTANDING COMPETITION

"Winning isn't everything. It's the only thing!"
Vince Lombardi

We do it on the tennis courts and putting greens, in the boardroom and the playing field, at the chalkboard, and on the dance floor. It is eulogized at business club luncheons and exalted at Junior Achievement pep rallies. It is ballyhooed by economists and politicians as the cure for our financial ills, and it is glorified in locker room sermons as preparation for life in the real world. Some of us do it in three-piece suits and turbo-charged automobiles, others in wet T-shirts and souped-up muscle cars. It even happens in classrooms! One of the most common examples of competition is a classroom situation involving Boris and Peggy reported by Jules Henry (1963):

The teacher turns to the class and says, "Well, who can tell Boris what the number is?" There is a forest of hands and the teacher calls on Peggy, who says that 4 should be divided into both the numerator and denominator. It is obvious that Boris' failure made it possible for Peggy to succeed, and, since the excited handwaving of the children indicates that they wanted to exploit Boris' predicament to succeed where he was failing, it appears that at least some of the children were learning to hope (covertly) for the failure of fellow students.

Competing with and defeating an opponent is one of the most widely recognized aspects of interpersonal interaction in our society. The language of business, politics, and even education is filled with "win–lose" terms. You "win" a promotion or raise, "beat" the opposition, "outsmart" a teacher, become a "superstar," and put competitors "in their place." The creed of competition as a virtue is woven deeply into our social fabric. Applause for it in sports dates back at least as far as the Greeks. Praise for it as an economic regulator of price and production reaches back to at least 1776 with the publication of Adam Smith's *The Wealth of Nations*. And Herbert Spencer's thoughts centered on it in the 1860s when he argued that Darwin's survival-of-the-fittest concept of evolution could be transposed to human society. In a society that stresses winning, it is no wonder that competition often gets out of hand and barriers arise to competing appropriately.

For competition to exist, there must be perceived scarcity. If I must defeat you in order to get what I want, then what I want is by definition scarce. Rewards are restricted so that only the few who are the best or highest performers are acknowledged as being successful or are rewarded in some way. Sometimes the scarcity is based on reality. Two hungry people may compete over one loaf of bread. Sometimes the scarcity is artificially created. Students may compete for a limited number of "A's," but how many "A's" there are is an arbitrary decision made by the teacher and the school. Schools create artificial shortages of "A's" in an attempt to motivate students through competition. Many competitions are based on such artificial shortages created for the contest.

Competitions vary as to how many winners there will be. Only one baseball team can be "world champions." Not everyone who applies to a college may be admitted, but how many applicants "win" by being accepted varies from college to college. *Competitions also vary as to the criteria for selecting a winner.* In many cases, such as art contests, winning is based on subjective judgment. In other cases, such as track races, winning is based on objective criteria. In either case, the criteria for success are uncertain in that what is needed for a win depends on the relative performance of the particular contestants. *Competitions vary as to the interaction that takes place among participants.* In a boxing match there is direct interaction between the two participants throughout the competition. In a track meet there is parallel interaction. Within college admissions, participants may never see each other. Two javelin throwers take turns doing the same thing and do not interfere with each other, whereas two chess players actively try to defeat each other. Finally, *competitions require social comparisons.* Competitive situations contain forced social comparisons in which participants are faced with information about their peers' performances, and this comparison information is both salient and obtrusive (Levine, 1983). Competitors get the information on how they performed relative to others whether they want it or not.*

Competition has been popular ever since Adam Smith, Herbert Spencer, and others proposed the Social Darwinism premise of survival of the fittest in human society. Four of the myths that supported its popularity were that competition is unavoidable because it is human nature, competition motivates people to do their best, competition is enjoyable, and competition builds character. Although very few people would accept these myths today, only a few years ago these myths supported the popularity of competition.

There are, on the other hand, individuals who believe competition is inherently destructive (Kohn, 1986). Any lesson can be structured competitively, but competition is appropriate only under a very limited set of conditions. Competition rarely increases student achievement and rarely facilitates the accomplishment of instructional goals. Constructive competition requires a number of skills and attitudes that must be carefully taught to students. And the teacher has to be skilled in using competition for instructional purposes. The conditions when competition may be used, the student skills and attitudes, and the teacher's role in using competition in instructional situations are discussed in Chapter 7.

UNDERSTANDING INDIVIDUALISTIC EFFORTS

Humans do not always interact with others. At times solitude is desired. A long hike to a mountain lake, a walk along a deserted seashore, recording thoughts in a journal, and even writing books are activities that often are done alone. There are times when individuals act independently from each other without any interdependence existing among them. In an *individualistic* situation, individuals work by themselves to accomplish goals unrelated to and independent from the goals of others. Individualistic efforts, too, have been supported by myths. The most notable myths are the frontiersmen who conquered the wilderness through isolated, individual, unrelated actions; the individual superhero or soldier who wins the war singlehandedly; the individual artist who creates masterpieces in isolation; and the individual scientist who makes great discoveries in isolation from the scientific community.

Any lesson can be structured individualistically, but individualistic learning is appropriate only under a very limited set of conditions. Individualistic efforts rarely increase student achievement and rarely facilitate the accomplishment of instructional goals. Constructive individualistic efforts require a number of skills and attitudes that must be carefully taught to students. And the teacher has to be skilled in structuring individualistic learning situations. The conditions when indi-

---

*For a heartrending but true life story of the misery of having to live with rabid competition among children, readers may write to our mother, Mrs. Frances W. Johnson.

When students commit themselves psychologically to achievement in school, two important factors are how likely they are to be successful in achieving academic goals and how challenging academic goals are to them. When teachers "grade on a curve" and receiving an A is defined as being successful—i.e., the goal—the vast majority of students will not expect to achieve the goal, whereas the high-ability students may see the goal as being too easy to be challenging. Thus a teacher may lose students because of a low likelihood of success and the superior students, whose resources make achievement too easy, all in one swoop!

Commitment to academic goals also require that students perceive the goals as being desirable and that they feel some satisfaction when the goals are achieved. There is consistent evidence that when classrooms are structured competitively or individualistically, success at academic tasks has little value for many students (Coleman, 1959; Bronfrenbrenner, 1970; DeVries, Muse, and Wells, 1971; Spilerman, 1971). Receiving recognition from one's peers is a source of satisfaction, yet there is recent evidence (as well as ancient folklore) that success on academic tasks in a competitively structured classroom has a negative effect on a student's sociometric status in the classroom (Slavin, 1974). Frequently doing well on quizzes resulted in losing friends!

The teacher's primary hope of inducing student commitment to academic goals is in structuring cooperative learning situations in the classroom. If you do not believe it now, keep reading, and by the time you finish this book you will!

vidualistic learning may be used, student skills and attitudes, and the teacher's role are discussed in Chapter 6.

UNDERSTANDING COOPERATION

The human species seems to have a *cooperation imperative.* We desire and seek out opportunities to operate jointly with others to achieve mutual goals. We are attached to others through a variety of "lifelines," and we alternate supporting and leading others to ensure a better life for ourselves, our colleagues and neighbors, our children, and all generations to follow. Cooperation is an inescapable fact of life. From cradle to grave we cooperate with others. Each day, from our first waking moment until sleep overtakes us again, we cooperate within family, work, leisure, and community by working jointly to achieve mutual goals. Throughout history, people have come together to (1) accomplish feats that any one of them could not achieve alone and (2) share their joys and sorrows. From conceiving a child to sending a rocket to the moon, our successes require cooperation among individuals.

Cooperation pervades human nature and human life. *Cooperation is the heart of our biology.* Each person's body is made up of several systems (such as the muscle, digestive, and nervous systems) all cooperating together to keep the person alive and healthy. Members of our species, furthermore, are divided into males and females, both of which are necessary to conceive a child. Biologically, we are a cooperative being.

Cooperation is the heart of family life. Frank and Jane Johnson, for example, are husband and wife, parents, and lovers. Each day they leave for work to ensure that their family has shelter, food, clothing, and other necessities for survival (as well as a number of luxuries). In the late afternoon they come home to play with their children, prepare dinner, help their children with their homework, read them a bedtime story, put the children to bed, chat with each other, make a number of decisions about who will do what tomorrow, make love, and then go to sleep. Family members work together to achieve mutual goals.

Cooperation is the heart of all economic systems. Helen Misener, for example, is a manager for the Lion Corporation. Today she meets with a group of managers to plan how to market a new product, meets with a subordinate who is dissatisfied with his job and is not performing well, and ensures that a rush order by a valued customer is filled on time. All members of the same company work together to achieve mutual goals. Different companies work together to move products from conception to manufacture to market to achieve mutual goals. Although it is not a personal relationship, cooperation exists among those who make cars and those who buy and use them, and among those who farm and those who manufacture, and among all participants within an economic system.

Cooperation is the heart of all legal systems. Laws specify how we are to cooperate with each other as we travel to and from work (e.g., drive on the right side of the street, stop at red lights, drive under certain specified speeds), how to transfer property and goods (e.g., deeds and contracts), how to determine responsibility for one's actions, and so forth. Keith Clement, for example, is a lawyer who today meets with a client to plan how best to present his case, meets with the judge and prosecutor and attempts to plea bargain for a lesser charge in exchange for a guilty plea, and then meets again with his client to discuss what the client's options are. Cooperation exists between those who make, enforce, and follow laws. Legal systems exist to define cooperative interactions among members of a society, ensure that cooperation runs smoothly, punish those who violate the norms for appropriate cooperative behavior, and reestablish cooperation among societal members who have conflicts.

Cooperation is the heart of our evolution as a species. Humans by their nature cooperate with each other. Just as the cheetah survives by speed and hawks survive by their eyesight, humans survive by their ability to "work together to get the job done." Among the hominids, the almost modern Homo sapiens appeared at least 300,000 years ago, and the anatomically modern Homo sapiens sapiens 40,000 years ago (Rensberger, 1984). As anatomically modern people appeared in Europe, suddenly so did sculpture, musical instruments, lamps, trade, and innovation. Insofar as there was any single moment when we could be said to have become human, it was at the time of this great leap forward in complexity of cooperation (Diamond, 1989). Only a few dozen millennia—a trivial fraction of our 6 to 10 million-year history—was needed for us to domesticate animals, develop agriculture and metallurgy, and invent writing. It was then only a short further step to the Mona Lisa, the Ninth Symphony, the industrial revolution, and the computer.

Cooperation is the heart of the worldwide community of humans. From small tribes to small communities to small states and countries to large countries to a worldwide community, there has been an unmistakable increase in the size of the "we-group" (Bigelow, 1972). We now live in a world increasingly characterized by interdependence, pluralism, conflict, and rapid change. Instead of being a member of a discrete society, we live in a multiboundary world characterized by a diversity of worldwide systems in which all people affect and are affected by others across the globe. Today there is no nation independent from the rest of the world. Raw materials, manufactured goods, consumers and markets, monetary systems, and preservation of the environment all cross national borders. The major problems faced by individuals (e.g., contamination of the environment, warming of the atmosphere, world hunger, international terrorism, nuclear war) increasingly are ones that cannot be solved by actions taken only at the national level.

The magnitude and scope of world interdependence has greatly increased the past forty years. Global interdependence is reflected in technological, economic, ecological, and political systems. *Technologically*, jet engines and rocketry, transistors and micro chips, nuclear fission and fusion, and many other technological advances are rapidly changing life on earth. Technologies know no boundaries. When scientists make a new discovery in one country, it is quickly picked up and utilized in other countries. Through advances in transportation technologies the earth has shrunk in the time it takes to cover distances. The increased ability to transport people and goods throughout the world has fundamentally changed the world's economy. Through advances in communication technologies the earth has expanded in terms of the number of people, places, events, and bits of information that are available to any one person.

Economically, we depend on other areas of the world to supply many of the raw materials used by our industries and the goods we consume daily. We also depend on other countries to buy our goods and services. Multinational assemblage of goods is common. Foreign investment by multinational corporations, international lending of money, and the buying and selling of foreign currencies has become the rule rather than the exception. When companies close plants in one part of the world, new jobs are created in other parts of the world. Rises or declines in interest rates have dramatic implications for debtor countries. Crop failures in one part of the world affect profits of farmers in another part of the world. Every country in the world is interdependent with other countries the distribution and exchange of raw materials and manufactured goods, the potential consumers and markets outside of national boundaries, and the worldwide monetary system. Such economic interdependence will continue to increase.

Ecologically, the pollution of one country most often affects the well-being of other countries, deforestation in one country affects the weather of many other countries, what affects the ecology in one part of the world affects the ecology in other parts of the world. *Politically*, an election in one country often has important

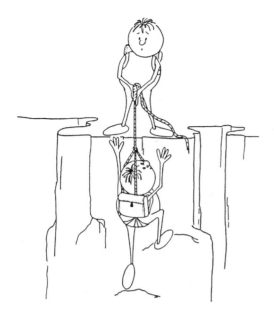

implications for the balance of power among the world's superpowers. By politically deciding to vary economic policy, countries can affect the stability of the governments of other countries. Technologically, economically, ecologically, and politically, we are all bound together on "spaceship earth."

Humans do not have a choice; we have to cooperate. Cooperation is an inescapable part of our lives. It is built into our biology and is the hallmark of our species. Cooperation is the building block of human evolution and progress. It is the heart of interpersonal relationships, families, economic systems, and legal systems. World interdependence is now a reality based on technology, economics, ecology, and politics that go beyond national boundaries and tie all countries in the world together. The management of human interdependence on global, national, regional, organizational, community, family, and interpersonal levels is one of the most pressing issues of our time. Understanding the nature of interdependent systems and how to operate effectively within them is an essential quality of future citizens. The question is not whether we will cooperate. The question is, "How well will we do it?"

MACRO AND MICRO COOPERATION

Cooperation to a human is like water to a fish; it is so pervasive that it remains unnoticed. Because we are immersed in it, social interdependence can escape our notice. Cooperation is a persuasive but *nonconscious* goal of education. Within most situations no alternative to cooperation seems possible to humans. Since we can barely imagine its absence, we do not often consider its presence.

Cooperation exists within the classroom on both a macro and a micro level. On a macro level, cooperation pervades the classroom and the school as social systems. In the classroom there are two complementary roles—teacher and student—that engage in specified role-related behaviors and conform to organizational norms and values concerning appropriate behavior. The teacher is a person who teaches students; students are persons who learn with the aid of a teacher. The roles are interrelated, reinforce each other, and are interdependent. Each cannot function or exist without the other. The individuals within the roles of both teacher and student must learn the role expectations of other members of the organization, accept them, and reliably fulfill them. Examples of teacher-role requirements are putting students into contact with the subject matter, specifying learning goals, creating specific instructional conditions, disciplining students, and evaluating students. Examples of student-role requirements are to be attentive, follow directions, exert effort to achieve assigned learning goals, arrive on time, and complete assignments. An example of a norm is that no physical violence takes place within the classroom, and an example of a value is that education is beneficial and worthwhile. Successful completion of the school's objectives depends on the fulfillment of the organizational role requirements and adherence to the norms and values of the school. When cooperation on this macro level breaks down, competitive and individualistic learning activities become completely ineffectual. If students refuse to be "role-responsible," for example, no effective instruction can take place regardless of how interdependence among students is structured.

On the micro level, cooperation is one of the three goal structures used to structure interdependence among students. Cooperative learning provides a context for the other two goal structures. Competition cannot exist if there is no underlying cooperation concerning rules, procedures, time, place, and criteria for determining the winner. Without this underlying cooperative system, no competition can take place. Most competitions have referees, umpires, judges, and teachers present to ensure that the basic cooperation over rules and procedures does not break down. Skills and information learned individualistically, furthermore, must at some time be contributed to a cooperative effort. No skill is learned without being enacted within a social system such as a family or business. Nothing is produced without being part of a larger economic system. What is learned alone today is enacted in cooperative relationships tomorrow, or else it has no meaning or purpose. Individualistic efforts, therefore, can be effectively used as part of a division of labor in which students master certain knowledge and skills that will later be used in cooperative activities. On the micro instructional level, cooperative learning must dominate. It has the most widespread and powerful effects on instructional outcomes, it is the most complex of the three goal structures to implement effectively, and it should be the one most frequently used. Competitive and individualistic learning should be used to supplement and enrich the basic cooperation taking place among students.

APPROACHES TO COOPERATIVE LEARNING

Approaches to implementing cooperative learning may be placed on a continuum with conceptual applications at one end and direct applications at the other. *Conceptual applications* are based on an interaction among theory, research, and practice. Teachers are taught a general conceptual model of cooperative learning that they use to tailor cooperative learning specifically for their circumstances, students, and needs. In essence, teachers are taught an *expert system* of how to implement cooperative learning that they use to create a unique adaptation. *Direct applications* are packaged lessons, curricula, and strategies that are used in a lock-step prescribed manner. The direct approach may be divided into three subcategories: strategy, curriculum package, and lesson approaches.

The difference between conceptual and direct applications may be illustrated by the following example. Practically everyone knows how to run a VCR. You tune the TV to the appropriate channel, turn on the VCR, insert the tape, and press "play." When the VCR breaks, very few of us know how to repair it. Most of the things we use, we use as technicians. We can follow the instructions (step 1, step 2, step 3), but we really do not understand how the thing works, we cannot adapt and modify it to our unique circumstances, and we cannot repair it when it breaks. A few of us are engineers in the sense that we have the conceptual knowledge required to modify and adapt the things we use and to repair them when they break. In training teachers to use cooperative learning, teachers may be trained to use cooperative learning like a technician (step 1, step 2, step 3) or an engineer (conceptually understand cooperative learning and how to adapt it to specific teaching circumstances).

These two approaches to implementing cooperative learning are not contradictory. They supplement and support each other. A carefully crafted approach to cooperative learning requires a combination of clear conceptual understanding of the essential components of cooperative learning, concrete examples of lessons and strategies, and continued implementation in classrooms and schools.

Conceptual Approach

The conceptual approach requires teachers to learn both a conceptual understanding of cooperative learning (its nature and essential components) and the skills to use that understanding to plan and teach cooperative learning lessons, strategies, and curriculum units uniquely tailored for their specific students and circumstances. Conceptual approaches to cooperative learning have been developed by Elizabeth Cohen (1986) and the authors of this article (Johnson, 1970; Johnson, Johnson, & Holubec, 1993). Cohen bases her conceptual principles on expectation-states theory; we base our conceptual principles on the theory of cooperation and competition that Morton Deutsch built from Kurt Lewin's field theory. The conceptual approach assumes that each teacher faces a complex and unique combination of circumstances, students, and needs, and, therefore, cooperative learning needs to be adapted and refined to uniquely fit each teacher's situations. Understanding the essential elements allows teachers to think metacognitively about cooperative learning and to create any number of strategies and lessons. The *goal of the conceptual approach* is to develop teacher expertise in cooperative learning so teachers can:

1. Take any lesson in any subject area and structure it cooperatively.
2. Practice the use of cooperative learning until they are at a routine (integrated) level of use and implement cooperative learning at least 60 percent of the time in their classrooms.
3. Describe precisely what they are doing and why they are doing it in order to (a) communicate to others the nature of cooperative learning and (b) teach them how to implement cooperative learning in their classrooms and settings.
4. Apply the principles of cooperation to other settings, such as colleagial relationships and faculty meetings.

The conceptual approach is used in all technological arts and crafts. An engineer designing a bridge, for example, applies validated theory to the unique problems imposed by the need for a bridge of a certain length, to carry specific loads, from a bank of one unique geological character to a bank of another unique geological character, in an area with specific winds, temperatures, and susceptibility to earthquakes. Teachers engage in the same process by (a) learning a conceptualization of essential components of cooperative learning and (b) applying that conceptual model to their unique teaching situation, circumstances, students, and instructional needs.

The conceptual approach to implementing cooperative learning is characterized by being based on theory that is validated by research and is operationalized through the elements identified as essential to cooperative efforts.

Direct Approaches

At the other end of the continuum are direct approaches to implementing cooperative learning that are relatively cheap and take very little time to implement (see Figure 1.2). Teachers may be trained to conduct a specific cooperative learning lesson, to use a specific cooperative learning curriculum, or to use a specific cooperative learning structure or script. These direct applications are basically atheoretical. The goal of the direct approaches is to train teachers to use lock-step (step 1, step 2, step 3) prescribed procedures and curriculum materials that have been successfully used in another classroom (i.e., *idiographic knowledge*). Trainees are told what the procedure is, the procedure is demonstrated or modeled, and then the trainee practices the procedure. Such training is based on a number of assumptions. All classrooms and students are assumed to be basically the same and, therefore, the same structure, curriculum package, or lesson is assumed to be

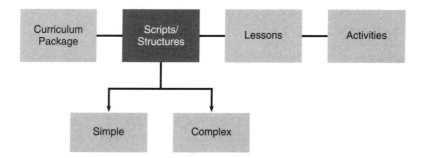

FIGURE 1.2   Direct approaches to cooperative learning

equally effective in all schools. Teachers are assumed to need to know only the steps involved in using cooperative learning. It is assumed that if teachers repeat the procedures dozens of times they will become quite skillful technicians. The problem with such technical competence is that it does not enable teachers to be flexible in their implementations and to adapt cooperative learning to new problems.

Direct approaches have focused on curriculum packages, scripts/structures, specific lessons, and specific activities. The *curriculum package approach* trains teachers to use a curriculum package within which lessons are structured cooperatively. Teachers are given a preset curriculum that contains all materials and procedures they need to implement it into their classrooms and are trained in how to use them. As with all curricula, the packages tend to be subject-area and grade-level specific. Dozens of curriculum packages that include instructions for using cooperative learning groups with the lessons are being published. This approach is best represented by the work of David DeVries, Keith Edwards, and Robert Slavin at Johns Hopkins University. The packages they have developed include Teams-Games-Tournament (TGT), Student-Team-Achievement Divisions (STAD), Team-Assisted-Individualization (TAI), and Cooperate Integrated Reading and Composition (CIRC). Although these curricula are a mixture of cooperative, competitive, and individualistic activities, they are built around or contain numerous cooperative lessons.

The *script/structure approach* trains teachers to use specific cooperative learning scripts. Scripts can be either simple or complex. Complex scripts are typically demonstrated with one or more specific lessons, and the steps required to implement the script are listed. Once the script is mastered, it may be used to build a number of cooperative lessons and be integrated into existing curriculums. Some of the most powerful complex scripts include the jigsaw method developed by Elliot Aronson and his colleagues (Aronson, 1978), the coop/coop strategy developed by Spencer Kagan (Kagan, 1988), the group project method developed by the Sharans (Sharan & Sharan, 1976), math groups-of-four developed by Marilyn Burns (Burns, 1981), and many more. The number increases yearly.

When teachers are trained in how to use cooperative learning from the *lesson approach*, they are given a specific lesson structured cooperatively (such as an

English lesson on punctuation, a math lesson on long division, or a science lesson on what sinks and what floats) and exposed to demonstrations on how the lesson is taught. Teachers are then expected to go back to their classrooms and conduct the lesson.

Finally, there are cooperative activities that may be used in the classroom that are related to cooperative learning. In the *cooperative activities approach,* teachers may use group-building activities (e.g., "favorite sports and hobbies," "pets I wish I had," and "team juggling") and cooperative games. Teachers may also have support groups within the classroom and promote classwide cooperation through class meetings. All of these activities enhance the effectiveness of cooperative learning activities, but they are not considered cooperative learning as there are no academic goals.

Integration of the Two Approaches

The conceptual and direct approaches to implementing cooperative learning are not contradictory. They supplement and support each other. A carefully crafted approach to cooperative learning requires a combination of a clear conceptual framework for engineering successful cooperative learning while utilizing the concrete examples of lessons and scripts. Cooperative learning is a complex instructional procedure that requires conceptual knowledge if it is to be implemented successfully and used with fidelity for the rest of a teacher's career. To gain real expertise, teachers have to conceptually understand cooperative learning well enough to tailor it to their unique circumstances, students, and needs. Direct approaches are helpful in getting teachers started with cooperative learning. As a starting point or a means to build toward conceptual understanding, direct procedures are very helpful. This book integrates the conceptual and direct approaches by presenting a conceptual framework of cooperative learning in which the direct curricula, scripts and structures, lessons, and activities can be used.

USING COOPERATIVE LEARNING

In order to achieve real expertise in using cooperative learning, you must first understand what cooperative learning is and the five basic elements that make cooperation work (see Figures 1.3 and 1.4). You must then know how to plan and implement formal cooperative learning lessons, informal cooperative learning lessons, cooperative base groups, and cooperative learning scripts or structures (for repetitive lessons and classroom routines). Once you plan, structure, and implement hundreds of cooperative learning lessons, you will achieve a routine level of implementation. Doing so will result in students' challenging each others' thinking, and utilizing their different points of view for learning. Your implementation of cooperative learning, furthermore, takes place within an organizational context that ideally is the cooperative school.

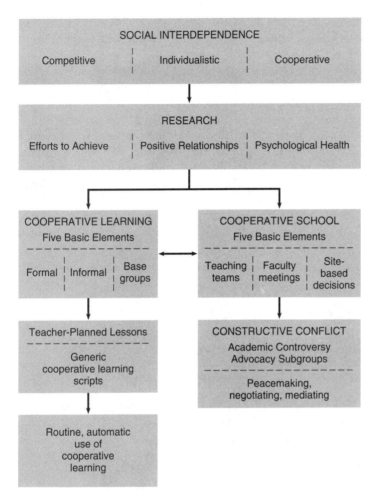

FIGURE 1.3 Overall framework: Circles of learning

Essential Components: What Makes Cooperation Work?

Together we stand, divided we fall.

Watchword of the American Revolution

There is more to cooperative learning than a seating arrangement. Placing students in groups and telling them to work together does not in and of itself result in cooperative efforts. Sitting in groups could instead result in competition at close quarters or individualistic efforts with talking. To structure lessons so students do in fact work cooperatively with each other requires an understanding of the components that make cooperation work. Mastering the essential components of cooperation allows teachers to:

1. Take their existing lessons, curricula, and courses and structure them cooperatively.
2. Tailor cooperative learning lessons to their unique instructional needs, circumstances, curricula, subject areas, and students.
3. Diagnose the problems some students may have in working together and intervene to increase the effectiveness of the student learning groups.

For cooperation to work well, teachers explicitly have to structure five essential elements in each lesson. The first and most important element is *positive interdependence.* Students must believe that they sink or swim together. Positive interdependence has been successfully structured when group members perceive that they are linked with each other in a way that one cannot succeed unless everyone succeeds. They realize, therefore, that each member's efforts benefit not only him- or herself, but all other group members as well. Students' vested interest in each other's achievement results in their sharing resources, helping and assist-

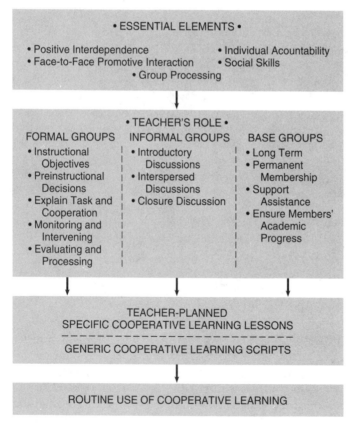

FIGURE 1.4   Conceptual approach to cooperative learning

ing each other's efforts to learn, providing mutual support, and celebrating their joint success. Positive interdependence is the heart of cooperative learning.

The second essential component of cooperative learning is *promotive interaction,* preferably face-to-face. Once teachers establish positive interdependence, they need to maximize the opportunity for students to promote each other's success by helping, assisting, supporting, encouraging, and praising one another's efforts to learn. There are cognitive activities and interpersonal dynamics that occur only when students get involved in promoting each other's learning. This includes orally explaining how to solve problems, discussing the nature of the concepts being learned, teaching one's knowledge to classmates, and connecting present with past learning.

The third essential component of cooperative learning is *individual accountability.* The purpose of cooperative learning groups is to make each member a stronger individual in his or her own right. Students learn together so that they can subsequently perform higher as individuals. To ensure that each member is strengthened, students are held individually accountable to do their share of the work. Individual accountability exists when the performance of each individual student is assessed and the results given back to the individual and the group. Individual accountability ensures that group members know (a) who needs more assistance, support, and encouragement in completing the assignment and (b) that they cannot "hitchhike" on the work of others.

The fourth essential component of cooperative learning is teaching students the required *interpersonal and small-group skills.* In cooperative learning groups, students are required to learn academic subject matter (*taskwork*) and also to learn the interpersonal and small-group skills required to function as part of a team (*teamwork*). Cooperative learning is inherently more complex than competitive or individualistic learning because students have to simultaneously engage in taskwork and teamwork. Contributing to the success of a cooperative effort requires social skills. Placing socially unskilled individuals in a group and telling them to cooperate does not guarantee that they will be able to do so effectively. Persons must be taught the social skills for high-quality cooperation and be motivated to use them. Leadership, decision-making, trust-building, communication, and conflict-management skills have to be taught just as purposefully and precisely as academic skills. Procedures and strategies for teaching students social skills may be found in Johnson (1991, 1993) and Johnson and F. Johnson (1991).

The fifth essential component of cooperative learning is *group processing.* Group processing exists when group members discuss how well they are achieving their goals and maintaining effective working relationships. Groups need to describe what member actions are helpful and unhelpful and make decisions about what behaviors to continue or change.

Real expertise in using cooperative learning is gained by learning how to structure the five essential components into instructional activities (Johnson & Johnson, 1989a). These essential elements, furthermore, should be carefully structured within all levels of cooperative efforts—learning groups, the class as a whole, the teaching team, the school, and the school district.

Types of Cooperative Learning

These problems are endemic to all institutions of education, regardless of level. Children sit for 12 years in classrooms where the implicit goal is to listen to the teacher and memorize the information in order to regurgitate it on a test. Little or no attention is paid to the learning process, even though much research exists documenting that real understanding is a case of active restructuring on the part of the learner. Restructuring occurs through engagement in problem posing as well as problem solving, inference making and investigation, resolving of contradictions, and reflecting. These processes all mandate far more active learners, as well as a different model of education than the one subscribed to at present by most institutions. Rather than being powerless and dependent on the institution, learners need to be empowered to think and learn for themselves. Thus, learning needs to be conceived of as something a learner does, not something that is done to a learner.

Catherine Fosnot (1989)

The ways cooperative learning may be used are quite varied. They include formal cooperative learning, informal cooperative learning, cooperative base groups, and cooperative scripts or structures. In order to understand cooperative learning and use it effectively, teachers have to be able to plan and implement formal cooperative lessons. *Formal cooperative learning* is students working together, from one class period to several weeks, to achieve shared learning goals by ensuring that they and their groupmates have successfully completed the learning task assigned. Any learning task in any subject area with any curriculum may be structured cooperatively. Any course requirement or assignment may be reformulated for formal cooperative learning. In formal cooperative learning groups, teachers (a) specify the objectives for the lesson, (b) make a number of preinstructional decisions, (c) explain the task and the positive interdependence, (d) monitor students' learning and intervene within the groups to provide task assistance or to increase students' interpersonal and group skills, and (e) evaluate students' learning and help students process how well their groups functioned.

Does the use of cooperative learning mean that teachers can no longer lecture, give demonstrations, show films, and use videotapes? No. Lectures, demonstrations, films, and videotapes may be used effectively when they are used with informal cooperative learning groups. *Informal cooperative learning* consists of having students work together to achieve a joint learning goal in temporary, ad hoc groups that last from a few minutes to a full class period. During a lecture, demonstration, or film, quick informal cooperative groupings are used to focus student attention on the material to be learned, set a mood conducive to learning, help set expectations as to what will be covered in a class session, ensure that students cognitively process the material being taught, and provide closure to an instructional session. During direct teaching the instructional challenge for the teacher is to ensure that students do the intellectual work of organizing material, explaining it, summarizing it, and integrating it into existing conceptual structures. Informal cooperative learning groups are often organized so that students engage in a three-to-five-minute focused discussion before and after a lecture and two-to-three-minute turn-to-your-partner discussions interspersed throughout a lecture.

Are all cooperative learning groups temporary, lasting only for a short period of time? No. One cooperative learning group should be permanent and serve as a base for all efforts to learn. *Cooperative base groups* are long-term, heterogeneous cooperative learning groups with stable membership whose purpose is for members to give each other the support, help, encouragement, and assistance each needs to make good academic progress (Johnson, Johnson, & Smith, 1991; Johnson, Johnson, & Holubec, 1992). Base groups provide students with permanent, long-term, committed relationships that last for at least a year and perhaps until all members are graduated. The purpose of the base group is to give the support, encouragement, and assistance each member needs to consistently work hard in school, make academic progress (attend class, complete all assignments, learn), and develop cognitively and socially in healthy ways. Base groups meet daily in elementary school and twice a week in secondary school (or whenever the class meets). They formally meet to discuss the academic progress of each member, provide help and assistance to each other, and verify that each member is completing assignments and progressing satisfactorily through the academic program. Base groups may also be responsible for letting absent group members know what went on in class when they miss a session. Informally, members interact every day within and between classes, discussing assignments and helping each other with homework. The use of base groups tends to improve attendance, personalizes the work required and the school experience, and improves the quality and quantity of learning. The larger the class or school and the more complex and difficult the subject matter, the more important it is to have base groups. Base groups are also helpful in structuring homerooms and when a teacher meets with a number of advisees.

For teachers to use cooperative learning the majority of the time, they must identify course routines and generic lessons that repeat over and over again and structure them cooperatively. *Cooperative learning scripts* are standard content-free cooperative procedures for either conducting generic, repetitive lessons (such as writing reports or giving presentations) or managing classroom routines (such as checking homework and reviewing a test) that proscribe student actions step by step. Scripted repetitive cooperative lessons and classroom routines provide a base on which the cooperative classroom may be built. Once planned and conducted several times, they will become automatic activities in the classroom. They may also be used in combination to form an overall lesson.

When teachers use formal, informal, and base cooperative base groups and generic cooperative learning scripts over and over again, they will gain expertise in doing so and will automatically use them as needed. The *routine-use level of teacher competence* is the ability to structure cooperative learning situations automatically without conscious thought or planning. Any lesson in any subject area with any set of curriculum materials may be reflexively and cooperatively structured to become

an automatic habit pattern. Cooperative learning can then be used in the long term with fidelity.

Resolving Conflicts Constructively

Once cooperative learning is implemented in classrooms and cooperative faculty teams are initiated at the school level, a major issue becomes, "How well do group members manage conflicts?" Cooperation and conflict go hand in hand. The more group members care about achieving the group's goals and the more they care about each other, the more frequently conflicts will occur. When conflicts are managed constructively, they add creativity, fun, and higher-level reasoning. When they are managed destructively, conflicts can result in anger, frustration, and hostility. In order to manage conflicts constructively, students and faculty need to learn the procedures for doing so and become skillful in their use.

In a *conflict-positive* school (or learning group), members promote and seek out conflicts in order to reap the many positive outcomes they can bring. Two types of conflicts are essential for cooperative groups to function effectively. The first type is *academic controversy*, where students challenge each other's intellectual reasoning and conclusions and argue the different sides of an issue (Johnson & Johnson, 1992). The second type is *peer mediation*, in which all students are taught how to negotiate solutions to their conflicts with schoolmates and faculty and how to mediate the conflicts among their peers (Johnson & Johnson, 1991). When conflicts are managed constructively within a group, class, or school, the stage is set for cooperative learning and for the cooperative school to achieve up to their potential.

The Cooperative School

Cooperative learning does not take place in a vacuum. It takes place within an organizational context. Currently, that context is a "mass-production" organizational structure that divides work into small component parts performed by individuals who work separately from and in competition with peers. The alternative context is a team-based, high-performance organizational structure in which individuals work cooperatively in teams that have responsibility for an entire product, process, or set of customers. The new organizational structure is known as the "cooperative school."

In a cooperative school, students work primarily in cooperative learning groups, teachers and building staff work in cooperative teams, and district administrators also work in cooperative teams (Johnson & Johnson, 1989b). The organizational structure of the classroom, school, and district are then congruent. Each level of cooperative teams supports and enhances the other levels. The cooperative school begins in the classroom. Students spend the majority of the day in cooperative learning groups. Cooperative learning is used to increase student achievement, create more positive relationships among students, and generally improve students' psychological well-being. What is good for students, furthermore, is even better for faculty.

The second level of the cooperative school is for faculty to work in colleagial support groups aimed at increasing teachers' instructional expertise and success. Teacher work teams are just as effective as student work teams. The use of cooperation to structure faculty and staff work involves colleagial support groups, school-based decision making, and faculty meetings. Just as the heart of the classroom is cooperative learning, the heart of the school is the colleagial support group. In addition, school-based decision making is implemented through the use of cooperative teams. First, a task force considers a school problem and proposes a solution to the faculty as a whole. Second, the faculty is divided into ad hoc decision-making groups that consider whether to accept or modify the proposal. Third, the decisions made by the ad hoc groups are summarized, and the entire faculty then decides on the action to be taken to solve the problem. The use of faculty colleagial support groups, task forces, and ad hoc decision-making groups tends to increase teacher productivity, cohesion, and professional self-esteem. Faculty meetings, furthermore, are structured to model cooperative procedures.

The third level is at the district level, where administrators are organized into support groups to increase their administrative expertise and success. Administrative task forces and ad hoc decision-making groups may dominate decision making at the district level as much as at the school level. Cooperation is more than an instructional procedure. It is a basic shift in organizational structure that extends from the classroom through the superintendent's office.

Gaining Expertise in Using Cooperative Learning

Knowledge about how to do something is not a skill. Being able to do something well is a skill. Skills take considerable time and effort to develop. Gaining expertise in using cooperative learning in the classroom and cooperative teams in the school and district takes at least one lifetime. *Expertise* is reflected in a person's proficiency, adroitness, competence, and skill in structuring cooperative efforts. Cooperation takes more expertise than do competitive or individualistic efforts, because it involves dealing with other people as well as dealing with the demands of the task. Expertise, furthermore, focuses attention on the transfer of what is learned within training sessions to the workplace and the long-term maintenance of new procedures throughout the person's career. Expertise in using cooperative learning is reflected in the teacher's being able to:

1. Take any lesson in any subject area and structure it cooperatively.
2. Practice the use of cooperative learning until a routine or integrated level of use has been reached and to implement cooperative learning at least 60 percent of the time in the classroom.
3. Describe precisely what he or she is doing and why in order to (a) communicate to others the nature of cooperative learning and (b) teach colleagues how to implement cooperative learning in their classrooms and settings.
4. Apply the principles of cooperation to other settings, such as colleagial relationships and at faculty meetings.

James Watson, who won a Nobel Prize as the co-discoverer of the double helix, stated, "Nothing new that is really interesting comes without collaboration." Gaining expertise in using cooperative learning is in itself a cooperative process that requires a team effort. Colleagial support groups encourage and assist teachers in a long-term, multiyear effort to continually improve their competence in using cooperative learning (Johnson & Johnson, 1989b). With only a moderately difficult teaching strategy, for example, teachers may require from twenty to thirty hours of instruction in its theory, fifteen to twenty demonstrations using it with different students and subjects, and an additional ten to fifteen coaching sessions to attain higher-level skills. For a more difficult teaching strategy such as cooperative learning, several years of training and support may be needed to ensure that teachers master it.

Harvey Firestone (of Firestone Tires) stated, "It is only when we develop others that we permanently succeed." To gain expertise in using cooperative learning, teachers have to help their colleagues gain expertise, primarily within support groups. In training sessions teachers learn about cooperative learning and the essential elements that make it work. Teachers then have to transfer this knowledge to their own classrooms and maintain their use of cooperative learning for years to come. The success of the training depends on transfer (teachers' trying out cooperative learning in their classrooms) and maintenance (long-term use of cooperative learning). As Aristotle said, "For things we have to learn before we can do them, we learn by doing them." Teachers have to use cooperative learning for some time before they begin to gain real expertise. This usually requires support, encouragement, and assistance from colleagues. Transfer and maintenance, therefore, depend largely on teachers themselves being organized into cooperative teams (colleagial support groups) that focus on helping each member progressively improve his or her competence in using cooperative learning.

SOCIAL INTERDEPENDENCE REVISITED

The first purpose of this book is to integrate cooperative, competitive, and individualistic learning into an overall instructional framework. Within any social situation, individuals may work together to achieve shared goals, compete to see who is best, or act independently without interacting with others. Competition is based on perceived scarcity and social comparisons. Competitions vary as to how many winners will result, the criteria used to select a winner, and the way contestants interact. Competitive learning can be effective under a very limited set of conditions. Individualistic efforts are based on independence and isolation from others. Cooperation is based on joint action to achieve mutual goals. It is the heart of human biology, family life, economic systems, legal systems, evolution, and community life.

Cooperation is also the heart of education. Teaching and learning are a cooperative enterprise in which faculty and students work together to achieve mutual goals. Approaches to implementing cooperation in schools have emphasized either teaching teachers a conceptual framework they can use to engineer a unique adaptation of cooperative learning to their specific circumstances, students, and needs or training teachers how to implement packaged curricula, scripts or structures, lessons, and activities in a lock-step manner. *The second purpose of this book is to integrate the conceptual and direct approaches to cooperative learning.*

Nothing is more basic in human life than working with, working against, and working separately from other people. Teachers must decide whether to structure students' learning goals to create competitive, individualistic, or cooperative efforts. Cooperation provides the foundation on which competitive and individualistic efforts are based. Competing for fun and enjoyment and individualistic learning are used as "changes of pace" to supplement the effectiveness of cooperative learning and to provide instructional variety. Cooperation and competition go hand in hand because they both involve relationships among individuals. Like hugging, cooperation or competition takes two (or more). You cannot cooperate or compete by yourself. Cooperation and competition take place among people. They both are opposites of individualistic efforts—the solitary striving for goals independent from all other humans.

For the past fifty years, competitive and individualistic goal structures have dominated American education. Students usually come to school with competitive expectations and pressures from their parents. Many teachers have tried to reduce classroom competition by switching from a norm-referenced to a criterion-referenced evaluation system. In both competitive and individualistic learning situations teachers try to keep students away from each other. "Do not copy!" "Move your desks apart!" "I want to see how well you can do, not your neighbor!" are all phrases that teachers commonly use in their classrooms. Students are repeatedly

Certainly, aggressiveness exists in nature, but there is also a healthy nonruthless competition, and there exist very strong drives toward social and cooperative behavior. These forces do not operate independently but together, as a whole, and the evidence strongly indicates that, in the social and biological development of all living creatures, of all these drives, the drive to cooperation is the most dominant, and biologically the most important. . . . It is probable that man owes more to the operation of this principle than to any other in his own biological and social evolution.
—*Ashley Montagu (1966)*

told, "Do not care about the other students in this class. Take care of yourself!" When a classroom is dominated by competition, students often experience classroom life as a "rat race" with the psychology of the one hundred–yard dash. When a classroom is dominated by individualistic efforts, students will concentrate on isolating themselves from each other, ignoring others, and focusing only on their own work. Many students begin to compete within individualistic situations, even though the structure does not require it.

There is a third option. Cooperative learning is the most important of the three ways of structuring learning situations, yet it is currently the least used. In most schools, class sessions are structured cooperatively only for 7 to 20 percent of the time (Johnson & Johnson, 1983a, 1989a). Research indicates, however, that cooperative learning should be used whenever teachers want students to learn more, like school better, like each other better, have higher self-esteem, and learn more effective social skills.

APPROPRIATELY USING INTERDEPENDENCE

Cooperative, competitive, and individualistic efforts are not in competition with each other. Survival of the fittest does not apply when it comes to structuring learning situations appropriately. When the three goal structures are used appropriately and in an integrated way, their sum is far more powerful than each one separately. When the goal structures are used inappropriately (such as the inappropriate use and overuse of competitive or individualistic learning), problems result for both students and teachers (see Table 1.3).

In the ideal classroom all three goal structures are used. This does not mean that they should be used equally, however. The basic foundation of instruction—the underlying context on which all instruction rests—is cooperation. Unless they are used within a context of cooperation, competitive and individualistic instruction lose much of their effectiveness. *A cooperative goal structure should dominate the classroom, being used 60 to 70 percent of the time.* The individualistic goal structure may

TABLE 1.3 Elements of Social Interdependence

ELEMENTS	COOPERATIVE	COMPETITIVE	INDIVIDUALISTIC
Interdependence	Positive	Negative	None
Importance of Goal	High	Low	Low
Interaction	Promotive	Oppositional	None
Accountability	Individual group	Individual	Individual
Social Skills	All	Comparison	None
Task	Any, including complex, divisible, new	Simple, unitary, nondivisible, overlearned	Simple, unitary, nondivisible, new
Procedures	Clear	Clear	Clear
Rules	Unclear		

be used 20 percent of the time, and a competitive goal structure may be used 10 to 20 percent of the time. All competitive and individualistic efforts take place within a broader cooperative framework. Cooperation is the forest; competitive and individualistic efforts are but trees.

Teachers have no choice but to choose a goal structure for each lesson they teach. If no overt choice is made, students will choose the goal structure they believe is most appropriate. When students are familiar with and have had experience learning within each type of goal structure, they will probably be very good judges as to which goal structure is most desirable for accomplishing specified learning goals. When students do not have past experience in each type of instructional situation, an informed and free choice cannot take place. Students' conceptions of the alternatives in a situation depend on their past experiences and their perceptions of the situational constraints. If students have rarely experienced a goal structure other than interpersonal competition in school, they will tend to assume competition when left to their own devices. If all the organizational pressures within the school are based on the traditional interpersonal competitive goal structure, students will tend to behave competitively whenever they are left "free" to choose. Under such conditions, implementing no goal structure at all or giving students a superficial choice among the three goal structures is to ask students subtly (or not so subtly) to place the traditional interpersonal competition goal structure on themselves.

BASIC PARTNERSHIP BETWEEN COOPERATIVE AND INDIVIDUALISTIC LEARNING

Probably the most frequent combination of goal structures used in classrooms is the combination of cooperative and individualistic learning situations. There are three major ways in which individualistic and cooperative goal structures may be

So wherever I am, there's always Pooh, there's always Pooh and me. "What would I do," I said to Pooh, "if it wasn't for you?" and Pooh said, "True! It isn't much fun for one, but two can stick together," says Pooh, says he. "That's how it is," says Pooh. —*A. A. Milne*

combined. The first is through task interdependence in which a division of labor is created. While working on a cooperative task, a group may arrive at a division of labor in which it is necessary for different students to master different skills or different information in order to provide the resources the group needs to achieve its goal successfully. An ideal teaching situation is to assign a cooperative project and provide individual tasks for various aspects of the problem so that different group members can master different skills and information for later integration into the group's product. An example of this approach is to assign the individual tasks of learning how to make a microscope slide, how to gather pondwater, and how to use a microscope and then assign the cooperative task of writing a group report on the microscopic life within swampwater.

A second possible combination is through resource interdependence. This procedure is commonly referred to as a "jigsaw." A list of vocabulary words may be given to a cooperative learning group and then subdivided so that each member is responsible for (1) learning a subset of words and (2) teaching the words to the other group members.

Finally, individualistic and cooperative goal structures may be combined through reward interdependence. Students can study material within a cooperative learning group, take an achievement test individually, and then be rewarded on the basis of a performance ratio such as:

1. Students receive 50 percent credit for every problem they solve correctly and 50 percent of the average performance of group members.
2. Students receive their individual score and then are given bonus points on the basis of whether all members of their group achieve above a preset criterion for excellence.

Conversely, students could be assigned to a cooperative group where they study material individualistically, are tested individualistically, receive their own score, and receive bonus points on the basis of how well the members of their group do when their scores are compared to a preset criterion for excellence. Since such a procedure does not include the interaction among group members that contributes to learning, this procedure should be used infrequently.

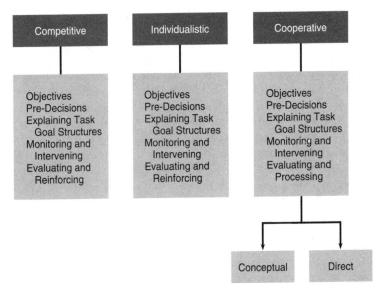

FIGURE 1.5   Teacher's role in structuring social interdependence

INTEGRATED USE OF ALL THREE GOAL STRUCTURES

All three methods of structuring interdependence among students may be used in an integrated way within classrooms. A typical schedule for doing so is:

1. Assign students to heterogeneous cooperative learning groups.
2. Give each member an individualistic assignment of learning a subsection of the material the group needs to complete its assignment.
3. Give each group a cooperative assignment of learning all of the material, with each member presenting his or her subsection to the entire group.
4. Conduct a competitive tournament to drill students on the material they have just learned.
5. Give a cooperative assignment to use the material learned to complete a group project.
6. Give an achievement test that each student takes individually and determine a group score on the basis of the performance of all group members.

An example of such an integrated unit follows.

1. Students are assigned to four-person heterogeneous cooperative learning groups.
2. Each group is given the cooperative assignment of ensuring that all group members learn a set of vocabulary words.

3. A list of thirty-two vocabulary words is given to each group. Each group member is given the individualistic assignment of mastering eight of the vocabulary words and planning how to teach the eight words to the other group members.

4. The group then meets with the cooperative goal of ensuring that all four members master all thirty-two vocabulary words. Each group member teaches his or her subset of eight words to the other members.

5. A competitive class tournament is conducted to drill students on the thirty-two words and to see which group has been most successful in mastering the vocabulary words.

6. Each group is given the cooperative assignment of writing a story in which 95 percent of the assigned vocabulary words are used appropriately and correctly. The group is to produce one story that contains contributions from all group members.

7. Students individually take a test on the thirty-two vocabulary words. All members of groups on which each member scored 95 percent or above receive an "A" on the unit.

When conducting an integrated unit, the important issues to keep in mind are:

1. Emphasize the underlying cooperation. The individualistic and competitive aspects of the unit are supplements to the overall cooperation among students. Individualistic and competitive learning activities should enhance, not detract from, cooperative learning.

2. Begin and end with a group meeting. At the initial group meeting the division of labor (or jigsaw) may be agreed on and the goal of individualistically learning material to contribute to the overall success of the group is emphasized. During the final meeting students should discuss how well the group functioned.

3. Remember that students will bring more to the competition than you want them to. They will want to make more of winning the competition than is appropriate. Remember to keep the reward for winning minor. In the students' past, winning has too often been a "life-or-death" matter. You will have to teach students to compete appropriately for fun. You may wish to have a class discussion about how enjoyable the competition was.

4. Vary the number of instructional periods according to the unit. The individualistic assignments could be done as homework. Cooperative tasks could take more than one instructional period.

SUMMARY

Social interdependence to humans is like water to fish. Because we are immersed in it, it can escape our notice. There are two types of social interdependence: cooperative and competitive. The absence of interdependence results in individualistic efforts. Teachers have a choice of structuring every learning task competitively, individualistically, or cooperatively. Which structure is chosen determines how students interact with each other, which in turn determines the outcomes achieved. For the past fifty years competitive and individualistic efforts have dominated classrooms. Cooperative learning has been relatively ignored and underutilized by teachers even though it is the most important and powerful way to structure learning situations. Chapter 2, which reviews the basic research that has been conducted on the three goal structures, makes this point clearly. This does not mean, however, that competitive and individualistic learning should be abandoned. Each goal structure has its place, and when they are used appropriately, they form an integrated whole. In Chapters 3 through 7, therefore, the appropriate use of each goal structure is discussed in depth.

Cooperation is by far the most pervasive and important type of social interdependence. We do not have a choice. We have to cooperate. Working together to accomplish shared goals pervades our biology and is the building block of human evolution and progress. Cooperation provides the foundation on which competitive and individualistic efforts are based. The topic is discussed thoroughly in Chapters 3 through 5. Competing for fun and enjoyment is frequently sought out as a "change of pace" from the pervasiveness of cooperation. It is discussed in Chapter 7. Cooperation and competition involve relationships with other people. Like hugging, it takes two or more. You cannot cooperate or compete by yourself. Both are opposites of individualistic efforts—the solitary striving for goals independent from those of others. Individualistic learning is discussed in Chapter 6.

Cooperation is the most powerful of the three ways to structure learning situations (see Chapter 2). It is also the most complex to implement. Besides knowing what cooperative learning is, teachers have to understand the various types of cooperative learning (see Chapters 4 and 5) and the essential elements that make cooperation work (Chapter 3). Thus, positive interdependence is discussed in Chapter 7 and the small-group and interpersonal skills required to work cooperatively with others is discussed in Chapter 8. Finally, the questions most frequently asked about the use of cooperative learning are discussed in Chapter 9.

FINAL NOTE

During one very difficult trek across an ice field in Don Bennett's hop to the top of Mount Rainer, his daughter stayed by his side for four hours and with each new hop told him, "You can do it, Dad. You're the best dad in the world. You can do it, Dad." There was no way Bennett would quit hopping to the top with his daughter yelling words of love and encouragement in his ear. The encouragement of his daughter kept him going, strengthening his commitment to make it to the top. The classroom is similar. With members of their cooperative group cheering them on, students amaze themselves and their teachers with what they can achieve.

2

Goal Structures, Interaction Among Students, and Instructional Outcomes

INTRODUCTION

No logic or wisdom or willpower could prevail to stop the ancient Greek sailors. Buffeted by the hardships of life at sea, voices came out of the mist to the sailors like a mystical, ethereal lovesong with tempting and seductive promises of ecstasy and delight. The voices and the song were irresistible. The mariners helplessly turned their ships to follow the Sirens' call with scarcely a second thought. Lured to their destruction, the sailors crashed their ships on the waiting rocks and drowned in the tossing waves, struggling with their last breath to reach the source of that beckoning song.

Centuries later, the Sirens still call. Educators seem drawn to competitive and individualistic learning, crashing their teaching on the rocks due to the seductive and tempting attractions of explicating knowledge to an adoring audience and teaching as they themselves were taught. Yet if you ask individuals who have made remarkable achievements during their lifetimes, they typically say their success came from cooperative efforts (Kouses & Posner, 1967). Not only is cooperation connected with success, competitiveness has been found to be detrimental to career success (Kohn, 1986). The more competitive a person is, the less chance he or she has of being successful. Perhaps the most definitive research on this issue has been conducted by Robert L. Helmreich and his colleagues (Helmreich, 1982; Helmreich, Beane, Lucker, & Spence, 1978; Helmreich, Sawin, & Carsrud, 1986; Helmreich, Spence et al., 1980). They first determined that high achievers, such as scientists, MBAs, and pilots, tend *not* to be very competitive individuals. Then

Helmreich and his associates examined the relationship between the competitive drive within individuals and career success. They conceptualized the desire to achieve as consisting of *competitiveness* (desire to win in interpersonal situations, where one tends to see that success depends on another's failure), *mastery* (desire to take on challenging tasks), and *work* (positive attitudes toward hard work). A sample of 103 male Ph.D. scientists was rated on the three factors based on a questionnaire. Achievement was defined as the number of times their work was cited by colleagues. The result was that the most citations were obtained by those high on the Work and Mastery scale but low on the Competitiveness scale. Startled by these results, Helmreich and his associates conducted follow-up studies with academic psychologists, businessmen working in "cutthroat" big business (measuring achievement by their salaries), undergraduate male and female students (using grade-point average as the achievement measure), fifth- and sixth-grade students (measuring achievement by performance on standardized achievement tests), airline pilots (measuring achievement by performance ratings), airline reservation agents (measuring achievement by performance ratings), and supertanker crews. In all cases they found a negative correlation between achievement and competitiveness. With regard to faculty members, the researchers proposed that competitive individuals focus so heavily on outshining others and putting themselves forward that they lose track of the scientific issues and produce research that is more superficial and less sustained in direction. As yet, Helmreich and his colleagues have not been able to identify a single professional arena where highly competitive individuals tend to be more successful.

Given that competitiveness seems to be detrimental to career success, why has it been so prevalent in classrooms? One answer may be that the preceding evidence is not enough. Interesting, but not conclusive. In this chapter, therefore, research directly comparing the relative effects of competitive, individualistic, and cooperative efforts is reviewed.

HISTORY OF COOPERATIVE LEARNING

Two are better than one, because they have a good reward for toil. For if they fall, one will lift up his fellow; but woe to him who is alone when he falls and has not another to lift him up. . . . And though a man might prevail against one who is alone, two will withstand him. A threefold cord is not quickly broken.

Ecclesiastes 4:9–12

Cooperative learning has been around a long time. It will probably never go away. Its rich history of theory, research, and actual use in the classroom makes it one of the most distinguished of all instructional practices. Theory, research, and practice all interact and enhance each other. Theory both guides and summarizes research. Research validates or disconfirms theory, thereby leading to its refinement and modification. Practice is guided by validated theory, and applications of the theory reveal inadequacies that lead to refining of the theory, conducting new research

> Let us put our minds together . . . and see what life we can make for our children.
> —*Sitting Bull*

studies, and modifying the application. The history of cooperative learning is reviewed here with the emphasis being on the theories that have guided the development of cooperative learning and the research they have generated.

Where We Have Been: Theoretical Roots

There are at least three general theoretical perspectives that have guided research on cooperative learning—social interdependence, cognitive-developmental, and behavioral. The *social interdependence perspective* began in the early 1900s, when one of the founders of the Gestalt School of Psychology, Kurt Kafka, proposed that groups were dynamic wholes in which the interdependence among members could vary. One of his colleagues, Kurt Lewin (1935, 1948), refined Kafka's notions in the 1920s and 1930s while stating that (1) the essence of a group is the interdependence among members (created by common goals) that results in the group's being a "dynamic whole" so that a change in the state of any member or subgroup changes the state of any other member or subgroup, and (2) an intrinsic state of tension within group members motivates movement toward the accomplishment of the desired common goals. One of Lewin's graduate students, Morton Deutsch, formulated a theory of cooperation and competition in the late 1940s (Deutsch, 1949, 1962). One of Deutsch's graduate students, David Johnson (working with his brother Roger Johnson), extended Deutsch's work into social interdependence theory (Johnson, 1970; Johnson & Johnson, 1974, 1989a).

The social interdependence perspective assumes that the way social interdependence is structured determines how individuals interact which, in turn, determines outcomes. Positive interdependence (cooperation) results in *promotive interaction* as individuals encourage and facilitate each other's efforts to learn. Negative interdependence (competition) typically results in *oppositional interaction* as individuals discourage and obstruct each other's efforts to achieve. In the absence of interdependence (individualistic efforts) there is *no interaction* as individuals work independently without any interchange with each other.

The *cognitive developmental perspective* is largely based on the theories of Jean Piaget and Lev Semenovich Vygotsky. From Piaget and related theories comes the premise that when individuals cooperate on the environment, sociocognitive conflict occurs that creates cognitive disequilibrium, which in turn stimulates perspective-taking ability and cognitive development. Piagetians argue that during cooperative efforts participants will engage in discussions in which cognitive conflicts will occur and be resolved, and inadequate reasoning will be exposed and modified. The work of Vygotsky and related theorists is based on the premise that

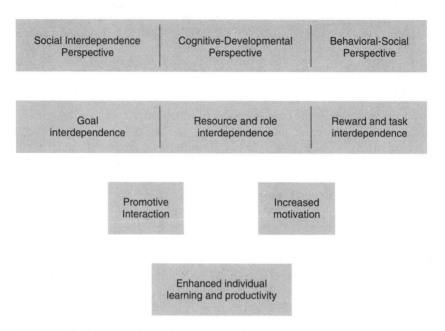

FIGURE 2.1 A general theoretical framework

knowledge is social, constructed from cooperative efforts to learn, understand, and solve problems. Group members exchange information and insights, discover weak points in each other's reasoning strategies, correct one another, and adjust their understanding on the basis of others' understanding.

Related to developmental theorists are the *controversy theorists* (Johnson & Johnson, 1979, 1992) who posit that being confronted with opposing points of view creates uncertainty or conceptual conflict, which creates a reconceptualization and an information search, which results in a more refined and thoughtful conclusion; and the *cognitive restructuring theorists* who state that in order for information to be retained in memory and incorporated into existing cognitive structures, the learner must cognitively rehearse and restructure the material (Wittrock, 1978). An effective way of doing so is explaining the material to a collaborator.

The *behavioral learning theory perspective* focuses on the impact of group reinforcers and rewards for learning. The assumption is that actions followed by extrinsic rewards are repeated. Skinner focused on group contingencies, Bandura focused on imitation, and Homans as well as Thibaut and Kelley focused on the balance of rewards and costs in social exchange among interdependence individuals. More recently, Slavin (1983) has emphasized the need for extrinsic group rewards to motivate efforts to learn in cooperative learning groups.

There are basic differences among the three theoretical perspectives. Social interdependence theory assumes that cooperative efforts are based on intrinsic motivation generated by interpersonal factors in working together and joint aspirations to achieve a significant goal. The behavioral-social perspective assumes that cooperative efforts are powered by extrinsic motivation to achieve group rewards. Social interdependence theory is made up of relational concepts dealing with what happens among individuals (e.g., cooperation is something that exists only among individuals, not within them), whereas the cognitive-developmental perspective is focused on what happens within a single person (e.g., disequilibrium, cognitive reorganization). The differences in basic assumptions among the perspectives create theoretical conflicts and disagreements that have yet to be fully explored or resolved. These three theoretical perspectives have, however, generated a considerable body of research to confirm or disprove their predictions.

Where We Have Been: Research

We know a lot about cooperation and we have known it for some time. In the late 1800s Triplett (1898) in the United States, Turner (1889) in England, and Mayer (1903) in Germany conducted a series of studies on the factors associated with competitive performance. Since then we have learned a lot about cooperation. In 1929 Maller wrote a book about it (*Cooperation and Competition: An Experimental Study in Motivation*). In 1936 Margaret Mead (*Cooperation and Competition Among Primitive Peoples*), and in 1937 May and Doob ("Competition and Cooperation") wrote research reviews on it. In 1949 Deutsch published a research study and a theory on it. In the 1950s Muzafer Sherif (Sherif & Hovland, 1961) conducted his famous studies on three summer camps in which he engineered intense intergroup competition and studied its resolution. Stuart Cook (1969), in collaboration with Shirley and Larry Wrightsman, conducted a study on the impact of cooperative interaction on relationships between black and white college students. James Coleman (1961) published an observational study of American schools in which a pervasive competitiveness was documented. In 1963 Miller and Hamblin reviewed twenty-four studies on cooperation and competition. From an anthropological perspective, Millard C. Madsen (1967) and his associates developed a series of dyadic games that allowed comparison of children's preferences for competitive and cooperative interaction, across ages and various cultures. One of Madsen's students, Spencer Kagan, began a series of studies on cooperation and competition in children. The research of Madsen and Kagan presents a consistent picture of rural children collaborating more than urban children, and middle-class urban American children being most strongly motivated to compete.

In the 1970s the authors of this book published comprehensive research reviews on cooperation and competition (e.g., *The Social Psychology of Education* [Johnson, 1970]; *Learning Together and Alone*, 1st ed. [Johnson & Johnson, 1975]). From then on the research review articles are too many to mention. Since 1898, over 550 experimental and 100 correlational research studies have been conducted on cooperative, competitive, and individualistic efforts (see Johnson & Johnson, 1989a, for a complete review of these studies).

The effectiveness of cooperative learning has been confirmed by both theoretical and demonstration research. There is a "scientific" literature and a "professional" literature on cooperative learning. The scientific literature is made up of carefully controlled research studies conducted to validate or disconfirm theory. Most of the studies are either laboratory or field experimental studies. The vast majority of the research on cooperative learning was conducted to validate or disconfirm theory. The theoretical studies typically are carefully controlled and have high internal validity—randomly assigning subjects to conditions, carefully operationalizing the independent variable, ensuring that the measures of the dependent variables are both reliable and valid. The theoretical studies have focused on a wide variety of dependent variables from achievement to higher-level reasoning to friendships between majority and minority individuals to accuracy of perspective taking to self-esteem to psychological health. The results of these theoretical studies are highly consistent in supporting the use of cooperative over competitive and individualistic learning. It is this combination of hundreds of studies producing validated theory that could be operationalized into practice that has created such interest in cooperative learning.

There are problems with theoretical studies. They lack credibility with many practitioners. Most of the theoretical studies on cooperative learning were conducted in social psychology laboratories using college students as subjects. Although they clarified the power of cooperative efforts, they did not in fact demonstrate that cooperative learning could work in the "real world."

The professional literature is made up of field quasi-experimental or correlational studies demonstrating that cooperative learning works in real classrooms for a prolonged period of time. Demonstration studies have tended to focus on external validity. The demonstration studies may be grouped into four categories.

1. *Summative evaluations.* By far the largest category of demonstration studies is straight-forward summative evaluation in which the central question is whether a particular cooperative learning program produces beneficial results. The comparison is typically between a cooperative learning method and "traditional" classroom learning. The Johns Hopkins research on specific cooperative learning programs (Teams-Games-Tournaments, Student Teams-Achievement Divisions, Team-Assisted Individualization) are examples that focused primarily on achievement on lower-level learning tasks. The reviews of these studies (Slavin, 1983, 1991) are organized around a particular method, not a particular skill or knowledge to be learned. This serves the advocates of the method, but users of cooperative learning may not be so concerned with whether STAD works or does not work; instead, they would like to know the best procedures for maximizing learning or higher-level reasoning. Although these evaluation studies are of interest, the information value of their conclusions is limited for designing effective instructional programs.

2. *Comparative summative evaluations.* Less research attention has been devoted to the comparative question of which of two or more cooperative learning methods produces the most beneficial effects when compared on the same criterion measures. The jigsaw method, for example, might be compared with Team-Assisted-Individualization. There is an inherent problem with such studies, as it is difficult if not

impossible to tell if both methods have been implemented at the same strength. The results can easily be biased through carefully implementing one method at full strength and implementing the other method at partial strength.

3. *Formative evaluations.* Very little research that focuses on where a cooperative learning program went wrong and how it could be improved makes its way into the literature. Formative evaluations are aimed at improving ongoing implementations of coopera- tion learning. The critical-incident method seems well suited to the diagnosis of training deficiencies or unintended consequences, as does a combination of surveys with follow-up interviews of a representative subsample of respondents.

4. *Survey studies.* A few studies have conducted large-scale surveys of the impact of cooperation on students (Johnson & Johnson, 1991d). These studies have (a) corre- lated attitudes toward cooperative, competitive, and individualistic learning with such variables as perceived social support, self-esteem, and attitudes toward learning and (b) compared the responses of students in high-use classrooms (where cooperative learning was frequently used) with the responses of students in low-use classrooms (where cooperative learning was never or rarely used) on a number of learning climate variables (e.g., Johnson & Johnson, 1983; Johnson, Johnson, & Anderson, 1983; Johnson, Johnson, Buckman, & Richards, 1986). Although these studies are not direct evaluations of cooperative learning procedures, they do provide interesting data about the long-term impact of cooperative learning on a variety of attitudinal and learning climate outcomes.

Demonstration studies have both weaknesses and strengths. First, like all case studies, demonstration studies simply indicate that a certain method worked at that time in those circumstances. Second, demonstration studies are always in danger of being biased because the researchers typically are evaluating programs they have developed themselves and have a professional and sometimes a financial stake in their success. By definition, such researchers favor cooperative learning. Reviews of demonstration studies, furthermore, suffer the same limitation; they are most often conducted by the researchers who invented the cooperative learning programs. The third problem with demonstration studies is that what is labeled as cooperative learning is not always cooperation. In many cases, the "cooperative learning method" being evaluated was only one element of a broader educational package and, therefore, cooperative learning was confounded with other variables. The original jigsaw procedure (Aronson, 1978), for example, is a combination of resource interdependence (cooperative) and individual reward structure (individualistic). Teams-Games-Tournaments (DeVries & Edwards, 1974) and Student-Teams-Achievement-Divisions (Slavin, 1980) are mixtures of cooperation and intergroup competition. Team-Assisted-Instruction (Slavin, Leavey, & Madden, 1982) is a mixture of individualistic and cooperative learning. It is difficult to interpret the results of studies evaluating the effectiveness of such mixtures as it is impossible to know which elements contributed which part of the effects found.

Fourth, demonstration studies often lack methodological rigor, focusing far more on external validity (such as length of study) than on internal validity (such as experimental control). In many demonstration studies, the comparison has been with an ambiguous and unknown "traditional classroom learning." When differences are found, it is not clear what has been compared with what. The lack of methodological quality to most demonstration studies adds further doubts as to how seriously their results can be taken. Finally, most demonstration studies have been conducted in elementary schools; very few have been conducted at the secondary and college levels. This reduces their relevance.

There are at least two strengths to demonstration studies. First, there is a clear value to demonstration studies when their results are viewed in combination with more controlled and more theoretical studies. When the results of the demonstration studies agree with and support the results of the theoretical studies, the demonstration studies strengthen the validity of the theory and make it more credible. Second, demonstration studies provide a model for teachers who wish to implement identical programs.

Cooperative learning can be used with some confidence at every grade level, in every subject area, and with any task. Research participants have varied as to economic class, age, sex, nationality, and cultural background. A wide variety of research

A human being is a part of the whole, called by us "Universe," a part limited in time and space. He experiences himself, his thoughts and feelings as something separated from the rest—a kind of optical delusion of consciousness. This delusion is a kind of prison for us, restricting us to our personal desires and to affection for a few persons nearest to us. Our task must be to free ourselves from this prison by widening our circle of compassion to embrace all living creatures and the whole nature in its beauty.
—*Albert Einstein*

tasks, ways of structuring cooperation, and measures of the dependent variables have been used. The research has been conducted by many different researchers with markedly different orientations working in different settings, countries, and decades. The research on cooperative learning has a validity and a generalizability rarely found in the educational literature.

Cooperation is a generic human endeavor that affects many different instructional outcomes simultaneously. Over the past ninety years researchers have focused on such diverse outcomes as achievement, higher-level reasoning, retention, achievement motivation, intrinsic motivation, transfer of learning, interpersonal attraction, social support, friendships, prejudice, valuing differences, social support, self-esteem, social competencies, psychological health, moral reasoning, and many others. These numerous outcomes may be subsumed within three broad categories (Johnson & Johnson, 1989a): effort to achieve, positive interpersonal relationships, and psychological health (see Figure 2.2 and Table 2.1).

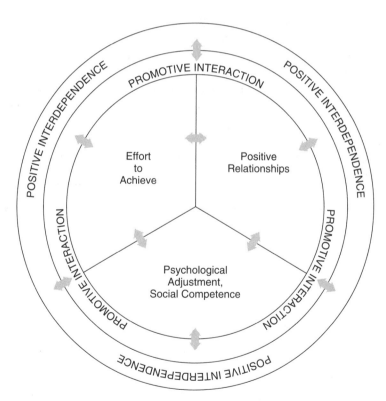

FIGURE 2.2   Outcomes of cooperation. (*Source:* D. W. Johnson & R. Johnson: *Cooperation and competition: Theory and research.* Edina, MN: Interaction, 1989. Reprinted with permission.)

History of Practical Use of Cooperative Learning

There is a rich and long history of practical use of cooperative learning. Thousands of years ago the Talmud stated that in order to understand the Talmud, one must have a learning partner. As early as the first century, Quintillion argued that students could benefit from teaching one another. The Roman philosopher Seneca advocated cooperative learning through such statements as "Qui Docet Discet" (when you teach, you learn twice). Johann Amos Comenius (1592–1679) believed that students would benefit both by teaching and by being taught by other students. In the late 1700s Joseph Lancaster and Andrew Bell made extensive use of cooperative learning groups in England, and the idea was brought to America when a Lancastrian school was opened in New York City in 1806. Within the Common School Movement in the United States in the early 1800s there was a strong emphasis on cooperative learning. Certainly, the use of cooperative learning is not new to American education. There have been periods in which cooperative learning had strong advocates and was widely used to promote the educational goals of that time.

One of the most successful advocates of cooperative learning in America was Colonel Francis Parker. In the last three decades of the nineteenth century, Colonel Parker brought to his advocacy of cooperative learning enthusiasm, idealism, practicality, and an intense devotion to freedom, democracy, and individuality in the public schools. His fame and success rested on the vivid and regenerating spirit that he brought into the schoolroom and on his power to create a classroom

TABLE 2.1   Mean Effect Sizes for Impact of Social Interdependence on Dependent Variables

	ACHIEVE	INTERA	SUPPORT	S-ESTEEM
Total Studies				
Coop vs. Comp	0.67	0.67	0.62	0.58
Coop vs. Ind	0.64	0.60	0.70	0.44
Comp vs. Ind	0.30	0.08	–0.13	–0.23
High-Quality Studies				
Coop vs. Comp	0.88	0.82	0.83	0.67
Coop vs. Ind	0.61	0.62	0.72	0.45
Comp vs. Ind	0.07	0.27	–0.13	–0.25
Mixed Operationalizations				
Coop vs. Comp	0.40	0.46	0.45	0.33
Coop vs. Ind	0.42	0.36	0.02	0.22
Pure Operationalizations				
Coop vs. Comp	0.71	0.79	0.73	0.74
Coop vs. Ind	0.65	0.66	0.77	0.51

Note: Coop = Cooperation, Comp = Competition, Ind = Individualistic, Achieve = Achievement, InterA = Interpersonal Attraction, Support = Social Support, S-Esteem = Self-Esteem

For a complete description of effect sizes and the data, see Johnson & Johnson (1989a).

atmosphere that was truly cooperative and democratic. When he was superintendent of the public schools at Quincy, Massachusetts (1875–1880), he averaged more than 30,000 visitors a year to examine his use of cooperative learning procedures (Campbell, 1965). Parker's instructional methods of structuring cooperation among students dominated American education through the turn of the century. Following Parker, John Dewey promoted the use of cooperative learning groups as part of his famous project method in instruction (Dewey, 1924). In the late 1930s, however, interpersonal competition began to be emphasized in public schools (Pepitone, 1980).

In the mid 1960s the authors began training teachers how to use cooperative learning at the University of Minnesota. The Cooperative Learning Center resulted from our efforts to synthesize existing knowledge concerning cooperative, competitive, and individualistic efforts (Johnson, 1970; Johnson & Johnson, 1974, 1978, 1983, 1989a), to formulate theoretical models concerning the nature of cooperation and its essential components, to conduct a systematic program of research to test our theorizing, to translate the validated theory into a set of concrete strategies and procedures for using cooperation in classrooms, schools, and school districts (Johnson & Johnson, 1989b, 1992b; Johnson, Johnson, & Holubec, 1984/1993, 1992a), and to build and maintain a network of schools and colleges implementing cooperative strategies and procedures throughout North America and many other countries.

In the early 1970s David DeVries and Keith Edwards at Johns Hopkins University developed Teams-Games-Tournaments (TGT), and Sholmo and Yael Sharan in Israel developed the group investigation procedure for cooperative learning groups. In the late 1970s Robert Slavin extended DeVries and Edwards' work at Johns Hopkins University by modifying TGT into Student Teams-Achievement Divisions (STAD) and modifying computer-assisted instruction into Team-Assisted Instruction (TAI). Concurrently, Spencer Kagan developed the Co-op Co-op procedure. In the 1980s Donald Dansereau developed a number of cooperative scripts, and many other individuals worked out further cooperative procedures.

RESEARCH ON SOCIAL INTERDEPENDENCE

Learning together to complete assignments can have profound effects. Building on the theorizing of Kurt Lewin and Morton Deutsch, the premise may be made that the type of interdependence structured among students determines how they interact with each other, which in turn largely determines instructional outcomes. Structuring situations cooperatively results in promotive interaction, structuring situations competitively results in oppositional interaction, and structuring situations individualistically results in no interaction among students. These interaction patterns affect numerous variables, which may be subsumed within the three broad and interrelated outcomes of effort exerted to achieve, quality of relationships among participants, and participants' psychological adjustment and social competence (see Figure 2.2) (Johnson & Johnson, 1989a). In most cases, references to individual studies are not included in this chapter. Rather, the reader is referred to the reviews that contain references to the specific studies that corroborate the point being made.

INTERACTION PATTERNS

Two heads are better than one.

Heywood

Simply placing students near each other and allowing interaction to take place does not mean that learning will be maximized, high-quality peer relationships will result, or student psychological adjustment, self-esteem, and social competencies will be maximized. Students can obstruct as well as facilitate each other's learning. Or they can ignore each other. The way students interact depends on how faculty members structure interdependence in the learning situation.

Positive interdependence results in students' promoting each other's learning and achievement. *Promotive interaction* may be defined as individuals' encouraging and facilitating each other's efforts to achieve, complete tasks, and produce in order to reach the group's goals. Whereas positive interdependence in and of itself may have some effect on outcomes, it is the face-to-face promotive interaction among individuals fostered by the positive interdependence that most powerfully influences efforts to achieve, caring and committed relationships, and psychological adjustment and social competence. Students focus both on increasing their own achievement and on increasing the achievement of their groupmates. Promotive interaction is characterized by individuals (Johnson & Johnson, 1989a):

1. Providing each other with efficient and effective help and assistance.
2. Exchanging needed resources such as information and materials, and processing information more efficiently and effectively.
3. Providing each other with feedback in order to improve the subsequent performance of their assigned tasks and responsibilities.
4. Challenging each other's conclusions and reasoning in order to promote higher-quality decision making and greater insight into the problems being considered.
5. Advocating the exertion of effort to achieve mutual goals.
6. Influencing each other's efforts to achieve the group's goals.
7. Acting in trusting and trustworthy ways.
8. Being motivated to strive for mutual benefit.
9. Having a moderate level of arousal characterized by low anxiety and stress.

Negative interdependence typically results in students' opposing each other's success. *Oppositional interaction* occurs as students discourage and obstruct each other's efforts to achieve. Students focus both on increasing their own achievement and on preventing other classmates from achieving higher than they do. *No inter-*

action exists when students work independently without any interaction or interchange with each other. Students focus only on increasing their own achievement and ignore as irrelevant the efforts of others.

Giving and Receiving Assistance and Help

Within most task situations, productivity is enhanced when individuals give each other relevant task-related help and assistance (see Johnson & Johnson, 1989a). Observational studies of actual learning groups consistently find more giving and receiving of help (including cross-ethnic and cross-handicap helping) in cooperative than in competitive or individualistic situations. In both social-psychological and applied behavior research, cooperative structures have enhanced helping and assistance among group members, whereas competitive structures have resulted in individuals' obstructing each other's efforts to achieve, refusing to help and share, and engaging in antisocial behaviors. These effects of competition are exacerbated by losing.

Information Exchange and Cognitive Processes

More efficient and effective exchange and processing of information takes place in cooperative than in competitive or individualistic situations (Johnson, 1974; Johnson & Johnson, 1989a). Although a wide variety of material resources may need to be exchanged in order to complete tasks and accomplish goals, the most common resource shared and exchanged within cooperative efforts is information.

Compared with competitive and individualistic situations, students who work cooperatively (Johnson & Johnson, 1989a):

1. Seek significantly more information from each other than do students working within a competitive goal structure.
2. Are less biased and have fewer misperceptions in comprehending the viewpoints and positions of other individuals.
3. More accurately communicate information by verbalizing ideas and information more frequently, attending to others' statements more carefully, and accepting others' ideas and information more frequently.
4. Are more confident about the value of their ideas.
5. Make optimal use of the information provided by other students.

In cooperative situations, students are bound together by their mutual fate, shared identity, and mutual causation and, therefore, celebrate (and feel benefited by) each other's successes. Relevant ideas, information, conclusions, and resources tend to be made available, exchanged, and utilized in ways that promote collective and individual insights and increase energy to complete the task. Such oral discussion of relevant information has at least two dimensions: oral explanation and listening. Both benefit the giver and the receiver. The *giver* benefits from the cognitive organizing and processing, higher-level reasoning, insights, and personal commitment to achieving the group's goals derived from orally explaining, elaborating, and summarizing information and teaching one's knowledge to others. The *receiver* benefits from the opportunity to utilize others' resources in his or her goal accomplishment efforts.

Information exchange and stimulation of cognitive processes may not occur in competitive or individualistic situations. In *competitive situations* communication and information exchange tends to be nonexistent or misleading and competition biases a person's perceptions and comprehension of viewpoints and positions of other individuals. *Individualistic situations* are usually deliberately structured to ensure that individuals do not communicate or exchange information at all.

Survey research indicates that fear of public speaking is quite common among the general population of adolescents and adults (Motley, 1988). College students, in particular, frequently experience communication apprehension in the classroom (Bowers, 1986). Such speech anxiety, however, can be significantly reduced if students are given the opportunity to first express themselves in the more comfortable social context of a small group of peers (Neer, 1987). Students whose primary language is not English may especially find their anxiety reduced by working in cooperative learning groups.

Peer Feedback

An important aspect of promotive interaction is the opportunity for group members to provide each other with feedback as to how they are fulfilling their responsibilities and completing their work. *Feedback* is information made available to individuals that makes possible the comparison of actual performance with some

standard of performance. *Knowledge of results* is information provided to the person about his or her performance on a given effort. It may be in the form of qualitative information in which the person is informed that a performance is either correct or incorrect. Or it may be quantitative information about how much discrepancy exists between the person's response and the correct response. Usually, quantitative information (i.e., process feedback) about (1) the size of the discrepancy existing between actual performance and some standard of performance or (2) how to improve one's reasoning or performance promotes achievement more effectively than does qualitative information (i.e., terminal feedback) about being right or wrong or what the correct answer is. Receiving personalized feedback from another person increases performance to a greater extent than does receiving impersonal feedback, and peer feedback from collaborators may be especially vivid and personalized. Frequent and immediate feedback serves to increase students' motivation to learn (Mackworth, 1970).

Challenge and Controversy

An important aspect of promotive interaction is *controversy*—the conflict that arises when involved group members have different information, perceptions, opinions, reasoning processes, theories, and conclusions, and they must reach agreement. When controversies arise, they may be dealt with constructively or destructively, depending on how they are managed and the level of interpersonal and small-group skills of the participants. When managed constructively, controversy promotes uncertainty about the correctness of one's views, an active search for more information, a reconceptualization of one's knowledge and conclusions, and, consequently, greater mastery and retention of the material being discussed. Individuals working alone in competitive and individualistic situations do not have the opportunity for such a process and, therefore, their productivity, quality of decision making, and achievement suffer.

Public Advocacy and Commitment

Promotive interaction includes advocating that cooperators increase their efforts to accomplish the group's goals and publicly committing oneself to do the same. *Commitment* may be defined as the binding or pledging of the individual to an act or a decision. To the extent that people act in the absence of coercion, commit themselves to act in front of others, or invest time, money, or personal prestige in an activity, they come to see themselves as believers in that sort of activity and develop a personal interest in it. Individuals become more committed to attitudes that are made public than to attitudes that remain private. People are particularly prone to increase their commitment to actions that they have attempted to persuade another to adopt.

Mutual Influence

During the information-exchange process individuals share ideas and information and utilize each other's resources in order to maximize their productivity and achievement. This entails mutual influence in which cooperators consider each other's ideas and conclusions and coordinate their efforts. Participants must be open to influence attempts aimed at facilitating the accomplishment of shared goals, must trust each other not to use the resources being shared in detrimental ways, and must form emotional bonds that result in commitment to each other's welfare and success. There are three ways in which influence takes place within social situations: direct influence, social modeling, and situational norms. Students will be receptive to the *direct influence* attempts of others to the extent that they perceive a cooperative relationship among goal attainments. In cooperative situations, students benefit from groupmates' *modeling* effective and committed behaviors, skills, and attitudes. Visible and credible models who demonstrate the recommended attitudes and behavior patterns and who directly discuss their importance are powerful influences. Finally, achievement is influenced by whether or not *group norms* favor high performance. Within cooperative situations everyone benefits from the efforts of cooperators and, therefore, group norms support efforts to achieve. There is evidence, furthermore, that in the generally competitive climate of most schools, success at academic tasks has little value for many individuals and may even be a deterrent to popularity with peers (see Johnson & Johnson, 1989a).

Achievement Motivation

Achievement is a *we* thing, not a *me* thing, always the product of many heads and hands.

J. W. Atkinson

Motivation to achieve is reflected in the effort individuals purposely commit to strive to acquire increased understandings and skills they perceive as being meaningful and worthwhile. Although humans may be born with a motivation to increase their competencies, achievement motivation is basically induced through interpersonal processes, through either internalized relationships or current interaction patterns within the learning situation. Depending on whether interaction takes place within a context of positive, negative, or no interdependence, different interaction patterns result, causing different motivational systems, which in turn affect achievement differentially, which determines expectations for future achievement. The motivational system promoted within cooperative situations includes intrinsic motivation, high expectations for success, high incentive to achieve based on mutual benefit, high epistemic curiosity and continuing interest in achievement, high commitment to achieve, and high persistence. The motivational system promoted within competitive situations includes extrinsic motivation to win, low expectations for success by all but the highest-ability individuals, an incentive to learn based on differential benefit, low epistemic curiosity and a lack of continuing interest to achieve, a lack of commitment to achieving, and low task persistence by most individuals. The motivational system promoted within individualistic situations includes extrinsic motivation to meet preset criteria of excellence, low expectations for success by all but the highest-ability individuals, an incentive to achieve based on self-benefit, low epistemic curiosity and continuing interest to achieve, low commitment to achieving, and low task persistence by most individuals.

Motivation is most commonly viewed as a combination of the perceived likelihood of success and the perceived incentive for success. The greater the likelihood of success and the more important it is to succeed, the higher the motivation. Success that is intrinsically rewarding is usually seen as being more desirable for learning than is having students believe that only extrinsic rewards are worthwhile. There is greater perceived likelihood of success, and success is viewed as more important, in cooperative learning situations than in competitive or individualistic (Johnson & Johnson, 1989a). Striving for mutual benefit results in an emotional bonding with collaborators' liking each other, wanting to help each other succeed, and being committed to each other's well-being. These positive feelings toward the group and the other members may have a number of important influences on *intrinsic motivation to achieve* and actual productivity. In many cases, the relationships among group members may become more important than the actual rewards given for the work being done. Consequences provided by group members (e.g., respect, liking, blame, rejection) may supplement or replace those produced by task performance (e.g., salary or grades). Such consequences might be important in sustaining behavior during periods in which no task-based reinforcement is received.

Interpersonal Trust

To disclose one's reasoning and information, one must trust the other individuals involved in the situation to listen with respect. Trust is a central dynamic of promotive interaction. Trust tends to be developed and maintained in cooperative situations and it tends to be absent and destroyed in competitive and individualistic situations (Deutsch, 1958, 1960, 1962; Johnson, 1971, 1973, 1974; Johnson & Noonan, 1972). Trust includes the following elements (Deutsch, 1962):

1. Risk—the anticipation of beneficial or harmful consequences.
2. Realization that others have the power to determine the consequences of one's actions.
3. Expectation that the harmful consequences are more serious than are the beneficial consequences.
4. Confidence that the others will behave in ways that ensure beneficial consequences for oneself.

Interpersonal trust is built through placing one's consequences in the control of others and having one's confidence in the others confirmed. Interpersonal trust is destroyed through placing one's consequences in the hands of others and having one's confidence in the others disconfirmed through their behaving in ways that ensure harmful consequences for oneself. Thus, trust is composed of two sets of behaviors: *Trusting* behavior is the willingness to risk beneficial or harmful consequences by making oneself vulnerable to another person. *Trustworthy* behavior is the willingness to respond to another person's risk taking in a way that ensures that the other person will experience beneficial consequences. In order to establish trust, two or more people must be trustworthy and trusting. Within cooperative situations, individuals tend to be both trusting and trustworthy. Within competitive situations, individuals tend to be distrusting and untrustworthy because they use information to promote their own success and the others' failure.

Anxiety and Performance

Cooperation typically produces less anxiety and stress and more effective coping strategies used to deal with the anxiety than does competition. Anxiety is one of the most pervasive barriers to productivity and positive interpersonal relationships. Anxiety generally leads to an egocentric preoccupation with oneself, disruption of cognitive reasoning, and an avoidance of the feared situation. This can mean skipping school or work, cutting classes or taking long breaks, or avoiding challenging learning and work situations. A continued experience of even moderate levels of anxiety over a number of years, furthermore, can produce psychological and physiological harm. Especially for individuals with a chronic high state of anxiety, cooperation promotes a better learning and work climate.

Summary of Promotive Interaction

Positive interdependence results in promotive interaction, which in turn promotes efforts to achieve, positive interpersonal relationships, and psychological health. *Promotive interaction* may be defined as individuals' encouraging and facilitating each other's efforts to achieve, complete tasks, and produce in order to reach the group's goals. Promotive interaction is characterized by individuals' providing each other with efficient and effective help and assistance, exchanging needed resources such as information and materials and processing information more efficiently and effectively, providing each other with feedback in order to improve the subsequent performance of their assigned tasks and responsibilities, challenging each other's conclusions and reasoning in order to promote higher-quality decision making and greater insight into the problems being considered, advocating the exertion of effort to achieve mutual goals, influencing each other's efforts to achieve the group's goals, acting in trusting and trustworthy ways, being motivated to strive for mutual benefit, and showing a moderate level of arousal characterized

> Cooperation, not conflict, was evidently the selectively most valuable form of behavior for man at any stage of his evolutionary history, and surely, quite as evidently never more so than today. . . . It is essentially the experience, the means, that fits human beings not to their external environment so much as to one another. It must never be forgotten that society is fundamentally, essentially, and in all ways a cooperative enterprise, an enterprise designed to keep men in touch with one another. Without the cooperation of its members society cannot survive, and the society of man has survived because the cooperativeness of its members made survival possible—it was not an advantageous individual here and there who did so, but the group. In human societies the individuals who are most likely to survive are those who are best enabled to do so by their group. —*Ashley Montagu (1965)*

by low anxiety and stress. Oppositional and no interaction results in the opposite pattern of interaction. Promotive interaction results in a number of important outcomes that may be subsumed under three broad categories.

LEARNING OUTCOMES

Different learning outcomes result from the student–student interaction patterns promoted by the use of cooperative, competitive, and individualistic goal structures (Johnson & Johnson, 1989a). The numerous outcomes of cooperative efforts may be subsumed within three broad categories: effort to achieve, positive interpersonal relationships, and psychological adjustment. Since research participants have varied as to economic class, age, sex, and cultural background, since a wide variety of research tasks and measures of the dependent variables have been used, and since the research has been conducted by many different researchers with markedly different orientations working in different settings and in different decades, the overall body of research on social interdependence has considerable generalizability.

EFFORT TO ACHIEVE

Achievement

Over 375 studies have been conducted over the past ninety years to give an answer to the question of how successful competitive, individualistic, and cooperative efforts are in promoting productivity and achievement (Johnson & Johnson,

> The highest and best form of efficiency is the spontaneous cooperation of a free people.
> —*Woodrow Wilson*

1989a). The results are summarized in Table 2.1. When all of the studies were included in the analysis, the average cooperating student performed at about two-thirds a standard deviation above the average student learning within a competitive (effect size = 0.67) or individualistic situation (effect size = 0.64). When only high-quality studies were included in the analysis, the effect sizes were 0.88 and 0.61, respectively. Cooperative learning, furthermore, resulted in more higher-level reasoning, more frequent generation of new ideas and solutions (i.e., process gain), and greater transfer of what is learned within one situation to another (i.e., group-to-individual transfer) than did competitive or individualistic learning.

Some cooperative learning procedures contained a mixture of cooperative, competitive, and individualistic efforts, and others were "pure." The original jigsaw procedure (Aronson, 1978), for example, is a combination of resource interdependence (cooperative) and individual reward structure (individualistic). Teams-Games-Tournaments (DeVries & Edwards, 1974) and Student-Teams-Achievement-Divisions (Slavin, 1980) are mixtures of cooperation and intergroup competition. Team-Assisted-Instruction (Slavin, Leavey, & Madden, 1982) is a mixture of individualistic and cooperative learning. When the results of "pure" and "mixed" operationalizations of cooperative learning were compared, the "pure" operationalizations produced higher achievement (cooperative vs. competitive, pure = 0.71 and mixed = 0.40; cooperative vs. individualistic, pure = 0.65 and mixed = 0.42).

The potential value of cooperative learning in large classes is highlighted by a 1987 study designed to identify what specific factors contributed to student learning in large classes. Wulff, Nyquist, and Abbott (1987) surveyed 800 college students and found that the second most frequently cited factor contributing to their learning in large classes was "other students." The researchers concluded that faculty may wish to use cooperative learning within the large-class context. Levin, Glass, and Meister (1984) concluded from a comparison of the cost-effectiveness of four academic strategies that working with classmates is the most cost-effective support system for increasing student achievement.

That working together to achieve a common goal produces higher achievement and greater productivity than does working alone is so well confirmed by so much research that it stands as one of the strongest principles of social and organizational psychology. Cooperative learning is indicated whenever the learning goals are highly important, mastery and retention are important, the task is complex or conceptual, problem solving is desired, divergent thinking or creativity is desired, quality of performance is expected, and higher-level reasoning strategies and critical thinking are needed.

Why does cooperation result in higher achievement—what mediates? The critical issue in understanding the relationship between cooperation and achievement is specifying the variables that mediate the relationship. Simply placing students in groups and telling them to work together does not in and of itself promote higher achievement. It is only under certain conditions that group efforts may be expected to be more productive than individual efforts. Those conditions are clearly perceived positive interdependence, considerable promotive (face-to-face) interaction, felt personal responsibility (individual accountability) to achieve the group's goals, frequent use of relevant interpersonal and small-group skills, and periodic and regular group processing (Johnson & Johnson, 1989a).

Critical Thinking Competencies

In many subject areas the teaching of facts and theories is considered to be secondary to the development of students' critical thinking and use of higher-level reasoning strategies. The aim of science education, for example, has been to develop individuals "who can sort sense from nonsense," or who have the critical thinking abilities of grasping information, examining it, evaluating it for soundness, and applying it appropriately. The application, evaluation, and synthesis of knowledge and other higher-level reasoning skills, however, are often neglected. *Cooperative learning promotes a greater use of higher-level reasoning strategies and critical thinking than do competitive or individualistic learning strategies* (Gabbert, Johnson, & Johnson, 1986; Johnson & Johnson, 1981a; Johnson, Skon, & Johnson, 1980; Skon, Johnson, & Johnson, 1981). Cooperative learning experiences, for example, promote more frequent insight into and use of higher-level cognitive and moral reasoning strategies than do competitive or individualistic learning experiences (effect sizes = 0.93 and 0.97, respectively).

Studies conducted by Laughlin and his colleagues (Laughlin, 1965, 1973; Laughlin & Jaccard, 1975; Laughlin, McGlynn, Anderson, & Jacobson, 1968; McGlynn, 1972) found more frequent use of a *focusing strategy* (used to figure out a concept underlying a set of numbers or words) in cooperative than in competitive or individualistic situations and, therefore, cooperators solved the problems faster. Studies conducted by Dansereau and his colleagues (Spurlin, Dansereau, Larson, & Brooks, 1984; Larson, Dansereau, O'Donnell, Hythecker, Lambiotte, & Rocklin, 1984) found that an *elaboration strategy* (integrating new information being learned with prior knowledge) was used more frequently by cooperators than by students working individualistically and, therefore, the cooperators performed at a higher level.

In addition to the research directly relating cooperative learning with critical thinking, there are lines of research linking critical thinking and cooperative learning. McKeachie (1988) concludes that at least three elements of teaching make a difference in students' gains in thinking skills: student discussion, explicit emphasis on problem-solving procedures and methods using varied examples, and verbalization of methods and strategies to encourage development of metacognition. He states, "Student participation, teacher encouragement, and student-to-student interaction positively relate to improved critical thinking. These three activities confirm other research and theory stressing the importance of active practice, motivation, and feedback in thinking skills as well as other skills. This confirms that discussions, especially in small classes, are superior to lectures in improving thinking and problem solving." Ruggiero (1988) argues that the explicit teaching of higher-level reasoning and critical thinking does not depend on *what* is taught, but rather on *how* it is taught. He states, "The only significant change that is required is a change in teaching *methodology*" (p. 12). Cooperative learning is such a methodological change.

Research conducted by Schoenfeld (1985, 1989), Brown, Collins and Duguid (1989), Lave (1988), and others indicates that cooperative learning is an important procedure for involving students in meaningful activities in the classroom and engaging in situated cognition. Higher-level writing assignments may also best be done by cooperative peer response groups (DiPardo and Freedman, 1988).

Attitudes Toward Subject Area

Cooperative learning experiences, compared with competitive and individualistic ones, promote more positive attitudes toward the subject area, more positive attitudes toward the instructional experience, and more continuing motivation to learn more about the subject area being studied (Johnson & Johnson, 1989a). McKeachie (1951) and Guetzkow, Kelley, and McKeachie (1954) found in a study comparing group discussion and lecturing that students in discussion sections were significantly more favorable than the other groups in attitude toward psychology, and a follow-up of the students three years later revealed that seven men each from the tutorial and discussion groups majored in psychology, whereas none of those in the recitation group did so. Bligh (1972) found that students who had in-class opportunities to interact actively with classmates and the teacher were more satisfied with their learning experience than were students who were taught exclusively by the lecture method. Kulik and Kulik (1979) reported from their comprehensive literature review on college teaching that students who participated in discussion groups in class were more likely to develop positive attitudes toward the course's subject matter. One of the major conclusions of the Harvard Assessment Seminars was that the use of cooperative learning groups resulted in a large increase in satisfaction with the class (Light, 1990). These findings have important implications for influencing female and minority students to enter science- and math-oriented careers.

Time on Task

Achievement consists of never giving up. . . . If there is no dark and dogged will, there will be no shining accomplishment; if there is no dull and determined effort, there will be no brilliant achievement.

Hsun Tzu, Chinese Confucian philosopher

One explanation for why cooperation promoted greater productivity than did competitive or individualistic efforts is that members of cooperative groups may have spent more time on task. Over thirty studies did in fact measure time on task (see Johnson & Johnson, 1989a). They found that cooperators spent more time on task than did competitors (effect size = 0.76) or students working individualistically (effect size = 1.17). Competitors also spent more time on task than did students working individualistically (effect size = 0.64). These effect sizes are quite large, indicating that members of cooperative learning groups do seem to spend considerably more time on task than do students working competitively or individualistically.

INTERPERSONAL RELATIONSHIPS

Interpersonal Attraction and Cohesion

The degree of emotional bonding that exists among students has a profound effect on the quality of the work that is performed. Evidence from a variety of fields links caring relationships and productivity; one of the most dramatic examples comes from the sport of sled-dog racing. The longest and most grueling sled race in the world is the Alaskan Iditarod, a 1,500-mile race from Anchorage to Nome that winds its way across frozen mountain paths and cuts across long open stretches of land subject to blinding snowstorms. The race was won by a woman in 1985, 1986, 1987, and 1990. When asked if they had any special advantage over men in this race, the winning women said that they developed a closer bond with their dogs and, consequently, their dogs worked harder. A second example may be found in the world of business. When asked about their success, the chief executives of the companies that have the best track records in North America state that they have been successful because they are able to create teams in which members care about each other on a personal as well as a professional level (Kouzes & Posner, 1987). The successful chief executives create a "family" within which members care deeply about each other and the mutual goals they are striving to achieve. Secondary schools should do likewise.

Cooperative learning experiences, compared with competitive, individualistic, and "traditional" instruction, promote considerably more liking among students (effect sizes = 0.66 and 0.60, respectively) (Johnson & Johnson, 1989a; Johnson, Johnson, & Maruyama, 1983) (see Table 2.1). This is true regardless of individual differences in ability level, sex, handicapping conditions, ethnic membership, social class differences, or task orientation. Students who studied cooperatively, compared with those who studied competitively or individualistically, developed considerably more commitment and caring for each other no matter what their initial impressions of and attitudes toward each other were. When only the high-quality studies were included in the analysis, the effect sizes were 0.82 (cooperative vs. competitive) and 0.62 (cooperative vs. individualistic), respectively. The effect sizes are higher for the studies using pure operationalizations of cooperative learning than for studies using mixed operationalizations (cooperative vs. competitive, pure = 0.79 and mixed = 0.46; cooperative vs. individualistic, pure = 0.66 and mixed = 0.36). Students who learned cooperatively also liked the teacher

The fundamental facts that brought about cooperation, society, and civilization and transformed the animal man into a human being are the facts that work performed under the division of labor is more productive than isolated work and that man's reason is capable of recognizing this truth. But for these facts men would have forever remained deadly foes of one another, irreconcilable rivals in their endeavors to secure a portion of the scarce supply of means of sustenance provided by Nature. Each man would have been forced to view all other men as his enemies; his craving for the satisfaction of his own appetites would have brought him into an implacable conflict with all his neighbors. No sympathy could possibly develop under such a state of affairs. . . . We may call consciousness of kind, sense of community, or sense of belonging together the acknowledgement of the fact that all other human beings are potential collaborators in the struggle for survival because the are capable of recognizing the mutual benefits of cooperation. . . . —*Ludwig Von Mises (1949)*

better and perceived the teacher as being more supportive and accepting academically and personally.

In order to be productive, a class of students has to cohere and have a positive emotional climate. As relationships within the class or school become more positive, absenteeism decreases, and increases may be expected in student commitment to learning, feeling of personal responsibility to do the assigned work, willingness to take on difficult tasks, motivation and persistence in working on learning tasks, satisfaction and morale, willingness to endure pain and frustration to succeed, willingness to defend the school against external criticism or attack, willingness to listen to and be influenced by peers, commitment to peers' success and growth, and productivity and achievement (Johnson & F. Johnson, 1991; Johnson & Johnson, 1989a; Watson & Johnson, 1972).

In addition, when students are heterogeneous with regard to social class, language, ethnic, and ability differences, cooperative learning experiences are a necessity for building positive peer relationships. Studies on desegregation indicated that cooperation promoted more positive cross-ethnic relationships than did competitive (effect size = 0.54) or individualistic (effect size = 0.44) learning experiences (Johnson & Johnson, 1989a). Cross-handicapped relationships were also more positive in cooperative than in competitive (effect size = 0.70) or individualistic (effect size = 0.64) learning experiences.

Social Support

A friend is one
to whom one may pour
out all the contents
of one's heart,

chaff and grain together
knowing that the
gentlest of hands
will take and sift it,
keep what is worth keeping
and with a breath of kindness
blow the rest away.

Arabian proverb

Social support may be defined as the existence and availability of people on whom one can rely for emotional, instrumental, informational, and appraisal aid. More specifically, social support involves:

1. Emotional concern such as attachment, reassurance, and a sense of being able to rely on and confide in a person, all of which contribute to the belief that one is loved and cared for.
2. Instrumental aid such as direct aid, goods, or services.
3. Information such as facts or advice that may help to solve a problem.
4. Appraisal such as feedback about the degree to which certain behavioral standards are met (information relevant to self-evaluation).

A *social support system* consists of significant others who collaboratively share people's tasks and goals, who provide individuals with resources (such as money, materials, tools, skills, information, and advice) that enhance their well-being or help people mobilize their resources in order to deal with the particular stressful situation to which they are exposed. Social support is most often reciprocated, and if reciprocity is prevented, the relationship is weakened. Since not all interpersonal interactions are positive, it is assumed that social support is intended by the giver and perceived by the recipient as beneficial to the recipient. Social support may be given by peers or by authority figures. It may be focused on encouraging and assisting efforts to achieve goals (i.e., productivity/achievement support) or it may be focused on personal caring and liking (i.e., personal support).

Social support involves the exchange of resources intended to enhance mutual well-being and the existence and availability of people on whom one can rely for assistance, encouragement, acceptance, and caring. Through providing emotional concern, instrumental aid, information, and feedback, supportive people directly and indirectly promote:

1. Academic achievement and productivity.
2. Physical health—individuals involved in close relationships live longer, get sick less often, and recover from illness faster than do isolated individuals.
3. Psychological health, adjustment, and development by preventing neuroticism and psychopathology, reducing distress, and providing resources such as confidants.
4. Constructive management of stress by providing the caring, resources, information, and feedback needed to cope with stress and by buffering the impact of stress on the individual.

Since the 1940s there have been 106 studies comparing the relative impact of cooperative, competitive, and individualistic efforts on social support. Cooperative experiences tended to promote greater social support than did competitive (effect size = 0.62) or individualistic (effect size = 0.70) efforts. Stronger effects were found for peer support than for superior (teacher) support. For methodologically higher-quality studies, the effect sizes for cooperation compared with competition and individualistic efforts are even stronger (effect sizes = 0.83 and 0.71, respectively). The pure cooperative operationalizations promoted significantly higher levels of social support than did the mixed operationalizations (competitive, mixed = 0.45 and pure = 0.73; individualistic, mixed = 0.02 and pure = 0.77).

Social support is perceived to extend to personal commitment and caring as well as task encouragement. Caring about how much a person achieves and wanting to be the person's friend were perceived to go hand in hand. There was little difference between the levels of task and personal support perceived from peers and superiors.

The importance of social support has been ignored within education over the past thirty years. *A general principle is that the pressure to achieve should always be matched with an equal level of social support.* Challenge and security must be kept in balance (Pelz & Andrews, 1976). Whenever increased demands and pressure to be productive are placed on students (and faculty), a corresponding increase in social support should be structured. Social support and stress are related in that the greater the social support individuals have, the less the stress they experience and the better able they are to manage the stresses involved in their lives. Whenever pressure is placed on individuals to achieve higher and to challenge their intellectual capacities, considerable social support should be provided to buffer the individuals from the stress inherent in the situation and to help them cope constructively with the stress.

Student Retention

Traditional classroom teaching practices in higher education favor the assertive student. But our analysis indicates that instructors should give greater attention to the passive or reticent student. . . . Passivity is an important warning sign that may reflect a lack of involvement that impedes the learning process and leads to unnecessary attrition.

National Institute of Education (1984)

Tinto (1975, 1987), synthesizing the retention research, concluded that the greater the degree of students' involvement in their learning experience, the more likely they were to persist to graduation. The social-networking processes of social involvement, integration, and bonding with classmates are strongly related with higher rates of student retention. Astin (1985), on the basis of research conducted over ten years, found that student involvement academically and socially in the school experience was the "cornerstone" of persistence and achievement. Astin and his associates (1972) had earlier concluded that active involvement in the learning experience was especially critical for "withdrawal-prone" students (such as disadvantaged minorities), who have been found to be particularly passive in academic settings.

Cooperative learning experiences tend to lower attrition rates in schools. Students working on open-ended problems in small groups of four to seven members were more likely to display lower rates of attrition and higher rates of academic achievement than those not involved in the group-learning approach (Wales & Stager, 1978). Treisman (1985) found that the five-year retention rate for black students majoring in math or science at Berkeley who were involved in cooperative learning was 65 percent (compared with 41 percent for black students who were not involved). The percentage of black students involved in cooperative learning experiences who graduated in mathematics-based majors was 44 percent (compared with only 10 percent for a control group of black students not participating in cooperative learning groups).

College students report greater satisfaction with courses that allow them to engage in group discussion (Bligh, 1972; Kulik & Kulik, 1979). Students are more likely to stay in school if they are satisfied with their learning experiences (Noel, 1985). Cooperative learning allows for significant amounts of meaningful student discussion that enhances students' satisfaction with the learning experience and, in so doing, promotes student retention.

Importance of Peer Relationships

There are numerous ways in which peer relationships contribute to social and cognitive development and to socialization. Some of the more important consequences correlated with peer relationships follow. (The specific supporting evidence may be found in Johnson [1980] and Johnson & Johnson [1989a].)

1. In their interaction with peers, individuals directly learn attitudes, values, skills, and information unobtainable from adults. In their interaction with each other, individuals imitate each other's behavior and identify with friends who possess admired competencies. Through providing models, reinforcement, and direct learning, peers shape a wide variety of social behaviors, attitudes, and perspectives.

2. Interaction with peers provides support, opportunities, and models for prosocial behavior. It is within interactions with peers that one helps, comforts, shares with, takes care of, assists, and gives to others. Without peers with whom to engage in such behaviors, many forms of prosocial values and commitments could not be developed. Conversely, whether individuals engage in problem or transition behavior (such as the use of illegal drugs and delinquency) is related to the perceptions of their friends' attitudes toward such behaviors. Being rejected by one's peers tends to result in antisocial behavioral patterns characterized by aggressiveness, disruptiveness, and other negatively perceived behaviors.

3. Individuals frequently lack the time perspective needed to tolerate delays in gratification. As they develop and are socialized, the focus on their own immediate impulses and needs is replaced with the ability to take longer time perspectives.

Peers provide models of, expectations of, directions for, and reinforcements of learning to control impulses. Aggressive impulses provide an example. Peer interaction involving such activities as rough-and-tumble play promotes the acquisition of a repertoire of effective aggressive behaviors and helps establish the necessary regulatory mechanisms for modulating aggressive feelings.

4. Students learn to view situations and problems from perspectives other than their own through their interaction with peers. Such perspective taking is one of the most critical competencies for cognitive and social development. All psychological development may be described as a progressive loss of egocentrism and an increase in ability to take wider and more complex perspectives. It is primarily in interaction with peers that egocentrism is lost and increased perspective taking is gained.

5. **Autonomy** *is the ability to understand what others expect in any given situation and to be free to choose whether to meet their expectations.* Autonomous people are independent of both extreme inner- and outer-directedness. When making decisions concerning appropriate social behavior, autonomous people tend to consider both their internal values and the situational requirements and to then respond in flexible and appropriate ways. Autonomy is the result of (a) the internalization of values (including appropriate self-approval) derived from caring and supportive relationships and (b) the acquisition of social skills and sensitivity. Relationships with peers are powerful influences on the development of the values and the social sensitivity required for autonomy. Individuals with a history of isolation from or rejection by peers often are inappropriately other-directed. They conform to group pressures even when they believe the recommended actions are wrong or inappropriate.

6. Although adults can provide certain forms of companionship, students need close and intimate relationships with peers with whom they can share their thoughts and feelings, aspirations and hopes, dreams and fantasies, and joys and pains. They need constructive peer relationships to avoid the pain of loneliness.

7. Throughout infancy, childhood, adolescence, and early adulthood, a person moves through several successive and overlapping identities. The physical changes involved in growth, the increasing number of experiences with other people, increasing responsibilities, and general cognitive and social development all cause changes in self-definition. The final result should be a coherent and integrated identity. In peer relationships children and adolescents become aware of the similarities and differences between themselves and others. They experiment with a variety of social roles that help them integrate their own sense of self. In peer relationships values and attitudes are clarified and integrated into an individual's self-definition. It is through peer relationships that a frame of reference for perceiving oneself is developed. Gender typing and its impact on one's identity is an example.

8. Coalitions formed during childhood and adolescence provide help and assistance throughout adulthood.

9. The ability to maintain independent, cooperative relationships is a prime manifestation of psychological health. Poor peer relationships in elementary school predict psychological disturbance and delinquency in high school, and poor peer relationships in high school predict adult pathology. The absence of any friendships during childhood and adolescence seems to increase the risk of mental disorder.

10. In both educational and work settings, peers have a strong influence on productivity. Greater achievement is typically found in collaborative situations where peers work together than in situations where individuals work alone.

11. Student educational aspirations may be more influenced by peers than by any other social influence. Similarly, ambition in career settings is greatly influenced by peers. Within instructional settings, peer relationships can be structured to create meaningful interdependence through learning cooperatively with peers. Within cooperative learning situations students experience feelings of belonging, acceptance, support, and caring, and the social skills and social roles required for maintaining interdependent relationships can be taught and practiced.

Through repeated cooperative experiences students can develop the social sensitivity of what behavior is expected from others and the actual skills and autonomy to meet such expectations if they so desire. Through holding each other accountable for appropriate social behavior, students can greatly influence the values they internalize and the self-control they develop. It is through belonging to a series of interdependent relationships that values are learned and internalized. It is through prolonged cooperative interaction with other people that healthy social development, with the overall balance of trust rather than distrust of other people, the ability to view situations and problems from a variety of perspectives, a meaningful sense of direction and purpose in life, an awareness of mutual interdependence with others, and an integrated and coherent sense of personal identity, takes place (Johnson, 1979; Johnson & Matross, 1977).

In order for peer relationships to be constructive influences, they must promote feelings of belonging, acceptance, support, and caring, rather than feelings of hostility and rejection (Johnson, 1980). Being accepted by peers is related to willingness to engage in social interaction, utilizing abilities in achievement situations, and providing positive social rewards for peers. Isolation from peers is associated with high anxiety, low self-esteem, poor interpersonal skills, emotional handicaps, and psychological pathology. Rejection by peers is related to disruptive classroom behavior, hostile behavior and negative affect, and negative attitudes toward other students and school. In order to promote constructive peer influences, therefore, teachers first must ensure that students interact with each other and, second, must ensure that the interaction takes place within a cooperative context.

PSYCHOLOGICAL HEALTH

Psychological Adjustment

When students leave school, they require psychological health and stability to build and maintain career, family, and community relationships, to establish a basic and meaningful interdependence with other people, and to participate effectively in society. We have conducted a series of studies on the relationship between coop-eration and psychological health. Our studies (see Johnson & Johnson, 1989a) indicate that *cooperativeness* is positively related to a number of indices of psycho-logical health, namely: emotional maturity, well-adjusted social relations, strong personal identity, and basic trust in and optimism about people. *Competitiveness* seems also to be related to a number of indices of psychological health, whereas *individualistic attitudes* tend to be related to a number of indices of psychological pathology, such as emotional immaturity, social maladjustment, delinquency, self-alienation, and self-rejection. Schools should be organized cooperatively to rein-force those traits and tendencies that promote students' psychological well-being.

Accuracy of Perspective Taking

Social perspective taking is the ability to understand how a situation appears to another person and how that person is reacting cognitively and emotionally to the situation. The opposite of perspective taking is *egocentrism*, the embeddedness in one's own viewpoint to the extent that one is unaware of other points of view and of the limitation of one's perspective. Cooperative learning experiences tend to promote greater cognitive and affective perspective taking than do competitive or individualistic learning experiences (Johnson & Johnson, 1989a). Bovard (1951a, 1951b) and McKeachie (1954) found that students participating in class discus-sions (as opposed to listening to lectures) showed greater insight (as rated by clinical psychologists) into problems of the young women depicted in the film "The Feeling of Rejection."

Self-Esteem

We must see our own goodness, appreciate our assets and abilities, and celebrate our humanness.

Dennis Wholey

A person is not born with a sense of self. It is during the first two or three years that a kind of crude self-awareness develops, such as being able to make distinctions between what is part of his or her body and what is part of something else. It takes many years of maturation before full adult self-awareness comes into being. As people develop self-awareness, they formulate a self-conception and build proc-esses through which they derive conclusions about their self-worth. *Self-esteem* is a judgment about one's self-worth, value, and competence based on a process of conceptualizing and gathering information about oneself and one's experiences (Johnson & Norem-Hebeisen, 1981). It has two components: the level of worth a person places on him- or herself and the processes through which individuals derive conclusions about their self-worth. Conclusions about self-esteem may be

derived through at least five processes (Johnson, 1979; Norem-Hebeisen, 1974, 1976; Norem-Hebeisen & Johnson, 1981): basic self-acceptance (the perceived intrinsic acceptability of oneself), conditional self-acceptance (the perceived acceptability of oneself resulting from outperforming others and meeting external standards and expectations), comparative self-evaluation (the estimate of how positively one's attributes compare with those of peers), reflected self-acceptance (seeing oneself as others see one), and real-ideal self-esteem (the correspondence between what one thinks one is and what one thinks one should be). The final conclusion has not been studied in connection with social interdependence. Many studies, furthermore, used academic self-esteem (the self-perception of one being a capable, competent, and successful student) as a dependent measure.

Since the 1950s there have been over eighty studies comparing the relative impact of cooperative, competitive, and individualistic experiences on self-esteem. Cooperative efforts promoted higher self-esteem than did competitive (effect size = 0.58) or individualistic (effect size = 0.44) efforts (Johnson & Johnson, 1989a). These findings are consistent across high-, medium-, and low-quality studies. The pure operationalizations of cooperation had a significantly stronger impact on self-esteem than did the mixed operationalizations (competitive, mixed = 0.33 and pure = 0.74; cooperative vs. individualistic, mixed = 0.22 and pure = 51). A similar pattern was found for academic self-esteem and reflected self-esteem. Our own research demonstrated that cooperative experiences tended to be related to beliefs that one is intrinsically worthwhile—believing that others see one in positive ways, comparing one's attributes favorably with those of one's peers, and judging that one is a capable, competent, and successful person (Johnson, 1979; Norem-Hebeisen, 1974, 1976; Norem-Hebeisen & Johnson, 1981). In cooperative efforts, students (a) realized that they were accurately known, accepted, and liked by one's peers (basic self-acceptance), (b) knew that they had contributed to their own, others', and the group's success (reflected self-esteem), and (c) perceived themselves and others in a differentiated and realistic way that allowed for multidimensional comparisons based on complementarity of their own and others' abilities (comparative self-evaluation). In cooperative situations, individuals tend to interact, promote each other's success, form multidimensional and realistic impressions of each other's competencies, and give accurate feedback. Such interaction tends to promote a basic self-acceptance of oneself as a competent person. Competitive experiences tend to be related to conditional self-esteem based on whether one wins or loses. Competitors' self-esteem tends to be based on the contingent view of one's competence that "if I win, then I have worth as a person, but if I lose, then I have no worth." Winners attribute their success to superior ability and attribute the failure of others to lack of ability, both of which contribute to self-aggrandizement. Losers, who are the vast majority, defensively tend to be self-disparaging, are apprehensive about evaluation, and tend to withdraw psychologically and physically. Individualistic experiences tend to be related to basic self-rejection. In individualistic situations, students are isolated from one another, receive little direct comparison with or feedback from peers, and perceive evaluations as inaccurate and unrealistic. A defensive avoidance, evaluation apprehension, and distrust of peers results.

Social Skills

If you want one year of prosperity, grow grain.
If you want ten years of prosperity, grow trees.
If you want one hundred years of prosperity, grow people.

Chinese proverb

Most people realize that education or vocational training improves their career opportunities. Many people are less aware that interpersonal skills may be the most important set of skills to their employability, productivity, and career success. A recent national survey found that employers value five types of skills: verbal communication skills, responsibility, interpersonal skills, initiative, and decision-making skills. In 1982, the Center for Public Resources published *Basic Skills in the U.S. Workforce*, a nationwide survey of businesses, labor unions, and educational institutions. They found that 90 percent of the people fired from their jobs were fired for poor job attitudes, poor interpersonal relationships, inappropriate behavior, and inappropriate dress. Being fired for lack of basic and technical skills was infrequent. Even in high-tech careers, the ability to work effectively with other high-tech personnel is essential, and so is the ability to communicate and work with people from other professions to solve interdisciplinary problems. In the real world of work, the heart of most jobs—especially the higher-paying, more interesting jobs—is getting others to cooperate, leading others, coping with complex power and influence issues, and helping solve people's problems in working with each other (Johnson & Johnson, 1989a).

Social competence is an essential aspect of psychological health. We are not born instinctively knowing how to interact effectively with others. Interpersonal and group skills do not magically appear when they are needed. Many individuals lack basic interpersonal skills such as correctly identifying the emotions of others and appropriately resolving a conflict, and often their social ineptitude seems to persist as they get older. Their lives typically do not go well. Individuals who lack social skills find themselves isolated, alienated, and at a disadvantage in vocational and career settings. The relationships so essential for living productive and happy lives are lost when the basic interpersonal skills are not learned.

Generally, students may be taught social skills more effectively in work contexts than in isolation from actually completing a meaningful task. Working together to learn increases students' social skills. To coordinate efforts to achieve mutual goals, students must get to know and trust each other, communicate accurately and unambiguously, accept and support each other, and resolve conflicts constructively (Johnson, 1993; Johnson & F. Johnson, 1991). Interpersonal and small-group skills form the basic nexus among individuals, and if individuals are to work together productively and cope with the stresses and strains of doing so, they must have a modicum of these skills.

There are a number of studies that have examined the impact of cooperative learning experiences on the mastery and use of social skills. Lew, Mesch, Johnson, and Johnson (1986a, 1986b) found that socially isolated and withdrawn students learned more social skills and engaged in them more frequently within cooperative than within individualistic situations, especially when the group was rewarded for their doing so. Slavin (1977) found that emotionally disturbed adolescents who experienced cooperative learning were more likely than traditionally taught students to interact appropriately with other students, and this effect was still present five months after the end of the project. Janke (1980) found enhancing effects of cooperative learning on appropriate interactions among emotionally disturbed students and also found that the program improved these students' attendance. More generally, cooperation promotes more frequent, effective, and accurate communication than do competitive and individualistic situations (Johnson, 1973, 1974). Within cooperative situations communication is more open, effective, and accurate, whereas in competitive situations communication will be closed, ineffective, and inaccurate (Bonoma, Tedeschi, & Helm, 1974; Crombag, 1966; Deutsch, 1949b, 1962; Deutsch & Krauss, 1962; Fay, 1970; French, 1951; Grossack, 1953; Krauss & Deutsch, 1966; Johnson, 1971, 1973, 1974).

One of the most important sets of social skills to master is conflict resolution. Involved participation in cooperative efforts inevitably produces conflicts. The more caring and committed the relationships, furthermore, the more intense conflicts tend to be (Johnson & Johnson, 1991a, 1992a). Cooperative efforts provide a context in which the structures and skills for managing conflicts constructively may be successfully implemented and learned. Cooperation, furthermore, promotes more constructive management of conflicts than do competitive and individualistic efforts (Deutsch, 1962, 1973; Johnson, 1971, 1973, 1974).

Inculcating Constructive Attitudes

From the standpoint of everyday life . . . there is one thing we do know; that man is here for the sake of other men—above all, for those upon whose smile and well-being our own happiness depends, and also for the countless unknown souls with whose fate we are connected by a bond of sympathy. Many times a day I realize how much my own outer and inner life is built upon the labors of my fellow men, both living and dead, and how earnestly I must exert myself in order to give in return as much as I have received.

Albert Einstein

There are many attitudes and behavioral patterns that are essential to psychological health that schools wish to inculcate in students. Students need to develop a love of learning, curiosity, the desire to distinguish between sense and nonsense, and the ability to use higher-level reasoning to solve problems. Students also need to develop a desire to do high-quality work, a desire to improve continuously, and a sense of pride and accomplishment in doing a good job. They need to develop self-respect, respect for other people, and respect for property. They need to learn how to reliably fulfill assigned roles. Students need to develop a meaningful purpose and direction in life, develop a desire to achieve, and aspire to contribute to making the world a better place. Students need to develop a love of democracy, liberty, and freedom; a high level of patriotism; and a desire to be a good citizen. They need to learn to value the diversity of people within our society. Furthermore, students need to develop lifelong good health habits such as nutritious eating patterns, adequate sleep each night, and regular exercise.

In many subject areas (such as health, art, music), educators have designed instructional programs aimed at promoting a lifelong pattern of attitudes and behavior. Yet the issues of creating enduring conceptual frameworks, positive attitudes, and behavioral habits have been slighted in most discussions of educational practice.

It is through interpersonal influences that attitudes are acquired and behavioral patterns are changed. And it is through the cognitive processing resulting from interpersonal interaction that conceptual frameworks are developed and retained over long periods of time. The factors involved in promoting learning, developing desirable attitudes, and establishing lifelong behavioral patterns are (Johnson & Johnson, 1985):

1. Adopting and conforming to the norms of the reference groups to which one belongs and aspires to belong, and with which one identifies.
2. Publicly committing oneself to adopt desired attitudes and behavior, and being held accountable by peers to fulfill one's public commitments.
3. Being exposed to visible and credible social models.
4. Being confronted with vivid and personalized information and appeals.
5. Discussing information with peers in ways that promote active cognitive processing and the development of enduring conceptual frameworks.
6. Teaching information one has learned to others.

7. Acquiring continuing motivation to learn.

8. Framing information received as a gain or a loss.

RECIPROCAL RELATIONSHIPS
AMONG THE THREE OUTCOMES

The reason we were so good, and continued to be so good, was because he [Joe Paterno] forces you to develop an inner love among the players. It is much harder to give up on your buddy, than it is to give up on your coach. I really believe that over the years the teams I played on were almost unbeatable in tight situations. When we needed to get that six inches, we got it because of our love for each other. Our camaraderie existed because of the kind of coach and kind of person Joe was.

Dr. David Joyner

Efforts to achieve, positive interpersonal relationships, and psychological health are reciprocally related (see Figure 2.2, earlier in this chapter). Within cooperative situations, the three outcomes are all bidirectional. Each induces and is induced by the others.

Joint efforts to achieve mutual goals create caring and committed relationships; caring and committed relationships among group members increase their effort to achieve (Johnson & Johnson, 1989a). From working together to accomplish academic tasks, students develop camaraderie and friendships. As students strive together, helping each other, sharing materials, exchanging ideas and information, and encouraging each other's efforts they get to know each other, become committed to each other, and develop friendships. Caring relationships come from mutual accomplishment, mutual pride in joint work, and the bonding that results from joint efforts. At the same time, caring and committed relationships promote joint efforts to achieve mutual goals. Individuals seek out opportunities to work with those they care about. As caring increases, so does regular attendance, commitment to learning and achievement, personal responsibility to do one's share of the work, willingness to take on difficult tasks, motivation and persistence in working toward goal achievement, willingness to listen to and be influenced by groupmates, and willingness to endure pain and frustration on behalf of the group (Johnson & F. Johnson, 1991; Johnson & Johnson, 1989a; Watson & Johnson, 1972). All of these contribute to group productivity. The most successful leaders in business and industry are ones who build teams with such personal closeness that team members feel like a family (Kouses & Posner, 1987).

Joint efforts to achieve mutual goals promote psychological health and social competence; the more psychologically healthy group members are, the more able they are to contribute to the joint effort (Johnson & Johnson, 1989a). Cooperating involves contributing to others' success and well-being, knowing there are others who contribute to your success and well-being, and being involved in a joint effort greater than oneself. Working together to complete academic tasks increases a person's social competencies, success, sense of meaning and purpose, ability to cope with failure and anxiety, self-esteem, and self-efficacy. Contributing to others' success has been found to cure the "blues" (decrease depression). Knowing that one's efforts contribute to the success of others as well as oneself gives added meaning and value to academic work. At the same time, the psychologically healthier individuals are, the better able they are to work with others to achieve mutual goals. States of depression, anxiety, guilt, shame, and fear interfere with ability to cooperate and decrease the energy a person has to devote to a cooperative effort. Joint efforts require coordination, effective communication, leadership, and conflict management, which in turn require social competencies.

The more caring and committed the relationships among group members, the greater their psychological health and social competencies tend to be; the healthier members are psychologically, the more able they are to build and maintain caring and committed relationships (Johnson & Johnson, 1989a). Psychological health is built on the internalization of the caring and respect received from loved ones. Through the internalization of positive relationships, direct social support, shared intimacy, and expressions of caring, psychological health and the ability to cope with stress are built. Friendships are developmental advantages that promote self-esteem, self-efficacy, and general psychological adjustment. Destructive relationships, and even the absence of caring and committed relationships, tend to increase psychological pathology. At the same time, the healthier people are psychologically (i.e., free of psychological pathology such as depression, paranoia, anxiety, fear of failure, repressed anger, hopelessness, and meaninglessness), the more they are able to initiate, build, and maintain caring and committed relationships.

REDUCING THE DISCREPANCY

Research results consistently indicate that cooperative learning will promote higher achievement, more positive interpersonal relationships, and higher self-esteem than will competitive or individualistic efforts. Although there may be a place for competitive and individualistic efforts in classrooms, there are those who believe that competition is inherently destructive (Kohn, 1986). From his review of the research, Alfie Kohn concludes that making others fail is not only an unproductive way to work and learn but also devastating to individuals and society, as competition (1) causes anxiety, selfishness, self-doubt, and poor communication; (2) poisons relationships among individuals, thereby making life more unpleasant than it needs to be; and (3) often results in outright aggression. Kohn (1990) also notes that competitive structures create a negative view of human nature as solitary individuals striving to maximize personal gain. He presents evidence that there is a brighter side to human nature based on our relationships with others characterized by altruism, empathy, caring, and commitment. Kohn would replace all competition in higher education with cooperative efforts.

With the amount of research evidence available, it is surprising that classroom practice is so oriented toward competitive and individualistic learning and schools are so dominated by competitive and individualistic organizational structures. *It is time for the discrepancy to be reduced between what research indicates is effective in teaching and what faculty actually do.* In order to do so, faculty must understand the role of the teacher in implementing cooperative learning experiences. In the next three chapters we focus on the essential elements of cooperative lessons and the teacher's role in using formal cooperative learning groups, informal cooperative learning groups, and cooperative base groups.

3

Basic Elements of Cooperative Learning

INTRODUCTION

The Killer Bees is a boys' high school basketball team from Bridgehampton, New York (a small, middle-class town on Long Island) (described in Katzenbach & Smith, 1993). Bridgehampton High School's total enrollment has declined since 1985 from sixty-seven to forty-one, with fewer than twenty males attending the high school. There have never been more than seven players on the team. Yet, since 1980 the Killer Bees have amassed a record of 164 wins and 32 losses, qualified for the state championship playoffs six times, won the state championship twice, and finished in the final four two other times. None of their players was ever really a star and the team members were never tall. Not one of the Killer Bees went on to play professional basketball. Although every Killer Bee graduated and most went to college, few had the talent to play basketball in college.

How did the Killer Bees become so successful with so few players and no star players? There are at least three reasons why the Killer Bees consistently won against bigger, supposedly more talented, opponents. The first is that the Killer Bees' game was "team basketball." They won not by superior talent but through superior teamwork. The second reason is that team members adopted an incredible work ethic. They practiced 365 days a year on skill development and teamwork. The third reason was their versatility and flexibility in how they played their opponents. The source of the Killer Bees' focus on team work, hard work, and versatility was a richness and depth of purpose that eludes most teams. Their mission was more than winning basketball games. They were committed to bringing honor and recognition to their community and protecting and enhancing their legacy. They were also committed to each other. The commitment of team members was reciprocated by the community, whose members came to every game and relentlessly cheered the team on.

It is the potential for such performances that make cooperative groups the key to successful education. Teamwork can do for learning what it did for the Killer Bees' basketball performance. *The truly committed cooperative learning group is probably the most productive instructional tool educators have.* Creating and maintaining truly committed cooperative learning groups, however, is far from easy. In most classrooms they are rare, perhaps because many educators:

1. Are confused about:
    a. What is (and is not) a cooperative learning group.
    b. The "basics" that make cooperative learning groups work.
2. Lack the discipline to implement the basics of cooperative efforts in a rigorous way.

In this chapter we shall differentiate cooperative learning groups from other types of groups, note the characteristics of pseudo and traditional classroom groups, and discuss the basic elements of cooperation. Finally, we note that educators need to develop the discipline to structure the basics of cooperation in every learning group.

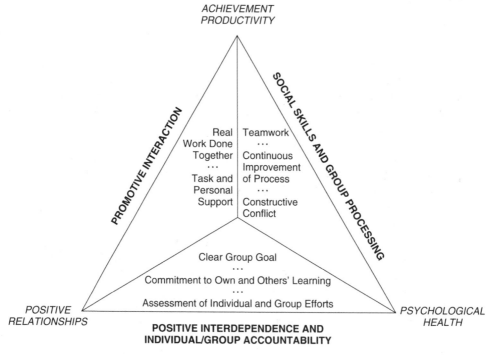

FIGURE 3.1 Cooperative efforts

MAKING POTENTIAL GROUP PERFORMANCE A REALITY

Not all groups are cooperative groups. Placing people in the same room and calling them a cooperative group does not make them one. Having a number of people work together does not make them a cooperative group. Study groups, project groups, lab groups, committees, task forces, departments, and councils are groups, but they are not necessarily cooperative. Groups do not become cooperative groups simply because that is what someone labels them.

The authors have studied cooperative learning groups for 30 years. We have interviewed thousands of students and teachers in a wide variety of school districts in a number of different countries over three different decades to discover how groups are used in the classroom and where and how cooperative groups work best. On the basis of our findings and the findings of other researchers such as Katzenbach and Smith (1993), we have developed a learning group performance curve to clarify the difference between traditional classroom groups and cooperative learning groups (Figure 3.2).

The learning group performance curve illustrates that how well any small group performs depends on how it is structured. On the performance curve four types of learning groups are described. It begins with the individual members of the group and illustrates the relative performance of these students to pseudo groups, traditional classroom groups, cooperative learning groups, and high-performance cooperative learning groups.

A *pseudo-learning group* is a group whose members have been assigned to work together but have no interest in doing so. They meet, but do not want to work

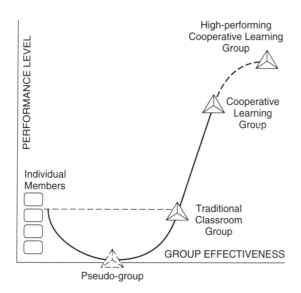

FIGURE 3.2 The learning group performance curve

together or help each other succeed. Members often block or interfere with each other's learning, communicate and coordinate poorly, mislead and confuse each other, loaf, and seek a free ride. The interaction among group members detracts from individual learning without delivering any benefit. The result is that the sum of the whole is less than the potential of the individual members. The group does not mature because members have no interest in or commitment to each other or the group's future.

A *traditional classroom learning group* (see Table 3.1) is a group whose members have accepted that they are to work together, but see little benefit from doing so. Interdependence is low. The assignments are structured so that very little if any joint work is required. Members do not take responsibility for anyone's learning other than their own. Members interact primarily to share information and clarify how the assignments are to be done. Then they each do the work on their own. And their achievements are individually recognized and rewarded. Students are accountable as separate individuals, not as members of a team. Students do not receive training in social skills, and a group leader who is in charge of directing members' participation is appointed. There is no processing of the quality of the group's efforts.

A *cooperative learning group* is more than a sum of its parts. It is a group whose members are committed to the common purpose of maximizing each other's learning. It has a number of defining characteristics. First, the group goal of maximizing all members' learning provides a compelling purpose that motivates members to roll up their sleeves and accomplish something beyond individual achievements. Each member takes responsibility for the performance of himself or herself, all teammates, and the group as a whole. Members believe that "they sink

TABLE 3.1   Traditional Learning Groups versus Cooperative Learning Groups

TRADITIONAL CLASSROOM GROUPS	COOPERATIVE LEARNING GROUPS
Low Interdependence. Members Take Responsibility Only For Self. Focus Is On Individual Performance Only.	High Positive Interdependence. Members Are Responsible For Own And Each Other's Learning. Focus Is On Joint Performance.
Individual Accountability Only.	Both Group And Individual Accountability. Members Hold Self And Others Accountable For High Quality Work.
Assignments Are Discussed With Little Commitment To Each Other's Learning.	Members Promote Each Other's Success, Doing Real Work Together, Helping And Supporting Each Other's Efforts To Learn.
Teamwork Skills Are Ignored. Leader Is Appointed To Direct Members' Participation.	Teamwork Skills Are Emphasized. Members Are Taught And Expected To Use Social Skills. Leadership Shared By All Members.
No Group Processing Of The Quality Of Its Work. Individual Accomplishments Are Rewarded.	Group Processes Quality Of Work And How Effectively Members Are Working Together. Continuous Improvement Is Emphasized.

or swim together," and "if one of us fails, we all fail." Second, in a cooperative group the focus is both on group and individual accountability. Group members hold themselves and each other accountable for doing high quality work. And they also hold themselves and each other accountable for achieving the overall group goals. Third, group members do real work together. They not only meet to share information and perspectives, they produce discrete work-products through members' joint efforts and contributions. And they give whatever assistance and encouragement is needed to promote each other's success. Through promoting each other's success, group members provide both academic and personal support based on a commitment to and caring about each other. Fourth, members are taught social skills and are expected to use them to coordinate their efforts and achieve their goals. Both taskwork and teamwork skills are emphasized. All members accept the responsibility for providing leadership. Finally, groups analyze how effectively they are achieving their goals and how well members are working together. There is an emphasis on continuous improvement of the quality of their learning and team-work processes.

A *high-performance cooperative learning group* is a group that meets all the criteria for being a cooperative learning group and outperforms all reasonable expectations, given its membership. What differentiates the high-performance group from the cooperative learning group is the level of commitment members have to each other and the group's success. Jennifer Futernick, who is part of a high-performing, rapid response team at McKinsey & Company, calls the emotion binding her teammates together a form of love (Katzenbach & Smith, 1993). Ken Hoepner of the Burlington Northern Intermodal Team (also described by Katzenbach & Smith, 1993) stated: "Not only did we trust each other, not only did we respect each other, but we gave a damn about the rest of the people on this team. If we saw somebody vulnerable, we were there to help." Members' mutual concern for each other's personal growth enables high-performance cooperative groups to perform far above expectations, and also to have lots of fun. The bad news about high-performance cooperative groups is that they are rare. Most groups never achieve this level of development.

FORCES HINDERING GROUP PERFORMANCE

Performance and small groups go hand-in-hand. Although cooperative groups outperform individuals working alone, there is nothing magical about groups. There are conditions under which groups function effectively and conditions under which groups function ineffectively. Potential barriers to group are effectiveness are (Johnson & F. Johnson, 1994):

1. *Lack of Group Maturity:* Group members need time and experience working together to develop into an effective group. Temporary, ad hoc groups usually do not develop enough maturity to function with full effectiveness.

2. *Uncritically Giving One's Dominant Response:* A central barrier to higher-level reasoning and deeper-level understanding is the uncritical giving of members' dominant response to academic problems and assignments. Instead, members should generate a number of potential answers and choose the best one.

3. *Social Loafing—Hiding in the Crowd:* When a group is working on an *additive task* (group product is determined by summing together individual group members' efforts), and individual members can reduce their effort without other members realizing that they are doing so, many people tend to work less hard. Such social loafing has been demonstrated on a variety of additive tasks such as rope pulling, shouting, and clapping.

4. *Free Riding—Getting Something for Nothing:* On *disjunctive tasks* (if one member does it, all members receive the benefit), there is the possibility of a free ride. When group members realize that their efforts are dispensable (group success or failure depends very little on whether or not they exert effort), and when their efforts are costly, group members are less likely to exert themselves on the group's behalf.

5. *Motivation Losses Due to Perceived Inequity—Not Being a Sucker:* When other group members are free riding, there is a tendency for the members who are working to reduce their efforts to avoid being a "sucker."

6. *Groupthink:* Groups can be overconfident in their ability and resist any challenge or threat to their sense of invulnerability by avoiding any disagreements and seeking concurrence among members.

7. *Lack of Sufficient Heterogeneity:* The more homogeneous the group members, the less each member adds to the group's resources. Groups must develop the right mix of taskwork and teamwork skills necessary to do their work. Heterogeneity ensures a wide variety of resources are available for the group's work.

8. *Lack of Teamwork Skills:* Groups with members who lack the small group and interpersonal skills required to work effectively with others often underperform their most academically able members.

9. *Inappropriate Group Size:* The larger the group, the fewer members that can participate, the less essential each member views their personal contribution, the more teamwork skills required, and the more complex the group structure.

Not every group is effective. Most everyone has been part of a group that wasted time, was inefficient, and generally produced poor work. But there are groups accomplish wondrous things. Educators must be able to spot the above characteristics of ineffective groups and take action to eliminate them. The hindering factors are eliminated by the basics of cooperation.

APPLYING THE BASICS OF COOPERATION

Educators fool themselves if they think well-meaning directives to "work together," "cooperate," and "be a team," will be enough to create cooperative efforts among students. *There is a discipline to creating cooperation.* The "basics" of structuring cooperation are not a series of elements that characterize good groups. They are a regimen that, if followed rigorously, will produce the conditions for effective cooperation. Cooperative learning groups are rare because educators (and students) seek shortcuts to quality groupwork and assume that "traditional classroom groups will do." Like persons who wish to lose weight without dieting, they seek easy alternatives to the disciplined application of the basics of effective groups.

The basics of cooperation are *not* new and startling to most educators. They already have a good idea of what the basics are. *The performance potential of learning groups, however, is frequently lost due to educators not applying what they know about cooperative efforts in a disciplined way.* The basic components of effective cooperative efforts are positive interdependence, individual and group accountability, face-to-face promotive interaction, appropriate use of social skills, and group processing.

POSITIVE INTERDEPENDENCE: "WE INSTEAD OF ME"

All for one and one for all.
    Alexandre Dumas

Within a football game, the quarterback who throws the pass and the receiver who catches the pass are positively interdependent. The success of one depends on the success of the other. It takes two to complete a pass. One player cannot succeed without the other. Both have to perform competently if their mutual success is to be assured. If one fails, they both fail.

The discipline of using cooperative groups begins with structuring positive interdependence (see Johnson & Johnson, 1992b, 1992c). Group members have to know that they "sink or swim together." It is positive interdependence that requires group members to roll up their sleeves and work together to accomplish something

beyond individual success. It is positive interdependence that creates the realization that members have two responsibilities: to learn the assigned material and to ensure that all members of their group learn the assigned material. When positive interdependence is clearly understood, it highlights (a) each group member's efforts are required and indispensable for group success (i.e., there can be no "free-riders") and (b) each group member has a unique contribution to make to the joint effort because of his or her resources and/or role and task responsibilities (i.e., there can be no social loafing).

There are three steps in structuring positive interdependence. *The first is assigning the group a clear, measurable task.* Members have to know what they are supposed to do. *The second step is to structure positive goal interdependence* so members believe that they can attain their goals if and only if their groupmates attain their goals. In other words, members know that they cannot succeed unless all other members of their group succeed. Positive goal interdependence ensures that the group is united around a common goal, a concrete reason for being, such as "learn the assigned material and make sure that all members of your group learn the assigned material." Positive goal interdependence may be structured by informing group members they are responsible for:

1. All members scoring above a specified criterion when tested individually.
2. The overall group score (determined by adding the individual scores of members together) being above a specified criterion.
3. One product (or set of answers) successfully completed by the group.

Individuals contribute more energy and effort to meaningful goals than to trivial ones. Being responsible for others' success as well as for one's own gives cooperative efforts a meaning that is not found in competitive and individualistic situations. The efforts of each group member, therefore, contribute not only to their own success, but also the success of groupmates. When there is meaning to what they do, ordinary people exert extraordinary effort. It is positive goal interdependence that gives meaning to the efforts of group members.

The third step is to supplement positive goal interdependence with other types of positive interdependence. Reward/celebration interdependence is structured when (a) each group member receives the same tangible reward for successfully completing a joint task (e.g., if all members of the group score 90 percent correct or better on the test, each will receive 5 bonus points) or (b) group members jointly celebrate their success. Regular celebrations of group efforts and success enhance the quality of cooperation. In order for students to look forward to working in cooperative groups, and enjoy doing so, they must feel that their efforts are appreciated and they are respected as an individual. Long-term commitment to achieve is largely based on feeling recognized and respected for what one is doing. Thus, students' efforts to learn and promote each other's learning need to be observed, recognized, and celebrated. The celebration of individual efforts and group success involves structuring reward interdependence. Ways of structuring positive reward interdependence include:

1. Celebrating their joint success when all members reach criterion.
2. Adding bonus points to all members' academic scores when everyone in the group achieves up to criterion or when the overall group score reaches criterion.
3. Receiving nonacademic rewards (such as extra free time, extra recess time, stickers, stars, or food) when all group members reach criterion.
4. Receiving a single group grade for the combined efforts of group members. This should be cautiously done until all students (and parents) are very familiar with cooperative learning.

Role interdependence is structured when each member is assigned complementary and interconnected roles (such as reader, recorder, checker of understanding, encourager of participation, and elaborator of knowledge) that specify responsibilities that the group needs in order to complete the joint task. Roles prescribe what other group members expect from a person (and therefore the person is obligated to do) and what that person has a right to expect from other group members who have complementary roles. In cooperative groups responsibilities are often divided into roles that help the group achieve its goals and roles that help members maintain effective working relationships with each other. Such roles are vital to high-quality learning. The role of checker, for example, focuses on periodically asking each groupmate to explain what is being learned. Rosenshine and Stevens (1986) reviewed a large body of well-controlled research on teaching effectiveness and found "checking for comprehension" to be one specific teaching behavior that was significantly associated with higher levels of student learning and achievement. While the teacher cannot continually check the understanding of every student (especially if there are thirty or more students in the class), the teacher can engineer such checking by having students work in cooperative groups and assigning one member the role of checker.

Resource interdependence is structured when each member has only a portion of the information, materials, or resources necessary for the task to be completed and members' resources have to be combined in order for the group to achieve its goal. Ways of structuring resource interdependence include:

1. Limiting the resources given to the group. Only one pencil, for example, may be given to a group of three students.
2. Jigsawing materials so that each member has part of a set of materials. A group could be given the assignment of writing a biography of Abe Lincoln and information on Lincoln's childhood given to one member, information on Lincoln's early political career given to another, information on Lincoln as president given to a third, and information on Lincoln's assassination given to the fourth member.

3. Having each member make a separate contribution to a joint product. Each member, for example, could be asked to contribute a sentence to a paragraph, an article to a newsletter, or a chapter to a "book."

Identity interdependence is structured when the group established a mutual identity through a name or a group symbol such as a motto, flag, or song. *Outside enemy interdependence* (striving to perform higher than other groups) and *fantasy interdependence* (striving to solve hypothetical problems such as how to deal with being shipwrecked on the moon.) *Task interdependence* is structured by creating a division of labor so that the actions of one group member have to be completed if the next group member is to complete his or her responsibilities. *Environmental interdependence* exists when group members are bound together by the physical environment in some way (such as a specific area to meet in).

The heart of cooperative efforts is positive interdependence. Without positive interdependence, cooperation does not exist. Positive interdependence may focus on joint outcomes or on the mutual effort required to achieve the group's goals. Positive goal and reward interdependence (with the related identity, outside enemy, fantasy, and environmental interdependence) result in members realizing that all group members (Johnson & Johnson, 1989a):

1. *Share a common fate* where they all gain or lose on the basis of the overall performance of group members. One result is a sense of personal responsibility for the final outcome and to do their share of the work.
2. *Are striving for mutual benefit* so that all members of the group will gain. There is recognition that what helps other group members benefits oneself and what promotes one's own productivity benefits the other group members.
3. *Have a long-term time perspective* so that long-term joint productivity is perceived to be of greater value than short-term personal advantage.
4. *Have a shared identity* based on group membership. Besides being a separate individual, one is a member of a team. The shared identity binds members together emotionally and creates an expectation for a *joint celebration* based on mutual respect and appreciation for the success of group members. The experience creates a positive cathexis so that group members like each other. Feelings of success are shared and pride is take in other members' accomplishments as well as one's own.

Positive resource, role, and task interdependence result in individuals realizing that the performance of group members is *mutually caused*. No member is on his or her own. Each person views himself or herself as instrumental in the productivity of other group members and views other group members as being instrumental in his or her productivity. Members realize that their efforts are required in order for the group to succeed (i.e., there can be no "free-riders") and that their potential contribution to the group as being unique (because of their role, resources, or task responsibilities). Each member shares responsibilities for other members' productivity (*mutual responsibility*) and is obligated to other members for their support and assistance (*mutual obligation*). As a result of the mutual causation, cooperative efforts are characterized by *positive inducibility* in that group members are open to being influenced by each other and *substitutability* in that the actions of group members substitute for each other so that if one member of the group has taken the action there is no need for other members to do so. There is a *mutual investment* in each other.

The authors have conducted a series of studies investigating the nature of positive interdependence and the relative power of the different types of positive interdependence (Frank, 1984; Hwong, Caswell, Johnson, & Johnson, 1993; Johnson, Johnson, Stanne, & Garibaldi, 1990; Johnson, Johnson, Ortiz, & Stanne, 1991; Lew, Mesch, Johnson, & Johnson, 1986a, 1986b; Mesch, Johnson, & Johnson, 1988; Mesch, Lew, Johnson, & Johnson, 1986). Six questions concerning positive interdependence have been addressed by our research. The first question is whether group membership in and of itself is sufficient to produce higher achievement and productivity or whether group membership and positive interdependence are required. The results of Hwong, Caswell, Johnson, and Johnson (1993) indicate that positive interdependence is necessary. Knowing that one's performance affects the success of groupmates seems to create "responsibility forces" that increase one's efforts to achieve.

The second question is whether interpersonal interaction is sufficient to increase productivity or whether positive interdependence is required. Debra Mesch and Marvin Lew conducted a series of studies in which they investigated whether the relationship between cooperation and achievement was due to the opportunity to interact with peers or positive goal interdependence. Their results are quite consistent. The individuals achieved higher under positive goal interdependence than when they worked individualistically but had the opportunity to interact with classmates (Lew, Mesch, Johnson, & Johnson, 1985a, 1985b; Mesch, Johnson, & Johnson, 1988; Mesch, Lew, Johnson, & Johnson, 1985).

The third question is whether goal or reward interdependence is most important in promoting productivity and achievement. The results of the Mesch and Lew studies indicate that while positive goal interdependence is sufficient to produce higher achievement and productivity than an individualistic effort, the combination of goal and reward interdependence is even more effective. The impact of the two types of outcome interdependence seem to be additive.

The fourth question is whether different types of reward interdependence have differential effects on productivity. Michael Frank's (1984) study indicates not. Both working to achieve a reward and working to avoid the loss of a reward produced higher achievement than did individualistic efforts.

The fifth question is whether goal or resource interdependence is most important in enhancing productivity and achievement. Johnson and Johnson (in press) found goal interdependence promoted higher achievement than did resource interdependence. The study by Johnson, Johnson, Stanne, and Garibaldi indicated that while goal interdependence in and of itself increased achievement, the combination of goal and resource interdependence increased achievement even further. Compared with individualistic efforts, the use of resource interdependence alone seemed to decrease achievement and lower productivity.

Finally, there is a question as to whether positive interdependence simply motivates individuals to try harder or facilitates the development of new insights and discoveries through promotive interaction. The latter position is supported by the fact that some studies have found that members of cooperative groups use higher level reasoning strategies more frequently than do individuals working individualistically or competitively.

In summary, our research indicates that positive interdependence provides the context within which promotive interaction takes place, group membership and interpersonal interaction among students do not produce higher achievement unless positive interdependence is clearly structured, the combination of goal and reward interdependence increased achievement over goal interdependence alone, and resource interdependence does not increase achievement unless goal interdependence is present also.

INDIVIDUAL ACCOUNTABILITY/PERSONAL RESPONSIBILITY

What children can do together today, they can do alone tomorrow.

Vygotsky

Among the early settlers of Massachusetts there was a saying, "If you do not work, you do not eat." Everyone had to do his or her fair share of the work. *The discipline of using cooperative groups includes structuring group and individual accountability. Group accountability* exists when the overall performance of the group is assessed and the results are given back to all group members to compare against a standard of performance. *Individual accountability* exists when the performance of each individual member is assessed, the results given back to the individual and the group to compare against a standard of performance, and the member is held responsible by groupmates for contributing his or her fair share to the group's success. On the basis of the feedback received, (a) efforts to learn and contribute to groupmates' learning can be recognized and celebrated, (b) immediate remediation can take place by providing any needed assistance or encouragement, and (c) groups can reassign responsibilities to avoid any redundant efforts by members.

The purpose of cooperative groups is to make each member a stronger individual in his or her own right. Individual accountability is the key to ensuring that all group members are in fact strengthened by learning cooperatively. After participating in a cooperative lesson, group members should be better prepared to complete similar tasks by themselves. There is a pattern to classroom learning. First, students learn knowledge, skills, strategies, or procedures in a cooperative group. Second, students apply the knowledge or perform the skill, strategy, or procedure alone to demonstrate their personal mastery of the material. Students learn it together and then perform it alone.

One can acquire everything in solitude—except character. —*Henri Beyle*

No man is an island, entire of itself; every man is a piece of the continent, a part of the main. —*John Donne*

Not vain the weakest, if their force unite. —*Homer*

Together we stand, divided we fall. —*Watchword of the American Revolution*

Union gives strength. —*Aesop*

Two heads are better than one. —*Heywood*

All for one and one for all, that is our device. —*Alexandre Dumas*

The true security is to be found in social solidarity rather than in isolated individual effort. —*Fyodor Dostoyevsky*

If we would seek for one word that describes society better than any other, the word is *cooperation.* —*Ashley Montagu*

There is no violent struggle between plants, no warlike killing, but a harmonious development on a share-and-share-alike basis. The cooperative principle is stronger than the competitive one. —*Frits W. Went*, Plants

Individual accountability results in group members knowing they cannot "hitch-hike" on the work of others. When it is difficult to identify members' contributions, when members' contributions are redundant, and when members are not responsible for the final group outcome, members sometimes engage in social loafing or seek a free ride (Harkins & Petty, 1982; Ingham, Levinger, Graves, & Peckham, 1974; Kerr & Bruun, 1981; Latane, Williams & Harkins, 1979; Moede, 1927; Petty, Harkins, Williams, & Latane, 1977; Williams, 1981; Williams, Harkins, & Latane, 1981). Common ways to structure individual accountability include:

1. Keeping the size of the group small. The smaller the size of the group, the greater the individual accountability.
2. Giving an individual test to each student.
3. Giving random oral examination. Students are randomly selected to present his or her group's work to you (in the presence of the group) or to the entire class.
4. Observing each group and recording the frequency with which each member contributes to the group's work.
5. Assigning one student in each group the role of checker. The *checker* asks other group members to explain the reasoning and rationale underlying group answers.
6. Having students teach what they learned to someone else. When all students do this, it is called simultaneous explaining.

Positive Interdependence and Individual Accountability

In cooperative situations, group members share responsibility for the joint outcome. Each group member takes personal responsibility for (a) contributing his or her efforts to accomplish the group's goals and (b) helping other group members do likewise. The greater the positive interdependence structured within a cooperative learning group, the more students will feel personally responsible for contributing their efforts to accomplish the group's goals. The shared responsibility adds the concept of ought to members' motivation—one ought to do one's share, contribute, and pull one's weight. The shared responsibility also makes each group member personally accountable to the other group members. Students will realize that if they fail to do their fair share of the work, other members will be disappointed, hurt, and upset.

FACE-TO-FACE PROMOTIVE INTERACTION

In an industrial organization it's the group effort that counts. There's really no room for stars in an industrial organization. You need talented people, but they can't do it alone. They have to have help.

John F. Donnelly, President, Donnelly Mirrors

The discipline of using cooperative groups includes ensuring that group members meet face-to-face to work together to complete assignments and promote each other's success. Group members need to do real work together. *Promotion interaction* exists when individuals encourage and facilitate each other's efforts to complete tasks in order to reach the group's goals. Through promoting each other's success, group members build both an academic and a personal support system for each member. There are three steps to encouraging promotive interaction among group members. *The first is to schedule time for the group to meet.* As simple as this step seems, many learning groups are not given sufficient meeting time to mature and develop. *The second step is to highlight the positive interdependence that requires members to work together to achieve the group's goals.* It is positive interdependence that creates the commitment to each other's success. *The third step is to encourage promotive interaction among group members.* Monitoring groups and celebrating instances of members' promotive interaction is one way to do so.

While positive interdependence in and of itself may have some effect on outcomes, it is the face-to-face promotive interaction among individuals fostered by the positive interdependence that most powerfully influences efforts to achieve, caring and committed relationships, and psychological adjustment and social competence (Johnson & Johnson, 1989a). Promotive interaction is characterized by individuals providing each other with efficient and effective help and assistance, exchanging needed resources such as information and materials and processing information more efficiently and effectively, providing each other with feedback in order to improve subsequent performance, challenging each other's conclusions and reasoning in order to promote higher-quality decision making and greater insight into the problems being considered, advocating the exertion of effort to achieve mutual goals, influencing each other's efforts to achieve the group's goals, acting in trusting and trustworthy ways, being motivated to strive for mutual benefit, and a moderate level of arousal characterized by low anxiety and stress. Members do real work together.

INTERPERSONAL AND SMALL GROUP SKILLS

I will pay more for the ability to deal with people than any other ability under the sun.

John D. Rockefeller

Placing socially unskilled students in a group and telling them to cooperate does not guarantee that they are able to do so effectively. We are not born instinctively knowing how to interact effectively with others. Interpersonal and small group skills do not magically appear when they are needed. Students must be taught the social skills required for high quality collaboration and be motivated to use them if cooperative groups are to be productive. The whole field of group dynamics is based on the premise that social skills are the key to group productivity (Johnson & F. Johnson, 1994).

The fourth arena in the disciplined use of cooperative groups is teaching group members the small group and interpersonal skills they need to work effectively with each other. In cooperative learning groups students are required to learn academic subject matter (*taskwork*) and also to learn the interpersonal and small group skills required to function as part of a group (*teamwork*). If the teamwork skills are not learned, then the taskwork cannot be completed. If group members are inept at teamwork, their taskwork will tend to be substandard. On the other hand, the greater the members' teamwork skills, the higher will be the quality and quantity of their learning. Cooperative learning is inherently more complex than competitive or individualistic learning because students have to simultaneously engage in taskwork and teamwork. In order to coordinate efforts to achieve mutual goals, students must (a) get to know and trust each other, (b) communicate accurately and unambiguously, (c) accept and support each other, and (d) resolve conflicts constructively (Johnson, 1991, 1993; Johnson & F. Johnson, 1994).

The more socially skillful students are, and the more attention teachers pay to teaching and rewarding the use of social skills, the higher the achievement that can be expected within cooperative learning groups. In their studies on the long-term implementation of cooperative learning, Marvin Lew and Debra Mesch (Lew, Mesch, Johnson, & Johnson, 1986a, 1986b; Mesch, Johnson, & Johnson, 1988; Mesch, Lew, Johnson, & Johnson, 1986) investigated the impact of a reward

contingency for using social skills as well as positive interdependence and a contingency for academic achievement on performance within cooperative learning groups. In the cooperative skills conditions students were trained weekly in four social skills and each member of a cooperative group was given two bonus points toward the quiz grade if all group members were observed by the teacher to demonstrate three out of four cooperative skills. The results indicated that the combination of positive interdependence, an academic contingency for high performance by all group members, and a social skills contingency promoted the highest achievement.

GROUP PROCESSING

Take care of each other. Share your energies with the group. No one must feel alone, cut off, for that is when you do not make it.

Willi Unsoeld, Renowned Mountain Climber

The final phase of the discipline of using cooperative groups is structuring group processing. Effective group work is influenced by whether or not groups reflect on (process) how well they are functioning. A *process* is an identifiable sequence of events taking place over time, and *process goals* refer to the sequence of events instrumental in achieving outcome goals (Johnson & F. Johnson, 1994). *Group processing* may be defined as reflecting on a group session to (a) describe what member actions were helpful and unhelpful and (b) make decisions about what actions to continue or change. The purpose of group processing is to clarify and improve the effectiveness of the members in contributing to the collaborative efforts to achieve the group's goals.

There are five steps in structuring group processing in order to improve continuously the quality of the group's taskwork and teamwork (see Johnson, Johnson, & Holubec, 1993a). *The first is to assess the quality of the interaction among group members as they work to maximize each other's learning.* The easiest way to conduct such assessments of the "process" of how the group gets its work done is for the teacher to observe the cooperative learning groups as they work. The teacher systematically moves from group to group and uses a formal observation sheet or checklist to gather specific data on each group. The frequency with which targeted social skills are used can be recorded.

Systematic observation allows teachers to attain a "window" into students' minds. Listening to students explain how to complete the assignment to group-mates provides better information about what students do and do not know and understand than do correct answers on tests or homework assignments. Listening in on students' explanations provides valuable information about how well the students understand the instructions, the major concepts and strategies being learned, and the basics of working together effectively. Wilson (1987, p. 18) conducted a three-year, teaching-improvement study as part of a college faculty development program. Both faculty and students agreed that faculty needed help on knowing if the class understood the material or not.

Teachers are not the only ones who can observe groups and record data about their functioning. A student observer can be appointed for each learning group (rotating the responsibility for each lesson). And at the end of a lesson, each group member can fill out a checklist as to the frequency with which they engaged in each targeted social skill. It is often helpful to assess the quality of the overall group product so groups can compare how well they performed with specific patterns of interaction among members.

The second step in examining the process by which the group does its work is to give each learning group feedback. Teachers need to allocate some time at the end of each class session for each cooperative group to process how effectively members worked together. Group members need to describe what actions were helpful and unhelpful in completing the group's work and make decisions about what behaviors to continue or change. The data collected can be taken from the checklists and placed in a Pareto chart to focus the discussion on current levels of effectiveness and how to improve the quality of the group's work. Individual efforts that

contribute to the group's success need to be recognized and celebrated. Such small group processing (a) enables learning groups to focus on maintaining good working relationships among members, (b) facilitates the learning of cooperative skills, (c) ensures that members receive feedback on their participation, (d) ensures that students think on the metacognitive as well as the cognitive level, and (e) provides the means to celebrate the success of the group and reinforce the positive behaviors of group members. Some of the keys to successful small group processing are allowing sufficient time for it to take place, providing a structure for processing (such as "List three things your group is doing well today and one thing you could improve"), emphasizing positive feedback, making the processing specific rather than general, maintaining student involvement in processing, reminding students to use their cooperative skills while they process, and communicating clear expectations as to the purpose of processing.

Group processing provides a structure for group members to hold each other accountable for being responsible and skillful group members. In order to contribute to each other's learning, group members need to attend class, be prepared (i.e., have done the necessary homework), and contribute to the group's work. A student's absenteeism and lack of preparation often demoralizes other members. Productive group work requires members to be present and prepared, and there should be some peer accountability to be so. When groups "process," they discuss any member actions that need to be improved in order for everyone's learning to be maximized.

The third step is for groups to set goals as to how to improve their effectiveness. Members suggest ways the teamwork could be improved and the group decides which suggestions to adopt. Discussing group functioning is essential. A common teaching error is to provide too brief a time for students to process the quality of their collaboration. Students do not learn from experiences that they do not reflect on. If the learning groups are to function better tomorrow than they did today, members must receive feedback, reflect on how their actions may be more effective, and plan how to be even more skillful during the next group session.

The fourth step is to process how effectively the whole class is functioning. In addition to small group processing, teachers should periodically conduct whole-class processing sessions. At the end of the class period the teacher can then conduct a whole-class processing session by sharing with the class the results of his or her observations. If each group had a student observer, the observation results for each group may be added together to get an overall class total.

The fifth step is to conduct small-group and whole-class celebrations. It is feeling successful, appreciated, and respected that builds commitment to learning, enthusiasm about working in cooperative groups, and a sense of self-efficacy about subject-matter mastery and working cooperatively with classmates.

Stuart Yager examined the impact on achievement of (a) cooperative learning in which members discussed how well their group was functioning and how they could improve its effectiveness, (b) cooperative learning without any group processing, and (c) individualistic learning (Yager, Johnson, & Johnson,

1985). The results indicate that the high-, medium-, and low-achieving students in the cooperation-with-group-processing condition achieved higher on daily achievement, post-instructional achievement, and retention measures than did the students in the other two conditions. Students in the cooperation-without-group-processing condition, furthermore, achieved higher on all three measures than did the students in the individualistic condition. Johnson, Johnson, Stanne, and Garibaldi (1990) conducted a follow-up study comparing cooperative learning with no-processing, cooperative learning-with-teacher processing (teacher specified co-operative skills to use, observed, and gave whole-class feedback as to how well students were using the skills), cooperative learning with teacher and student processing (teacher specified cooperative skills to use, observed, gave whole-class feedback as to how well students were using the skills, and had learning groups discuss how well they interacted as a group), and individualistic learning. Forty-nine high ability Black American high school seniors and entering college freshmen at Xavier University participated in the study. A complex computer-assisted problem-solving assignment was given to the students. All three cooperative conditions performed higher than the individualistic condition. The combination of teacher and student processing resulted in greater problem-solving success than did the other cooperative conditions. Julie Archer-Kath (Archer-Kath, Johnson, & Johnson, in press) studied the impact of the combination of group and individual feedback with group feedback only on student performance and attitudes. Fifty-six eighth-grade midwestern students studying German were used as subjects. The investigators found that the combination of group and individual feedback resulted in higher achievement motivation, actual achievement, and more positive attitudes toward each other, the subject area, the teacher, and themselves.

POSITIVE INTERDEPENDENCE AND INTELLECTUAL CONFLICT

The greater the positive interdependence within a learning group, the greater the likelihood of intellectual disagreement and conflict among group members. When members of a cooperative learning group become involved in a lesson, their different information, perceptions, opinions, reasoning processes, theories, and conclusions will result in intellectual disagreement and conflict. When such controversies arise, they may be dealt with constructively or destructively, depending on how they are managed and the level of interpersonal and small group skills of the participants. When managed constructively, controversy promotes uncertainty about the correctness of one's conclusions, an active search for more information, a reconceptualization of one's knowledge and conclusions and, consequently, greater mastery and retention of the material being discussed and the more frequent use of higher-level reasoning strategies (Johnson & Johnson, 1979, 1989a, 1992a). Individuals working alone in competitive and individualistic situations do

not have the opportunity for such intellectual challenge and, therefore, their achievement and quality of reasoning suffer.

REDUCING PROBLEM BEHAVIORS

When students first start working in cooperative learning groups they sometimes engage in unhelpful behaviors. Whenever inappropriate student behavior occurs, the teacher's first move should be toward strengthening the perceived interdependence within the learning situation. When you see students not participating or not bringing their work or materials, you may wish to increase positive interdependence by jigsawing materials, assigning the student a role that is essential to the group's success, or rewarding the group on the basis of their average performance (thus increasing the peer pressure on the student to participate).

When a student is talking about everything but the assignment, you may wish to give a reward that this student or group finds especially attractive and structure the task so that all members must work steadily and contribute in order for the group to succeed and attain the reward.

When you see a student working alone and ignoring the group discussion, you may wish to limit the resources in the group (if there is only one answer sheet or pencil in the group, the member will be unable to work independently) or jigsaw materials so that the student cannot do the work without the other members' information.

When you see a student refusing to let other members participate or bullying other members you may wish to jigsaw resources, assign roles so that other group members have the most powerful roles, or reward the group on the basis of the lowest two scores by group members on a unit test.

SUMMARY

Cooperative learning groups and student learning are inextricably connected. The truly committed cooperative learning group is probably the most productive instructional tool teachers have at their disposal, provided that teachers know what cooperative efforts are and have the discipline to structure them in a systematic way. Despite the fact that most educators are familiar with cooperative learning groups, many educators are imprecise in their thinking about cooperative efforts. For that reason, gaining a clear understanding of what a cooperative learning group is and is not and the basics of making cooperative efforts effective, can provide insights useful for strengthening the performance of cooperative learning groups. Imprecise thinking about cooperative learning groups, however, pales in comparison to the lack of discipline most educators bring to using cooperative learning groups in instructional situations.

Not all groups are cooperative groups. Groups can range from pseudo learning groups to traditional classroom groups to cooperative learning groups to high-performance cooperative learning groups. High-performance cooperative learning groups are rare. Most cooperative groups never reach this level. Many educators who believe that they are using cooperative learning are, in fact, using traditional classroom groups. There is a crucial difference between simply putting students in groups to learn and in structuring cooperation among students. Cooperation is *not* having students sit side-by-side at the same table to talk with each other as they do their individual assignments. Cooperation is *not* assigning a report to a group of students where one student does all the work and the others put their names on the product as well. Cooperation is *not* having students do a task individually with instructions that the ones who finish first are to help the slower students. Cooperation is much more than being physically near other students, discussing material with other students, helping other students, or sharing material among students, although each of these is important in cooperative learning.

Educators can examine any learning group and decided where on the group performance curve it now is. Pseudo learning groups and traditional classroom groups are characterized by group immaturity, members uncritically giving their dominant response in completing assignments, members engaging in social loafing and free riding, members losing motivation to learn, groupthink, homogeneity of skills and abilities, and inappropriate group size and resources. Cooperative learning groups are characterized by members perceiving clear positive interdependence, holding each other personally and individually accountable to do his or her fair share of the work, promoting each other's learning and success, appropriately using the interpersonal and small group skills needed for successful cooperative efforts, and processing as a group how effectively members are working together. These five essential components must be present for small group learning to be truly cooperative.

Creating cooperative learning groups is not easy. It takes daily, disciplined application of the basics of cooperative efforts. These basics are tough standards and present a difficult implementation challenge to teachers. At the same time, working hard to ensure that the basics are present in each learning group will accelerate teachers' efforts to ensure that all students are achieving up to their full potential. In structuring the five basic elements into cooperative efforts, teachers must differentiate between three types of cooperative learning groups. The use of cooperative formal, informal, and base groups is discussed in the following chapters.

4

Formal Cooperative Learning

INTRODUCTION

A number of years ago, a speeding car carrying five teenagers slammed into a tree, killing three of them. It was not long before small, spontaneous memorials appeared at the tree. A yellow ribbon encircled its trunk. Flowers were placed nearby on the ground. There were a few goodbye signs. Such quiet testimonies send an important message: When it really matters, we are part of a community, not isolated individuals. We define ourselves in such moments as something larger than our individual selves—as friends, classmates, teammates, and neighbors.

Many students have the delusion that each person is separate and apart from all other individuals. It is easy to be concerned only with yourself. But when classmates commit suicide and when cars slam into trees, the shock waves force us out of the shallowness of self into the comforting depth of community. An important advantage of placing students in cooperative learning groups and having them work together with a wide variety of peers to complete assignments is the resultant sense of belonging, acceptance, and caring. In times of crisis, such community may mean the difference between isolated misery and deep personal talks with caring friends.

Being part of a community does not "just happen" when a person enters school. Being known, being liked and respected, and being involved in relationships that provide help and support do not magically happen. School life can be lonely. Although many students are able to develop the relationships with classmates and fellow students to provide themselves with support systems, other students are unable to do so. Schools have to carefully structure student experiences to build a learning community. A learning community is characterized by two types of social support. The first is an academic support group that provides any needed assistance and helps students succeed academically. The second is a personal support group made up of people who care about and are personally committed to the student. Both academic and personal support systems result from the use of all three types of cooperative learning.

TYPES OF COOPERATIVE LEARNING GROUPS

Cooperative learning may be incorporated into courses through the use of *formal learning groups,* which stay together until the task is done (triad that ensures all members master the information assigned about the Revolutionary War); *informal learning groups,* which are short term (check the person next to you to see if he or she understood); and *base groups,* which are long-term groups whose role is primarily one of peer support and long-term accountability. Gaining expertise in using formal cooperative learning groups provides the foundation for using the other two. This chapter, therefore, focuses on formal cooperative learning groups. Informal cooperative learning groups and base groups are discussed in Chapter 5.

FORMAL COOPERATIVE LEARNING GROUPS

One of Roger's favorite demonstration science lessons is to ask students to determine how long a candle burns in a quart jar. He assigns students to groups of two, making the pairs as heterogeneous as possible. Each pair is given one candle and one quart jar (resource interdependence). He gives the instructional task of timing how long the candle will burn and the cooperative goal of deciding on one answer that both pair members can explain. Students are to encourage each other's participation and relate what they are learning to previous lessons (social skills). Students light their candle, place the quart jar over it, and time how long the candle burns. The answers from the pairs are announced. Roger then gives the pairs the task of generating a number of answers to the question, "How many factors make a difference in how long the candle burns in the jar?" The answers from the pairs are written on the board. The pairs then repeat the experiment in ways that test which of the suggested factors do in fact make a difference in how long the candle burns. The next day students individually take a quiz on the factors affecting the time a candle burns in a quart jar (individual accountability) and their scores are totaled to determine a joint score that, if high enough, earns them bonus points (reward interdependence). They spend some time discussing the helpful actions of each member and what they could do to be even more effective in the future (group processing).

In formal cooperative learning groups students work together, from one class period to several weeks, to achieve shared learning goals and to complete specific

TABLE 4.1 Appropriate Cooperation

Interdependence	Positive.
Type of Instructional Activity	Any instructional task. The more conceptual and complex the task, the greater the cooperation.
Perception of Goal Importance	Goal is perceived to be important.
Teacher–Student Interaction	Teacher monitors and intervenes in learning groups to teach cooperative skills.
Student–Materials Interaction	Materials are arranged according to purpose of lesson.
Student–Student Interaction	Prolonged and intense interaction among students, helping and sharing, oral rehearsal of material being studied, peer tutoring, and general support and encouragement.
Student Expectations	Group to be successful. All members to contribute to success. Positive interaction among group members. All members master the assigned material.
Room Arrangement	Small groups.
Evaluation Procedures	Criterion-referenced.

tasks and assignments. Formal cooperative learning groups may be used in a wide variety of ways. They may be structured specifically for learning of information, concept learning, problem solving, conducting science experiments, or composition. Before exploring each of these structures, the aspects of the teacher's role common to all are described.

Interdependence

Cooperative learning exists when students' goal attainments are positively correlated; when one student obtains his or her goal, all other students with whom he or she is cooperatively linked obtain their goals (Deutsch, 1949a). The learning goal is perceived to be important and students expect to achieve the goal with some help and assistance from fellow group members.

Appropriate Tasks

Cooperation is appropriate for any instructional task. The more conceptual the task, the more problem solving and decision making required, and the more creative answers need to be, the greater the superiority of cooperative over competitive and individualistic learning. Whenever problem solving is desired, whenever divergent thinking or creativity is desired, whenever quality of performance is expected, whenever higher-level reasoning strategies are needed, whenever long-term retention is desired, whenever the task is complex or conceptual, when the learning goals are highly important, and when the social development of students is one of the major instructional goals, cooperative learning should be used.

Teacher–Student Interaction

The teacher is used infrequently as a source for ideas and solutions. The teacher monitors the functioning of the learning groups and intervenes to teach collaborative skills and provide task assistance when it is needed. The teacher is more a consultant to promote effective group functioning than a technical expert. Typical statements a teacher may make are, "Check with your group," "Does anyone in your group know?" "Make sure everyone in your group understands."

Student–Materials Interaction

Depending on the instructional goals, each student may receive an individual set of materials, the group may receive one set of materials, or students may receive part of the required materials and be responsible for teaching their portion to the other group members.

Student–Student Interaction

Other students are perceived to be the major resource for assistance, feedback, reinforcement, and support. Students should be sitting so that each student can see all the other members of the group and can be heard without needing to shout (and disturb the other groups). These small groups should be spaced in the classroom in such a way as to maximize the distance between them.

Student Role Expectations

Students expect to interact with other students, to share ideas and materials, to support and encourage academic achievement, and to hold each other accountable for learning. Students will expect their group to be successful and for every member to contribute in some way to that success.

Evaluation System

A criteria-referenced evaluation system is used within cooperative learning situations.

THE TEACHER'S ROLE: BEING "A GUIDE ON THE SIDE"

In each class session teachers must make the choice of being "a sage on the stage" or "a guide on the side." In doing so they might remember that the challenge in teaching is not covering the material for the students; it's uncovering the material with the students.

Within cooperative learning situations, the teacher forms the learning groups, teaches the basic concepts and strategies, monitors the functioning of the learning groups, intervenes to teach small-group skills, provides task assistance when it is needed, evaluates students' learning using a criterion-referenced system, and ensures that the cooperative groups process how effectively members worked together. Students look to their peers for assistance, feedback, reinforcement, and support.

The teacher's role in using formal cooperative learning groups includes five parts (Johnson, Johnson, & Holubec, 1993):

1. Specifying the objectives for the lesson.
2. Making decisions about placing students in learning groups before the lesson is taught.
3. Explaining the task and goal structure to the students.
4. Monitoring the effectiveness of the cooperative learning groups and intervening to provide task assistance (such as answering questions and teaching task skills) or to increase students' interpersonal and group skills.
5. Evaluating the students' achievement and helping students discuss how well they collaborated with each other.

SPECIFYING THE INSTRUCTIONAL OBJECTIVES

There are two types of objectives that a teacher needs to specify before the lesson begins. The *academic objective* needs to be specified at the correct level for the students and matched to the right level of instruction according to a conceptual or task analysis. The *social skills objective* details what interpersonal and small-group skills are going to be emphasized during the lesson. Every lesson has both academic objectives that define what students are to learn and social skills objectives needed to train students to cooperate effectively with each other.

PREINSTRUCTIONAL DECISIONS

Deciding on the Size of the Group

Group size may vary according to the specific objectives and circumstances. Cooperative learning groups typically range in size from two to four. The basic rule of thumb about group size is, "the smaller the better." When in doubt, go with pairs or triads. In selecting the size of a cooperative learning group, remember:

1. As the size of the learning group increases, the range of abilities, expertise, and skills increase, as does the number of minds available for acquiring and processing information.
2. The larger the group, the more skillful group members must be in providing everyone with a chance to speak, coordinating the actions of group members, reaching

consensus, ensuring explanation and elaboration of the material being learned, keeping all members on task, and maintaining good working relationships. Within a pair students have to manage two interactions. Within a group of three there are six interactions to manage. Within a group of four there are twelve interactions to manage. As the size of the group increases, the interpersonal and small-group skills required to manage the interactions among group members become far more complex and sophisticated. Very few students have the social skills needed for effective group functioning even for small groups. A common mistake made by many teachers is to have students work in groups of four, five, and six members before the students have the skills to do so competently.

3. The materials available or the specific nature of the task may dictate a group size.

4. The shorter the period of time available, the smaller the learning group should be. If there is only a brief period of time available for the lesson, then smaller groups will be more effective because they take less time to get organized, they operate faster, and there is more "air time" per member.

Assigning Students to Groups

There are a number of ways to assign students to groups (see Johnson, Johnson, & Holubec, 1993). *Perhaps the easiest and most effective way is to assign students to groups randomly.* A teacher can divide the number of students in the class by the size of the group desired (thirty students divided by group size three equals counting off by ten). Variations on this procedure include counting off in languages other than English (Spanish or French, for example), or randomly handing out cards with the names of states and capitals on them and asking students to find their partner.

A *related procedure is stratified random assignment* where, for example, a pretest is given; the class is divided into high, medium, and low scorers; and one student from each category is randomly assigned to a triad. Or students' learning styles can be diagnosed and one student from each category randomly assigned to each learning group.

A *third method is teacher-selected groups.* Teachers can usually put together optimal combinations of students. The teacher can ensure that nonachievement-oriented students are a minority in each group or that students who trigger disruptive behavior in each other are not together.

One of our favorite methods is asking students to list three classmates with whom they would like to work. From their lists, the classroom isolates (whom no one wants to work with) can be identified. The teacher builds a group of skillful and supportive students around each isolated student.

The least-recommended procedure is to have students select their own groups. Student-selected groups often are homogeneous, with high-achieving students working with other high-achieving students, white students working with other white students, minority students working with other minority students, and males working with other males. Often there is less on-task behavior in student-selected than in teacher-selected groups. A useful modification of the "select your own group" method is to have students list whom they would like to work with and then place them in a learning group with one person they choose and one or two (or more) students that the teacher selects.

Teachers often ask three questions about assigning students to groups.

1. Should students be placed in learning groups that are homogeneous or heterogeneous in member ability? There are times when cooperative learning groups that are homogeneous in ability may be used to master specific skills or to achieve certain instructional objectives. Generally, however, in heterogeneous groups there is more elaborative thinking, more frequent giving and receiving of explanations, and greater perspective taking in discussing material, all of which increase the depth of understanding, the quality of reasoning, and the accuracy of long-term retention.

2. Should non-task-oriented students be placed in learning groups with task-oriented peers or be separated? To keep non-academically oriented students on task, it often helps to place them in a cooperative learning group with task-oriented peers.

3. How long should the groups stay together? Actually, there is no formula or simple answer to this question. Some teachers keep cooperative learning groups together for an entire semester or year. Other teachers like to keep a learning group together only long enough to complete a task, unit, or chapter. Sooner or later, however, every student should work with every other classmate. Our best advice is to allow groups to remain stable long enough for them to be successful. Breaking up groups that are having trouble functioning effectively is often counterproductive as the students do not learn the skills they need to resolve problems in collaborating with each other.

Arranging the Room

How the teacher arranges the room is a symbolic message of what is appropriate behavior, and it can facilitate the learning groups within the classroom. Room arrangement can foster or interfere with on-task efforts. Members of a learning group should sit eye-to-eye, knee-to-knee or, in other words, close enough to each other that they can share materials, maintain eye contact with all group members, talk to each other quietly without disrupting the other learning groups, and exchange ideas and materials in a comfortable atmosphere. The groups need to be far enough apart so that they do not interfere with each other's learning. Finally, the groups should be arranged so that the teacher has a clear access lane to every group.

Planning the Instructional Materials

The choice of materials is determined by the type of task students are required to complete. Once the teacher decides what materials are needed, the materials need to be distributed among group members so that all members participate

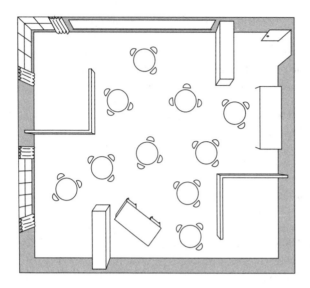

and achieve. When a group is mature and experienced and group members have a high level of interpersonal and small-group skills, the teacher may not have to arrange materials in any specific way. When a group is new or when members are not very skilled, however, teachers may wish to distribute materials in carefully planned ways to communicate that the assignment is to be a joint (not an individual) effort and that the students are in a "sink or swim together" learning situation.

Teachers can create *materials interdependence* by giving each group only one copy of the materials. The students will then have to work together in order to be successful. This is especially effective the first few times the group meets. After students are accustomed to working cooperatively, teachers can give a copy of the materials to each student.

Teachers can create *information interdependence* by giving each group member different books or resource materials to be synthesized. Or the materials may be arranged like a *jigsaw puzzle* so that each student has part of the materials needed to complete the task. Such procedures require that every member participate in order for the group to be successful.

Teachers can create *interdependence from outside enemies* by structuring materials into an intergroup tournament format and having groups compete to see who has learned the most. Such a procedure was introduced by DeVries and Edwards (1973). In the Teams-Games-Tournament format, students are divided into heterogeneous cooperative learning teams to prepare members for a tournament in which they compete with the other teams. During the intergroup competition the students individually compete against members of about the same ability level from other teams. The team whose members do the best in the competition is pronounced the winner by the teacher.

Assigning Roles to Ensure Interdependence

In planning the lesson, teachers think through what actions need to occur in order for student learning to be maximized. Teachers can then define those actions as "roles" and assign a role to each group member. Examples of roles include *summarizer* (who restates the group's major conclusions or answers), a *checker of understanding* (who ensures that all group members can explicitly explain how to arrive at an answer or conclusion), an *accuracy coach* (who corrects any mistakes in another member's explanations or summaries), an *elaborator* (who relates current concepts and strategies to material studied previously), a *researcher-runner* (who gets needed materials for the group and communicates with the other learning groups and the teacher), a *recorder* to write down the group's decisions and edit the group's report, an *encourager of participation* who ensures that all members are contributing, and an *observer* who keeps track of how well the group is cooperating. Assigning complementary and interconnected roles to group members is an effective method of teaching students social skills and fostering positive interdependence.

Roles such as checking for understanding and elaborating are vital to high-quality learning but are often absent in classrooms. The role of checking for understanding, for example, focuses on periodically asking each groupmate to explain what he or she is learning. From their research review, Rosenshine and Stevens (1986) concluded that "checking for comprehension" was significantly associated with higher levels of student learning and achievement. Wilson (1987) conducted a three-year teaching-improvement study and found that the frequency with which checking for understanding occurred was highly correlated with overall effectiveness as a teacher. The teacher cannot continually check the understanding of every student in the class; however, he or she can engineer such checking by having students work in cooperative groups and assigning one member the role of checker.

STRUCTURING THE TASK AND POSITIVE INTERDEPENDENCE

Explaining the Academic Task

At the beginning of a lesson, the teacher must explain the academic task so that students are clear about the assignment and understand the objectives of the lesson. *First, the teacher explains what the assignment is and the procedures students are to follow in completing it.* Instructions that are clear and specific are crucial in warding off student frustration. One advantage of cooperative learning groups is that students who do not understand what they are to do can clarify the assignment and the procedures with each other before asking the teacher.

Second, the teacher explains the objectives of the lesson and relates the concepts and information to be studied to students' past experience and learning to ensure maximum transfer and retention. The teacher may give examples to help students understand what they are to learn and do in completing the assignment. The objectives are sometimes given as outcomes—"At the end of this lesson you will be able to explain the causes of the Civil War." Explaining the intended outcomes of the lesson increases the likelihood that students will focus on the relevant concepts and information throughout the lesson.

It is often helpful to ask class members specific questions to check their understanding of the assignment. Such questioning ensures thorough two-way communication, that the assignment has been given effectively, and that the students are ready to begin completing it.

A focused discussion (see Chapter 5) may be used to help students organize in advance what they know about the content to be studied and to set students' expectations about the lesson.

Once the procedures and objectives are clear, direct teaching of concepts, principles, and strategies may take place. Relevant concepts may be defined. Teachers may wish to answer any questions students have about the concepts or facts they are to learn or apply in the lesson.

Explaining Criteria for Success

Students need to know what level of performance is expected of them. Academic expectations are expressed in preset criteria that establish what is and is not acceptable work (rather than grading students on a curve). In other words, evaluation within cooperatively structured lessons needs to be criterion-referenced. A teacher may say, "Everyone who earns 95 points or more will get an A, scores between 90 and 94 points will be given a B, and scores between 85 and 89 points will be given a C. The group is not finished until all members score above 85." Or he or she may say, "The group is not finished until every member has demonstrated mastery." Sometimes improvement (doing better this week than one did last week) may be set as the criterion of excellence. To promote intergroup cooperation, teachers may also set criteria for the whole class to reach.

Structuring Positive Interdependence

To ensure that students think *We,* not *me,* teachers say to students, "You have three responsibilities. You are responsible for learning the assigned material. You are responsible for making sure that all other members of your group learn the assigned material. And you are responsible for making sure that all other class members successfully learn the assigned material." Positive interdependence is the heart of cooperative learning. Without positive interdependence, cooperation does not exist. Students must believe that they are in a "sink or swim together" learning situation. Teachers can create positive interdependence in several ways (see Johnson & Johnson, 1992b, 1992c).

The first step in creating positive interdependence is structuring positive goal interdependence. Every cooperative lesson begins with positive goal interdependence. A group goal may be established in four ways:

1. The goal is for all members to score above the criteria specified when tested individually: "Make sure you score over 90 percent correct on the test and make sure everyone else in your group scores over 90 percent correct on the test."
2. The goal is for all members to improve their performance over their previous scores: "Make sure each member of your group does better this week than he or she did last week."
3. The goal is for the overall group score to reach the criterion specified when tested individually: "Each member of your triad can score up to 100. I will add your individual scores together to make a total group score. That score must be over 270 for you to be successful."
4. The goal is for the group to produce one product (or set of answers) successfully: "Each group is to conduct one science experiment and turn in one report that each member has signed to indicate that he or she agrees with the report and can explain what was done, why, and how."

The second step in creating positive interdependence is to supplement positive goal interdependence with other types of positive interdependence (such as reward, role, resource, or identity). Positive reward interdependence, for example, may be structured through providing group rewards—"If all members of your group score above 90 percent on the test, each of you will receive five bonus points." Usually, the more ways positive interdependence is structured in a lesson, the better.

Positive interdependence creates peer encouragement and support for learning. Such positive peer pressure influences underachieving students to become academically involved. Members of cooperative learning groups should give two interrelated messages, "Do your work—we're counting on you!" and "How can I help you to do better?"

Structuring Individual Accountability

An underlying purpose of cooperative learning is to make each group member a stronger individual in his or her own right. This is usually accomplished by maximizing the learning of each member. A group is not truly cooperative if members are "slackers" who let others do all the work. A group is not truly cooperative if members tell each other the answers without teaching each other how to get the answers. To ensure that all members learn, and that groups know which members to provide with encouragement and help, teachers need to frequently assess the level of performance of each group member. Ways of ensuring individual accountability include observing the participation patterns of each group member, giving practice tests, randomly selecting members to explain answers, having members edit each other's work, having students teach what they know to someone else, and having students use what they have learned on a different problem.

Structuring Intergroup Cooperation

The positive outcomes resulting from cooperative learning can be extended throughout a whole class by structuring intergroup cooperation. Class goals can be established as well as group and individual goals. Bonus points may be given if all members of a class reach a preset criterion of excellence. When a group finishes its work, the teacher should encourage the members to (a) find other groups who are finished and compare and explain answers and strategies or (b) find other groups who are not finished and help them understand how to complete the assignment successfully.

Specifying Desired Behaviors

The word *cooperation* has many different connotations and uses. Teachers need to define cooperation operationally by specifying the behaviors that are appropriate and desirable within the learning groups. There are beginning (forming) behaviors, such as "stay with your group and do not wander around the room," "use quiet voices," "take turns," and "use each other's names." When groups begin to function effectively, expected behaviors may include:

1. Having each member explain how to get the answer.
2. Asking each member to relate what is being learned to previous learnings.
3. Checking to make sure everyone in the group understands the material and agrees with the answers.
4. Encouraging everyone to participate.
5. Listening accurately to what other group members are saying.
6. Not changing your mind unless you are logically persuaded. (Majority rule does not promote learning.)
7. Criticizing ideas, not people.

Be specific. Operationally define each social skill through the use of a "T-Chart" (see Chapter 8). *Start small.* Do not overload your students with more social skills than they can learn at one time. One or two behaviors to emphasize for a few lessons is enough. Students need to know what behavior is appropriate and desirable within a cooperative learning group, but they should not be subjected to information overload. *Emphasize overlearning.* Having students practice skills once or twice is not enough. Keep emphasizing a skill until the students have integrated it into their behavioral repertoires and do it automatically and habitually.

THE COOPERATIVE LESSON

During the lesson students work together to complete the assignment. Their actions can be loosely or highly prescribed. Students can improvise procedures as they go along or they can follow explicit scripts (Johnson, Johnson, & Holubec 1991). Different teachers like to provide different degrees of structure. And they have a wide range of possibilities.

At one end of the continuum, cooperative learning can be given minimal structure. Cooperative lessons can be structured with only positive goal interdependence and individual accountability specified, a few social skills thrown in, and some group processing at the end of the lesson. Additional structure can be added by specifying complementary roles for students to engage in as they work together or arranging materials so that students must depend on each other's resources to complete the assignment. In essence, teachers are taught an *expert system* (a conceptual understanding of the five basic elements and the teacher's role) of how to implement cooperative learning that they use to create lessons uniquely tailored to their students, curriculum, needs, and teaching circumstances. The use of cooperative learning is based on a conceptual, metacognitive understanding of its nature.

At the other end of the continuum are highly structured direct approaches to cooperative learning that must be used in a prescribed lock-step manner. They include cooperative scripts, structures, and curriculum packages that specify step by step what each student is to do throughout the lesson. Donald Dansereau and his colleagues have

developed a number of *cooperative scripts* that structure student interaction as they work together. One of their most well known is MURDER, a simple text-processing script (Dansereau, 1985). In this script, students are assigned to pairs and first *M*obilize their resources for learning by (a) establishing an appropriate mood and (b) surveying the text to establish cooperative action points (asterisks in the margin to indicate where they will stop reading and will engage in cooperative information processing). Both partners then silently read for *U*nderstanding until they reach the first action point. One partner *R*ecalls/recites what has been learned to that point while the other partner *D*etects and corrects errors and omissions. Both partners then collaboratively *E*laborate on the material by forming images, analogies, and direct connections to other information. They then continue reading silently for understanding until they reach the next action point where they reverse roles and repeat the Recall, Detect, and Elaboration steps. The partners proceed through the material, alternating roles until they have completed the assignment. They then cooperatively *R*eview and organize the entire body of information, once again alternating active and monitoring roles.

Spencer Kagan (1988) has identified a number of *cooperative learning structures,*—ways of organizing the interaction of students by prescribing student behavior step by step to complete the assignment. Structures can be simple or complex. A simple structure is a *three-step interview,* in which students are assigned to pairs—student A interviews student B, student B interviews student A, and the two share the results in a group of four (made up of two pairs).

A complex structure is *Group Investigation* (Sharan & Hertz-Lazarowitz, 1980), in which students form cooperative groups according to common interests in a topic. All group members help plan how to research their topic. Then they divide the work among themselves, and each group member carries out his or her part of the investigation. The group synthesizes and summarizes its work and presents these findings to the class.

Similar to group investigation, in *Co-op Co-op* (Kagan, 1985) students are assigned to heterogeneous cooperative learning groups, each group is assigned one part of a learning unit, and each group member is assigned a mini-topic that is completed individualistically and then presented to the group. Each group then synthesizes the mini-topics of its members into a group presentation made to the whole class.

In *Jigsaw* (Aronson, 1978) students are assigned to cooperative groups, all groups are assigned the same topic, and each member is given one unique section of the topic to learn and then teach to the other members of the group. Members study the topic individualistically and then make a presentation to the group. The group synthesizes the presentations of the members into the whole picture. In studying the life of Sojourner Truth (a black abolitionist and women's rights activist), for example, each student is given material on a part of Truth's life and, therefore, group members cannot learn her total life unless all members teach their parts.

A *cooperative curriculum package* is a set of curriculum materials specifically designed to contain cooperative learning as well as academic content. *Teams-Games-*

Tournament (TGT) is a combination of in-group cooperation, intergroup competition, and instructional games (DeVries & Edwards, 1974). It begins with the teacher directly teaching a lesson. Students then meet in cooperative learning teams of four or five members (a mixture of high, medium, and low achievers) to complete a set of worksheets on the lesson. Students then play academic games as representatives of their teams. Who competes with whom is modified each week to ensure that students compete with classmates who achieve at a similar level. The highest-scoring teams are publicly recognized in a weekly class newsletter. Grades are given on the basis of individual performance.

TGT's development was followed by the development of a number of other curriculum packages by one of David DeVries' doctoral students, Robert Slavin. *Student Teams-Achievement Divisions* (STAD) (Slavin, 1980) is a modification of TGT that is basically identical except that instead of playing an academic game, students take a weekly quiz. Teams receive recognition for the sum of the improvement scores of team members.

Team-Assisted-Individualization (TAI) is a highly individualized math curriculum for grades 3 to 6 in which students work individualistically to complete math assignments using self-instructional (programmed learning) curriculum materials (Slavin, 1985). Students are assigned to four- or five-member teams, but team members do not work together. They check each other's answers, administer tests, and provide help if another member requests it. Because the curriculum units are designed to be self-explanatory and because team members are usually working at quite different levels, cooperative interaction is held to a minimum. Team scores are computed weekly and team members are given certificates on the basis of how much work each member completed. Students are graded strictly on their own individual work.

Cooperative Integrated Reading and Composition (CIRC) consists of a set of curriculum materials to supplement basal readers and ensure that cooperative learning is applied to reading, writing, spelling, and language mechanics (Stevens, Madden, Slavin, & Farnish, 1987). The class is divided into two reading groups of eight to fifteen members; one group focuses on phonic decoding and comprehension skills (code/meaning) and the other focuses on comprehension and inference skills (meaning). Students are assigned to a pair within their own reading group and then are combined with a pair from the other reading group. Assignments are given to the groups of four which they complete either as pairs or as a whole group. Students' scores on all quizzes, compositions, and book reports contribute to a team score that results in certificates. Students are graded individualistically on their own work.

MONITORING AND INTERVENING

Whether the lesson is loosely or very tightly structured cooperatively, the teacher's role is to monitor students' interaction in the learning groups and intervene to help students learn and interact more skillfully.

Monitoring Students' Behavior

The teacher's job begins in earnest when the cooperative learning groups start working. Resist that urge to get a cup of coffee or to grade papers. Teachers observe the interaction among group members to assess students' academic progress and appropriate use of interpersonal and small-group skills. Observations can be formal (with an observation schedule on which frequencies are tallied) or anecdotal (informal descriptions of students' statements and actions). Based on their observations, teachers can then intervene to improve students' academic learning or interpersonal and small-group skills.

In monitoring cooperative learning groups, there are a number of guidelines for teachers to follow. First, teachers should use a formal observation sheet to count the number of times they observe appropriate behaviors being used by students. The more concrete the data, the more useful it is to the teacher and to students. A variety of observation instruments and procedures that can be used for these purposes can be found in Johnson and F. Johnson (1991) and in Johnson, Johnson, and Holubec (1993). Second, teachers should not try to count too many different behaviors at one time, especially when they first start formal observation. At first they may just want to keep track of who talks in each group to get a participation pattern for the groups. Our current list of behaviors (though rather long) includes contributing ideas, asking questions, expressing feelings, active listening, expressing support and acceptance (toward ideas), expressing warmth and liking (toward group members and group), encouraging all members to participate, summarizing, checking for understanding, relieving tension by joking, and giving direction to group's work. Third, sometimes teachers should use a simple checklist in addition to a systematic observation form. Some questions to ask on the checklist might be:

1. Do students understand the task?
2. Have students accepted the positive interdependence and the individual accountability?
3. Are students working toward the criteria, and are those criteria for success appropriate?
4. Are students practicing the specified behaviors, or not?

Fourth, teachers should focus on positive behaviors that are to be celebrated when they are present and a cause for discussion when they are missing. Fifth, teachers should supplement and extend the frequency data with notes on specific student actions. Especially useful are skillful interchanges that can be shared with students later as objective praise and perhaps with parents in conferences or telephone conversations.

Sixth, teachers should train students to be observers, as student observers can obtain more complete data on each group's functioning. For very young students the system must be kept very simple, perhaps only "Who talks?" Many teachers have had good success with student observers, even in kindergarten. One of the more important things for the teacher to do is to make sure that the class is given adequate instructions (and perhaps practice) on gathering the observation data and sharing it with the group. The observer is in the best position to learn about the skills of working in a group. We can remember one first-grade teacher who had a student who talked all the time (even to himself while working alone). He tended to dominate any group he was in. When she introduced student observers to the class, she made him an observer. One important rule for observers was not to interfere in the task but to gather data without talking. He was gathering data on who talks and he did a good job, noticing that one student had done quite a bit of talking in the group whereas another had talked very little. The next day when he was a group member, and there was another observer, he was seen starting to talk, clamping his hand over his mouth, and glancing at the observer. He knew what was being observed for and he didn't want to be the only one with marks. The teacher said that he may have listened for the first time in the year. So the observer often benefits in learning about group skills. Seventh, when student observers are used, teachers should allocate several minutes at the end of each group session for the group to teach the observer what members of the group have just learned. Often important changes are made during this review. Finally, teachers may wish to use cooperative learning enough so that students understand what it is and how they should behave in helping each other learn before introducing student observers. Whether student observers are used or not, however, teachers should always monitor cooperative learning groups while they work.

Providing Task Assistance

Cooperative learning groups provide teachers with a "window" into students' minds. From carefully listening to students' explanations to each other of what they are learning, teachers can determine what students do and do not understand. Through working cooperatively, students make hidden thinking processes overt and subject to observation and commentary. Teachers are able to observe how students are constructing their understanding of the assigned material and intervene when necessary to help students understand what they are studying.

In monitoring the groups as they work, teachers will wish to clarify instructions, review important procedures and strategies for completing the assignment,

answer questions, and teach task skills as necessary. In discussing the concepts and information to be learned, teachers will wish to use the language or terms relevant to the learning. Instead of saying, "Yes, that is right," teachers will wish to say something more specific to the assignment, such as, "Yes, that is one way to find the main idea of a paragraph." The use of the more specific statement reinforces the desired learning and promotes positive transfer by helping the students associate a term with their learning.

One way to intervene is to interview a cooperative learning group by asking them (a) What are you doing? (b) Why are you doing it? and (c) How will it help you?

Intervening to Teach Social Skills

Cooperative learning groups provide teachers with a picture of students' social competencies. While monitoring the learning groups, teachers may find students who do not have the necessary social skills to be effective and positive group members. In these cases the teacher will wish to intervene to suggest more effective procedures for working together and specific social skills to use. Teachers may also wish to intervene and reinforce particularly effective and skillful behaviors that they notice. The social skills required for productive group work, along with activities that may be used in teaching them, are covered in Johnson and F. Johnson (1991) and Johnson (1991, 1993).

Teachers should not intervene any more than is absolutely necessary in the groups. Most of us as teachers are geared to jumping in and solving problems for students to get them back on track. With a little patience, we would find that cooperative groups can often work their way through their own problems (task and maintenance) and acquire not only a solution, but also a method of solving similar problems in the future.

Choosing when to intervene and when not to is part of the art of teaching. Even when intervening, teachers can turn the problem back to the group to solve. Many teachers intervene in a group by having members set aside their task, pointing out the problem, and asking the group to create three possible solutions and decide which solution they are going to try first.

In one third-grade class, the teacher noticed when distributing papers that one student was sitting back away from the other three. A moment later the teacher glanced over and only three students were sitting where four were a moment before. As she watched, the three students came marching over to her and complained that Johnny was under the table and wouldn't come out. "Make him come out!" they insisted (the teacher's role: police officer, judge, and executioner). The teacher told them that Johnny was a member of their group and asked what they had tried to solve their problem. "Tried?" the puzzled reply. "Yes, have you asked him to come out?" the teacher suggested. The group marched back and the teacher continued distributing papers to groups. A moment later the teacher glanced over to their table and saw no heads above the table (which is one way to solve the problem). After a few more minutes, four heads came struggling out from under the table and the group (including Johnny) went back to work with great energy. We don't know what happened under that table, but whatever it was, it was effective. What makes this story even more interesting is that the group received a 100 percent on the paper and later, when the teacher was standing by Johnny's desk, she noticed he had the paper clutched in his hand. The group had given Johnny the paper and he was taking it home. He confided to the teacher that this was the first time he could ever remember earning a 100 on anything in school. (If that was your record, you might slip under a few tables yourself.)

EVALUATING LEARNING AND PROCESSING INTERACTION

Providing Closure to the Lesson

Informal cooperative learning procedures often are used to provide closure to lessons by having students summarize the major points in the lesson, recall ideas, and identify final questions for the teacher (see Chapter 5). At the end of the lesson students should be able to summarize what they have learned and to understand where they will use it in future lessons.

Evaluating the Quality and Quantity of Students' Learning

Tests should be given and papers and presentations should be graded. The learning of group members must be evaluated by a criterion-referenced system for cooperative learning to be successful.

Processing How Well the Group Functioned

When students have completed the assignment, or run out of time, they should have time to describe what member actions were helpful (and unhelpful) in completing the group's work and make decisions about what behaviors to continue or change. Group processing occurs at two levels—in each learning group and in the class as a whole. In *small-group processing* members discuss how effectively they worked together and what could be improved. In *whole-class processing* teachers give the class feedback and have students share incidents that occurred in their groups. In structuring small-group processing teachers should avoid questions that can be answered "yes" or "no." Instead of saying, "Did everyone help each other learn?" the teacher should ask, "How frequently did each member (a) explain how to solve a problem and (b) correct or clarify other members' explanations?" Feedback given to students should be descriptive and specific, not evaluative and general (see Johnson, 1993).

Discussing group functioning is essential. *A common teaching error is to provide too brief a time for students to process the quality of their cooperation.* Students do not learn from experiences that they do not reflect on. If the learning groups are to function better tomorrow than they did today, students must receive feedback, reflect on how their actions may be more effective, and plan how to be even more skillful during the next group session.

BACK TO THE BASICS

The importance of cooperative learning goes beyond maximizing outcomes such as achievement, positive attitudes toward subject areas, and the ability to think critically, although these are worthwhile outcomes. Knowledge and skills are of no use if the student cannot apply them in cooperative interaction with other people. Being able to perform technical skills such as reading, speaking, listening, writing, computing, and problem solving are valuable but of little use if the person cannot apply those skills in cooperative interaction with other people. It does no good to train an engineer, secretary, accountant, teacher, or mechanic if the person does not have the cooperative skills needed to apply the knowledge and technical skills in cooperative relationships on the job.

Much of what students learn in school is worthless in the real world. Schools teach that work means performing tasks largely by oneself, helping and assisting others is cheating, technical competencies are the only thing that matters, attendance and punctuality are secondary to test scores, motivation is up to the teacher, success depends on performance on individual tests, and promotions are received no matter how little one works. In the real world of work, things are altogether different. Most employers do not expect people to sit in rows and compete with colleagues without interacting with them. The heart of most jobs—especially the higher-paying, more interesting jobs—is teamwork, which involves getting others to cooperate, leading others, coping with complex power and influence issues, and helping solve people's problems in working with each other. Teamwork, communication, effective coordination, and divisions of labor characterize most real-life settings. It is time for schools to leave the ivory tower of working alone and sitting in rows to see who is best and to more realistically reflect the realities of adult life.

Students increasingly live in a world characterized by interdependence, pluralism, conflict, and rapid change. Because of technological, economic, ecological, and political interdependence, the solution of most problems cannot be achieved by one country alone. The major problems faced by individuals (e.g., contamination of the environment, warming of the atmosphere, world hunger, international terrorism, nuclear war) are increasing ones that cannot be solved by actions taken only at the national level. Our students will live in a complex, interconnected world in which cultures collide every minute and dependencies limit the flexibility of individuals and nations. The internationalization of problems will increase so that there will be no clear division between domestic and international problems. Students need to learn the competencies involved in managing interdependence, resolving conflicts within cooperative systems made up of parties from different countries and cultures, and personally adapting to rapid change.

Quality of life depends on having close friends who last a lifetime, building and maintaining a loving family, being a responsible parent, caring about others, and contributing to the well-being of the world. These are things that make life worthwhile. Grades in school do not predict which students will have a high quality of life after they have graduated. The ability to work cooperatively with others does. The ability of students to work collaboratively with others is the keystone to building and maintaining the caring and committed relationships that largely determine quality of life.

SUMMARY AND CONCLUSIONS

At this point you know what cooperative learning is and how it is different from competitive and individualistic learning. You know that there are three types of cooperative learning groups—formal cooperative learning groups, informal cooperative learning groups, and cooperative base groups. You know that the essence of cooperative learning is positive interdependence, where students recognize that "we are in this together, sink or swim." Other essential components include individual accountability (where every student is accountable for both learning the assigned material and helping other group members learn), face-to-face interaction among students within which students promote each other's success, students appropriately using interpersonal and group skills, and students processing how effectively their learning group has functioned. These five essential components of cooperation form the conceptual basis for constructing cooperative procedures. You know that the research supports the proposition that cooperation results in greater effort to achieve, more positive interpersonal relationships, and greater psychological health and self-esteem than do competitive or individualistic efforts. You know the teacher's role in implementing formal cooperative learning. Any assignment in any subject area may be structured cooperatively. In using formal cooperative learning, the teacher decides on the objectives of the lesson, makes a number of preinstructional decisions about the size of the group and the materials required to conduct the lesson, explains to students the task and the cooperative goal structure, monitors the groups as they work, intervenes when it is necessary, and then evaluates. What is covered in the next chapter is the teacher's role in implementing informal cooperative learning groups and base groups.

One of the things we have been told many times by teachers who have mastered the use of cooperative learning is, "Don't say it is easy!" We know it's not. It can take years to become an expert. There is a lot of pressure to teach like everyone else, to have students learn alone, and not to let students look at each other's papers. Students will not be accustomed to working together and are likely to have a competitive orientation. You may wish to start small by using cooperative learning for one topic or in one class until you feel comfortable, and then expand into other topics or classes. In order to implement cooperative learning successfully, you will need to teach students the interpersonal and small-group skills required to collaborate, structure and orchestrate intellectual inquiry within learning groups, and form collaborative relations with others. Implementing formal cooperative learning in your classroom is not easy, but it is worth the effort.

"A threefold cord is not quickly broken."

Ecclesiastes 4:12

5

Informal Cooperative Learning and Cooperative Base Groups

INTRODUCTION

It is 12,896 B.C. A small group of hunters surround a band of reindeer as they ford an icy river. The hunters are armed with harpoons tipped with spearheads carved from reindeer antler. As the reindeer wallow in the water the hunters run in and slaughter them. It is the coordinated action of the group of Cro-Magnon hunters that makes them more successful than their Neanderthal cousins, who hunt as individuals.

Our origins are somehow linked with the fate of the Neanderthals. We have never been proud of our extinct predecessors, partly because of their looks. Nevertheless, the Neanderthals represent a high point in the human story. Their lineage goes back to the earliest members of the genus *Homo*. They were the original pioneers. Over thousands of years, Neanderthals moved out of Africa by way of the Near East into India and China and Malaysia, and into southern Europe. In recent times, 150,000 or so years ago, they pioneered glacial landscapes. The Neanderthals were the first to cope with climates hospitable only to woolly mammoths and reindeer.

There is no anatomical evidence that the Neanderthals were inferior to us (the Cro-Magnons) cerebrally, and no doubt whatever that they were our physical superiors. Their strongest individuals could probably lift weights of half a ton or so. Physically, we are quite puny in comparison. But we gradually replaced the Neanderthals during an overlapping period of a few thousand years. It may have mainly been a matter of attrition and population pressure. As the glaciers from

Scandinavia advanced, northern populations of Neanderthals moved south while our ancestors were moving north out of Africa. We met in Europe. They vanished about 30,000 years ago.

There are numerous explanations for the disappearance of the Neanderthals. Perhaps they evolved into us. Perhaps we merged. Perhaps there was an intergroup competition for food, with the Neanderthals unable to meet our challenge and dying off in marginal areas. Perhaps the Neanderthals were too set in their ways and were unable to evolve and refine better ways to cooperate, whereas we were continually organizing better cooperative efforts to cope with changing climatic conditions. There seems to be little doubt that we were more able to form and maintain cooperative efforts within small groups.

During the time we (the Cro-Magnons) overlapped with the Neanderthals, our ancestors developed highly sophisticated cooperative effects characterized by social organization, group hunting procedures, creative experimentation with a variety of materials, sharing of knowledge, divisions of labor, trade, and transportation systems. We sent out scouts to monitor the movements of herds of animals we preyed on. The Neanderthals probably did not. We cached supplies and first aid materials to aid hunting parties far away from our home bases. The Neanderthals did not. Neanderthals apparently engaged their prey chiefly in direct combat. We learned more efficient ways of hunting, such as driving animals over cliffs, that fundamentally changed our relationship with the rest of the animal kingdom (i.e., instead of behaving like lions and other carnivores, going after young, old, and sick animals to weed out the less fit, large-scale game drives wiped out entire herds and perhaps entire species). We developed more sophisticated tools and weapons to kill from a distance, such as the spear-thrower and the bow and arrow. The Neanderthals probably did not. The Neanderthals used local materials to develop tools. We were more selective, often obtaining special fine-grained and colorful flints from quarries as far as 250 miles away. This took a level of intergroup cooperation and social organization that the Neanderthals did not develop. We improved the tool-making process through experimentation and sharing knowledge. The Neanderthals did not. The Neanderthals used stone almost exclusively for tools. We used bone and ivory to make needles and other tools. We "tailored" our clothes and made ropes and nets. Our ability to obtain more food than we needed resulted in trading and the formation of far-ranging social networks. Status hierarchies, the accumulation of wealth, artistic efforts, laws, and story telling to preserve traditions followed, as more complex forms of cooperation were developed. Whether we replaced or evolved from the Neanderthals, our ingenuity was especially evident in organizing cooperative efforts to increase our standard of living and the quality of our lives. We excelled at organizing effective small-group efforts.

Humans are small-group beings. We always have been and we always will be. As John Donne said, "No man is an island, entire of itself." Throughout the history of our species we have lived in small groups. For 200,000 years humans lived in small hunting and gathering groups. For 10,000 years humans lived in small farming communities. It is only recently, the past one hundred years or so, that large cities have become the rule rather than the exception.

THE COOPERATIVE CLASSROOM

Classrooms perhaps should primarily be small-group places. And there is more to using cooperative learning groups than formal cooperative learning. Teachers also use informal cooperative learning and cooperative base groups. Informal cooperative learning is used with direct teaching. Base groups involve long-term cooperative efforts. The three types of cooperative learning are then integrated into coherent lessons.

DIRECT TEACHING

Our survey of teaching methods suggests that . . . if we want students to become more effective in meaningful learning and thinking, they need to spend more time in active, meaningful learning and thinking—not just sitting and passively receiving information.

McKeachie (1986)

Direct teaching includes lecturing, showing films and videos, giving demonstrations, and having guest speakers. Lecturing is currently the most common teacher behavior in secondary and elementary schools (as well as colleges and universities). Even in training programs within business and industry, lecturing dominates. A *lecture* is an extended presentation in which the speaker presents factual information in an organized and logically sequenced way. It typically results in long periods of uninterrupted teacher-centered, expository discourse that relegates students to the role of passive "spectators" in the classroom. A lecture has three parts: the introduction, the body, and the conclusion. Proponents of lecturing advise teachers, "Tell them what you are going to tell them; then tell them; then tell them what you told them." First you describe the learning objectives in a way that alerts students to what is to be covered in the lecture. You then present the material to be learned in small steps organized logically and sequenced in ways that are easy to follow. You end with an integrative review of the main points. Normally, lecturing includes using reference notes, occasionally using visuals to enhance the information being presented, and responding to students' questions as the lecture progresses or at its end. Occasionally, students are provided with handouts to help them follow the lecture. The lecturer presents the material to be learned in more or less final form, gives answers, presents principles, and elaborates the entire content of what is to be learned.

Appropriate Use

Two reasons lecturing is so popular are that it can be adapted to different audiences and time frames and it keeps the teacher at the center of all communication and attention in the classroom. There are conditions under which lecturing and other forms of direct teaching are appropriate. From the research directly evaluating lecturing (see reviews by Bligh, 1972; Costin, 1972; Eble, 1983; McKeachie, 1967; and Verner & Dickinson, 1967) it may be concluded that lecturing is appropriate when the purpose is to:

1. *Disseminate information.* Lecturing is appropriate when faculty wish to communicate a large amount of material to many students in a short period of time, when faculty wish to supplement curriculum materials that need updating or elaborating, when the material has to be organized and presented in a particular way, or when faculty want to provide an introduction to an area.

2. *Present material that is not available elsewhere.* Lecturing is appropriate when information is not available in a readily accessible source, the information is original, or the information might be too complex and difficult for students to learn on their own.

3. *Expose students to content in a brief time that might take them much longer to locate on their own.* Lecturing is appropriate when faculty need to teach information that must be integrated from many sources and students do not have the time, resources, or skills to do so.

4. *Arouse students' interest in the subject.* When a lecture is presented by a highly authoritative person or in a skillful way with lots of humor and examples, students may be intrigued and want to find out more about the subject. Skillful delivery of a lecture includes maintaining eye contact, avoiding distracting behaviors, modulating voice pitch and volume, and using appropriate gestures. Achievement is higher when presentations are clear (Good & Brouws, 1977; Smith & Land, 1981), delivered with enthusiasm (Armento, 1977), and delivered with appropriate gestures and movements (Rosenshine, 1968).

5. *Teach students who are primarily auditory learners.*

Problems with Direct Teaching

Although direct teaching may be appropriately used, there are also problems with direct teaching that must be kept in mind. Much of the research on lecturing has compared lecturing with group discussion. Whereas the conditions under which lecturing is more successful than group discussion have not been identified, a number of problems with lecturing have been found.

The first problem with lectures is that *students' attention to what the teacher is saying decreases as the lecture proceeds.* Research in the 1960s by D. H. Lloyd at the University of Reading in Berkshire, England, found that students' attention during lectures followed the pattern of five minutes of settling in, five minutes of readily assimilating material, confusion and boredom with assimilation falling off rapidly and remaining low for the bulk of the lecture, and some revival of attention at the end of the lecture (Penner, 1984). The concentration of medical students, who presumably are highly motivated, during lectures rose sharply and peaked ten to fifteen minutes after the lecture began, and then fell steadily thereafter (Stuart & Rutherford, 1978). J. McLeish in a research study in the 1960s analyzed the percentage of content contained in student notes at different time intervals throughout the lecture (reported in Penner, 1984). He found that students wrote notes on 41 percent of the content presented during the first fifteen minutes, 25 percent presented in a thirty-minute time period, and only 20 percent of what had been presented during forty-five minutes.

The second problem with lecturing is that *it takes an educated, intelligent person oriented toward auditory learning to benefit from listening to lectures.* Verner and Dickinson (1967) found that in general, very little of a lecture can be recalled except in the case of listeners with above average education and intelligence. Even under optimal conditions, when intelligent, motivated people listen to a brilliant scholar talk about an interesting topic there can be serious problems with a lecture. Verner and Dickinson (1967, p. 90) give this example:

> . . . ten percent of the audience displayed signs of inattention within fifteen minutes. After eighteen minutes one-third of the audience and ten percent of the platform guests were fidgeting. At thirty-five minutes everyone was inattentive; at forty-five minutes, trance was more noticeable than fidgeting; and at forty-seven minutes some were asleep and at least one was reading. A casual check twenty-four hours later revealed that the audience recalled only insignificant details, and these were generally wrong.

The third problem with lecturing is that *it tends to promote only lower-level learning of factual information.* Bligh (1972), after an extensive series of studies, concluded that although lecturing was as effective as (but not more effective than) reading or other methods in transmitting information, lecturing was clearly less effective in promoting thinking or in changing attitudes. A survey of fifty-eight studies conducted between the years of 1928 and 1967, comparing various characteristics of lectures versus discussions, found that lectures and discussions did not differ significantly on lower-level learning (such as learning facts and principles), but discussion appeared superior in developing higher-level problem-solving capabilities and positive attitudes toward the course (Costin, 1972). McKeachie and Kulik (1975) separated studies on lecturing according to whether they focused on factual learning, higher-level reasoning, attitudes, or motivation. Lecture was found to be superior to discussion for promoting factual learning, but discussion was found to be superior to lecture for promoting higher-level reasoning, positive attitudes, and motivation to learn. Lecturing at best tends to focus on the lower level of cognition and learning. When the material is complex, detailed, or abstract; when students need to analyze, synthesize, or integrate the knowledge being studied; or when long-term retention is desired, lecturing is not such a good idea. Formal cooperative learning groups should be used to accomplish goals such as these.

Fourth, there are problems with lecturing as *it is based on the assumptions that all students need the same information—presented orally, at the same pace, without dialogue with the presenter, and in an impersonal way.* Students have different levels of knowledge about the subject being presented, yet the same information is presented to all. The material covered in a lecture often may be communicated just as well in a text assignment or a handout. Lectures can waste student time by telling them things that they could read for themselves. Although students learn and comprehend at different paces, a lecture proceeds at the lecturer's pace. Students who listen carefully and cognitively process the information will have questions that need to be answered; but lectures typically are one-way communication situations, and the large number of classmates inhibits asking questions. If students cannot ask questions, misconceptions, incorrect understanding, and gaps in understanding cannot be identified and corrected. Stones (1970), for example, surveyed

over 1,000 college students and found that 60 percent stated that the presence of a large number of classmates would deter them from asking questions, even if the teacher encouraged them to do so. Lecturing by its very nature impersonalizes learning. There is research indicating that personalized learning experiences have more impact on achievement and motivation.

The fifth problem with lecturing is that *students tend not to like it.* Costin's (1972) review of literature indicates that students like the course and subject area better when they learn in discussion groups than when they learn by listening to lectures. This is important in introductory courses where disciplines often attempt to attract majors.

Finally, there are problems with lecturing as *it is based on a series of assumptions about the cognitive capabilities and strategies of students.* When you lecture you assume that all students learn auditorially, have high working memory capacity, have all the required prior knowledge, have good note-taking strategies and skills, and are not susceptible to information-processing overload.

Enemies of the Lecture

Besides the identified problems with lecturing and direct teaching, there are obstacles to making direct teaching and lecturing effective. We call these obstacles the enemies of the lecture. They are as follows.

1. Preoccupation with what happened during the previous hour or with what happened on the way to class. In order for lectures to succeed, faculty must take students' attention away from events in the hallway or campus and focus their attention on the subject area and topic being dealt with in class.

2. Emotional moods that block learning and cognitive processing of information. Students who are angry or frustrated about something are not open to new learning. For lectures to work, faculty must set a constructive learning mood. Humor helps.

3. Disinterest by students who go to sleep or who turn on a tape recorder while they write letters or read comic books. For lectures to work, faculty must focus student attention on the material being presented and ensure that they cognitively process the information and integrate it into what they already know.

4. Failure to understand the material being presented in the lecture. Students can learn material incorrectly and incompletely because of lack of understanding. There has to be some means of checking the accuracy and completeness of students' understanding of the material being presented.

5. Student feelings of isolation and alienation and beliefs that no one cares about them as persons or about their academic progress. Students have to believe that there are other people in the class who will provide help and assistance because they care about the students as people and about the quality of their learning.

6. Entertaining and clear lectures that misrepresent the complexity of the material being presented. Although entertaining and impressing students is nice, it often does not help students understand and think critically about complex material. Students must think critically and use higher-level reasoning in cognitively processing course content. One of our colleagues is a magnificent lecturer. His explanation of the simplex algorithm for solving linear-programming problems is so clear and straightforward that the students go away with the view that it is very simple. Later when they try to solve a problem on their own, they find that they don't have a clue as to how to begin. Our colleague used to blame himself for not explaining well enough. Sometimes he blamed the students. Now he puts small cooperative groups to work on a simple linear-programming problem, circulates and checks the progress of each student, provides help where he feels it is appropriate, and only gives his brilliant lectures when the students understand the problem and are ready to hear his proposed solution. Both he and the students are much happier with their increased understanding.

After considering these problems and barriers, it may be concluded that alternative teaching strategies have to be interwoven with lecturing if the lecture method is to be effective. Lecturing and direct teaching traditionally have been conducted within competitive and individualistic structures, but they can be made cooperative. Perhaps the major procedure to interweave with lecturing is informal cooperative learning groups.

INFORMAL COOPERATIVE LEARNING GROUPS

There are times when teachers need to lecture, show a movie or videotape, give a demonstration, or have a guest speaker. In such cases, informal cooperative learning may be used to ensure that students are active (not passive) cognitively. *Informal cooperative learning* consists of having students work together to achieve a joint learning goal in temporary, ad hoc groups that last from a few minutes to a full class period. Their purposes are to focus student attention on the material to be learned, set a mood conducive to learning, help organize in advance the material to be covered in a class session, ensure that students cognitively process the material being taught, and provide closure to an instructional session. Informal cooperative learning groups also ensure that misconceptions, incorrect understanding, and gaps in understanding are identified and corrected, and learning experiences are personalized. They may be used at any time, but are especially useful during a lecture or direct teaching.

During lecturing and direct teaching the instructional challenge for the teacher is to ensure that students do the intellectual work of organizing material, explaining it, summarizing it, and integrating it into existing conceptual networks. This may be achieved by having students do the advance organizing, cognitively process what they are learning, and provide closure to the lesson. Breaking up lectures with short cooperative processing times will give you slightly less lecture time, but will help counter what is proclaimed as the main problem of lectures: "The information passes from the notes of the professor to the notes of the student without passing through the mind of either one."

LECTURING WITH INFORMAL COOPERATIVE LEARNING GROUPS

The following procedure will help you plan a lecture that keeps students more actively engaged intellectually. It entails having focused discussions before and after the lecture (i.e., bookends) and interspersing pair discussions throughout the lecture. Two important aspects of using informal cooperative learning groups are to (1) make the task and the instructions explicit and precise and (2) require the groups to produce a specific product (such as a written answer). The procedure is as follows.

1. *Introductory focused discussion.* Assign students to pairs. The person nearest them will do. You may wish to require different seating arrangements each class period so that students will meet and interact with a number of other students in the class. Then give the pairs the cooperative assignment of completing the initial (advance organizer) task. Give them only four or five minutes to do so. The discussion task is aimed at promoting advance organizing of what the students know about the topic to be presented and establishing expectations about what the lecture will cover.

2. *Lecture segment 1.* Deliver the first segment of the lecture. This segment should last from ten to fifteen minutes. This is about the length of time a motivated adult can concentrate on a lecture. For unmotivated adolescents, the time may be shorter.

3. *Pair discussion 1.* Give the students a discussion task focused on the material you have just presented that may be completed within three or four minutes. Its purpose is to ensure that students are actively thinking about the material being presented. The discussion task may be to (a) give an answer to a question posed by the teacher, (b) give a reaction to the theory, concepts, or information being presented, or (c) relate material to past learning so that it gets integrated into existing conceptual frameworks (i.e., elaborate the material being presented). Discussion pairs respond to the task in the following way:

   a. Each student *formulates* his or her answer.

   b. Students *share* their answer with their partner.

   c. Students *listen* carefully to partner's answer.

   d. Pairs *create* a new answer that is superior to each member's initial formulation through the process of association, building on each other's thoughts, and synthesizing.

   Randomly choose two or three students to give thirty-second summaries of their discussions. It is important that students are randomly called on to share their answers after each discussion task. Such individual accountability ensures that the pairs take the tasks seriously and check each other to ensure that both are prepared to answer.

4. *Lecture segment 2.* Deliver the second segment of the lecture.

5. *Pair discussion 2.* Give a discussion task focused on the second part of the lecture.

6. Repeat this sequence of lecture segment and pair discussion until the lecture is completed.

7. *Closure-focused discussion.* Give an ending discussion task to summarize what students have learned from the lecture. Students should have four or five minutes to summa-

rize and discuss the material covered in the lecture. The discussion should result in students' integrating what they have just learned into existing conceptual frameworks. The task may also point students toward what the homework will cover or what will be presented in the next class session. This provides closure to the lecture.

Process the procedure with students regularly to help them increase their skill and speed in completing short discussion tasks. Processing questions may include (a) How well prepared were you to complete the discussion tasks? and (b) How could you come even better prepared tomorrow?

The informal cooperative learning group not only is effective for getting students actively involved in understanding what they are learning, it also provides time for you to gather your wits, reorganize your notes, take a deep breath, and move around the class listening to what students are saying. Listening to student discussions can give you direction and insight into how well the concepts you are teaching are being grasped by your students (who, unfortunately, may not have graduate degrees in the topic you are presenting).

Besides the use of formal and informal cooperative learning groups, there is a need for a permanent cooperative base group that provides relatively long-term relationships among students. It is to this use of cooperative learning that we next turn.

COOPERATIVE BASE GROUPS

Jim stands at the school door. "In this school," he thinks, "no one really knows me, no one cares about me, and no one will miss me when I am gone." Jim is a student *at risk* for academic failure, interpersonal isolation, and psychological maladjust-

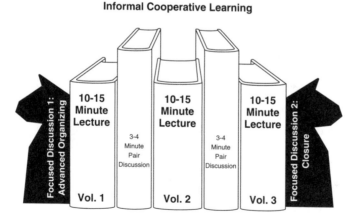

FIGURE 5.1 Informal cooperative learning

ment and social incompetence. There are many such students at risk—students who feel alone in the school, outside of its purposes, connected to no faculty member, and liked by few if any of their classmates. Many of these students drop out of school. They are not missed by anyone and are grieved by no one.

Schools can only influence students who are physically present. Children and youth must attend school if they are to achieve valuable knowledge, form constructive peer relationships, and develop personally and socially in healthy ways. Attending school, however, comes primarily from the heart, not the head. It is caring and committed relationships that keep students in school. Students must believe that they belong. They must believe that their friends are in school. Students' membership in the school must be promoted through social bonding and attachment to teachers and classmates. If attachment is weak or absent, students can act without regard for the feelings of others. Without attachment it is easy to say, "I do not care" and to believe that others "do not care about me." It is then a short step to not coming to school at all.

Caring and committed relationships cannot be created from memos and announcements over the loudspeaker that "in this school you are required to like each other." Caring and committed relationships evolve from working together to get the job done. It is out of being part of a joint effort to accomplish something worthwhile that friendships evolve. There must be a meaningful job to do, and the efforts of others must contribute to your success and your efforts must benefit others as well as yourself. *At-risk students must exert mental and physical effort to learn if they are to commit themselves to gaining an education.* They must realize that schooling requires hard work but it is worth it because it (a) contributes to others' success as well as their own and (b) prepares them to succeed later in life. Schools are the practice field for later careers and informed citizenship in a community, society, and world. Students must be willing to follow the adages of "Teamwork!" and "You have to sweat on the practice field before you can perform on the playing field." Unless students participate, exert effort, and succeed in the activities school offers, it is unlikely that commitment to achieve academically can be sustained. To provide all students with the long-term caring and committed relationships with classmates that are required to motivate them to achieve in school, teachers will wish to utilize cooperative base groups.

Cooperative base groups are long-term, heterogeneous cooperative learning groups with stable membership whose primary responsibilities are to provide support, encouragement, and assistance in completing assignments and hold each other accountable for striving to learn. Typically, cooperative base groups (a) are heterogeneous in membership (especially in terms of achievement motivation and task orientation), (b) meet regularly (for example, daily or biweekly), and (c) last for the duration of the class (a semester or a year) and preferably until the students are graduated. When students know that the cooperative base group will stay together until each member is graduated, they become committed to find ways to motivate and encourage their groupmates. Problems in working with each other cannot be ignored or waited out.

The agendas for base groups can include:

1. *Academic support tasks,* such as checking to see what assignments each member has and what help is needed to complete them. Members can give each other advice on how to take tests and "survive" in school. Members can prepare each other to take tests and go over the questions missed afterwards. Members can share their areas of expertise (such as art or computers) with each other. Above all, members monitor each other's academic progress and make sure all members are achieving.
2. *Routine tasks,* such as taking attendance or collecting homework.
3. *Personal support tasks,* such as listening sympathetically when a member has problems with parents or friends, having general discussions about life, giving each other advice about relationships, and helping each other solve nonacademic problems. Teachers may increase the likelihood of personal support by conducting trust-building exercises with the base groups, such as sharing their favorite movie, a childhood experience, a memory from high school, and so forth.

There are two ways base groups may be used. The first is to have a base group in each course. Class base groups stay together only for the duration of the course. The second is to organize all students within the school into base groups and have the groups function as an essential component of school life. School base groups stay together for at least a year and preferably until all members are graduated.

Class Base Groups

The larger the class and the more complex the subject matter, the more important it is to have base groups. The members of base groups should exchange phone numbers and information about schedules so they can meet outside of class. At the beginning of each session, class members meet in their base groups to:

1. Congratulate each other for showing up and check to see that none of their group is under undue stress. The two questions to discuss are: "Are we all prepared for this class period?" and "How are you today?"
2. Check to see if members have completed their homework or need help and assistance in doing so. The questions to discuss are: "Did you do your homework?" "Is there

anything you did not understand?" If there is not time to help each other during the base group meeting, an appointment is made to meet again during free time or lunch. Periodically, the base groups may be given a checklist of academic skills and assess which ones each member needs to practice more.

3. Review what members have read and done since the previous class session. Members should be able to give a succinct summary of what they have read, thought about, and done. They may come to class with resources they have found and want to share, or copies of work they have completed and wish to distribute to their base group members.

4. Get to know each other better and provide positive feedback by discussing such questions as: "What do you like about each other?" "What do you like about yourself?" and "What is the best thing that has happened to you this week?"

Class base groups are available to support individual group members. If a group member arrives late, or occasionally must leave, the group can provide information about what that student missed. Additionally, group members may assist one another in writing required papers. Assignments may be discussed in the base group; papers may be planned, reviewed, and edited in the base group; and any questions regarding the course assignments and class sessions may be first addressed in the base group. If the group is not able to resolve the issue, it should be brought to the attention of the teacher or the teaching assistant.

Some attention should be paid to building a base group identity and group cohesion. The first week the base groups meet, for example, groups can pick a name, design a flag, or choose a motto. If a teacher with the proper expertise is available, the groups will benefit from participating in a "challenge course" involving ropes and obstacles. This type of physical challenge that the groups complete together builds cohesion quickly.

All members are expected to contribute actively to the class discussion, work to maintain effective working relationships with other participants, complete all assignments, assist classmates in completing their assignments, express their ideas, not change their minds unless they are persuaded by logic or information to do so, and indicate agreement with the base group's work by signing the weekly contract.

School Base Groups

At the beginning of the academic year, students should be assigned to school base groups (or the base groups from the previous year should be reconvened). Class schedules should be arranged so that members of base groups are assigned to as many of the same classes as possible. School base groups should stay together for at least a year and, ideally, for four years.

During the year, base groups meet either twice each day or twice a week, or some variation in between. *When base groups meet twice each day,* they meet first thing in the morning and last thing in the afternoon. At the beginning of each day students meet in their base groups to welcome each other to school, check to see if everyone has completed and understands the homework, and get to know each other better.

At the end of the day members meet in their base groups to see that everyone is taking their homework home, understands the assignments to be completed, and has the help and assistance they need to do their work. Base groups may also wish to discuss what members have learned during the day and check to see if all members have plans to do something fun and interesting that evening. During the evening students can confer on the telephone or even study together at one house.

When base groups meet twice each week (perhaps first thing on Monday and last thing on Friday), they meet to discuss the academic progress of each member, provide help and assistance to each other, and hold each member accountable for completing assignments and progressing satisfactorily through the academic program. The meeting on Monday morning refocuses the students on school, provides any emotional support required after the weekend, reestablishes personal contact among base group members, and helps students set their academic goals for the week (what is still to be done on assignments that are due, and so forth). Members should carefully review each other's assignments and ensure that other members have the help and assistance needed. In addition, they should hold each other accountable for committing serious effort to succeed in school. The meeting on Friday afternoon helps students review the week, set academic goals for the weekend (what homework has to be done before Monday), and share weekend plans and hopes.

The Advisee or Homeroom Base Group

In many schools it will seem difficult to implement base groups. Two opportunities are advisor–advisee groups or homerooms. Teachers may take their advisees and divide students into base groups and then plan an important agenda for them to follow during a daily or a weekly meeting. Or homeroom time can be spent in having students meet in base groups.

In a school we work with, all students are assigned an advisor. The teacher then meets once a week with all of his or her advisees. The meeting lasts for thirty minutes. The base groups are given four tasks:

1. A quick *self-disclosure task* such as: "What is the most exciting thing you did over the vacation break? What is the worst thing that happened to you last weekend? What is your biggest fear? What is your favorite ice cream?"
2. An *administrative task* such as what classes to register for next semester.
3. An *academic task* such as: "You have midterms coming up. As a group, write out three pieces of advice for taking tests. I will type up the suggestions from each group and hand them out next week."
4. A *closing task* such as wishing each other good luck for the day or week.

Need for Long-Term, Permanent Relationships

Long-term, permanent relationships among students are needed for several reasons. First, most relationships in schools are, at best, shipboard romances. Relationships are temporary because in most schools it is assumed that classmates and teachers are replaceable parts in the education machine and, therefore, any classmate or teacher will do. It is important that some of the relationships built in schools are permanent. The longer a cooperative group exists, the more influence members will have over each other, the more caring their relationships will be, the greater the social support they will provide for each other, and the more committed they will be to each other's success. Permanent cooperative base groups provide the arena in which caring and committed relationships can be created that improve attendance, personalize the school experience, increase achievement, and improve the quality of life within the classroom.

Second, long-term relationships promote concern for others as well as oneself and an opportunity to work for the well-being of others as well as oneself. A balance between concern for self and concern for others is increasingly important. Among many current high school and college students, their own pleasures and pains, successes and failures, occupy center stage in their lives (Conger, 1988; Seligman, 1988). Each person tends to focus on gratifying his or her own ends without concern for others. Physical, psychological, and material self-indulgence has become a primary concern (Conger, 1988; National Association of Secondary School Principals, 1984). Over the past twenty years, self-interest has become more important than commitment to community, country, or God. Young adults have turned away from careers of public service to careers of self-service. Many young adults have a delusion of individualism, believing that (a) they are separate and apart from all other individuals and, therefore, (b) others' frustration, unhappiness, hunger, despair, and misery have no significant bearing on their own well-being. With the increase in the past two decades in adolescents' and youths' concern for personal well-being, there has been a corresponding diminished

concern for the welfare of others (particularly the less advantaged) and of society itself (Astin, Green, & Korn, 1987; Astin, Green, Korn, & Schalit, 1986). Self-orientation interferes with consideration of others' needs in that it actively prevents concern for others as equally deserving persons.

Third, cooperative base groups create the relationships that can motivate students to work hard and do their best, and hold them accountable for doing so. Numerous students spend very little time studying, avoid hard subjects, and simply coast along, doing far less than they are capable of doing. Long-term, hard, persistent efforts to achieve come from the heart, not from the head. And the heart is reached through relationships, not intellectual appeals.

Fourth, cooperative base groups create the relationships that can change students' attitudes about academic work. Students need to value education, have aspirations for postsecondary education, and want to learn. Such attitudes are changed primarily through personal relationships (not information), in groups, as the result of discussions that lead to public commitment to study hard and take education more seriously, and as the result of personal appeals made by friends whose opinions are valued (Johnson & F. Johnson, 1991).

Finally, cooperative base groups provide a means of both preventing and combating dropping out of school. Any student who believes that "in this school, no one knows me, no one cares about me, no one would miss me when I'm gone" is at risk of dropping out. Base groups provide a set of personal and supportive relationships that may prevent many students from dropping out of school. Dropping out often results from being alienated from the school and the other students. Base groups also provide a means of fighting a student's inclination to drop out. A teacher may approach a base group and say, "Roger thinks he is dropping out of school. Go find and talk to him. We're not going to lose Roger without a fight."

INTEGRATED USE OF ALL TYPES OF COOPERATIVE LEARNING

We need schools in which great lessons are commonplace occurrences. Great lessons result from the hard work of teachers; and to have a school in which great lessons are commonplace, teachers have to be skilled in using formal and informal cooperative learning procedures as well as cooperative base groups. For such schools to exist, teachers must adopt a set of beliefs, prepare lessons carefully, and then polish and polish and polish and polish each lesson until the lesson flows smoothly from beginning to middle to end (Stevenson & Stigler, 1992).

Stevenson and Stigler compared teaching methods in the United States, Japan, Taiwan, and China. They concluded that great lessons were far more commonplace in Japan, Taiwan, and China than in the United States and identified a number of *destructive teaching patterns*. The first is giving students solitary work. Students in the United States were found to spend nearly 50 percent of their time working alone, isolated from classmates and the teacher. They worked on their own, at their desks, doing solitary activities such as filling in workbooks or handout sheets and reading. In Japan, Taiwan, and China, students worked in a whole class as a unit with the teacher as a leader, and in small groups. The second destructive pattern is thirty minutes of teacher lecturing followed by twenty minutes of having students individually complete worksheets. The Asian teachers rarely lectured. Instead, they planned lessons in which there was a continual flow and change from whole class to small groups to individual practice to small groups to whole class, and so forth. All classroom activities were logically sequenced to ensure that the academic objectives of the lesson were reached.

On the basis of their comparison of these schools, Stevenson and Stigler (1992) concluded that there are a number of *pre-beliefs* that differentiate good from poor teachers. *First,* good teachers believe that high-achieving students are made, not born. (They avoid the genetic fallacy.) They see achievement being determined by student (a) effort (not ability) and (b) sustained time-on-task in (c) teacher-led lessons presented in a thoughtful, relaxed, and nonauthoritarian manner. Second, good teachers believe that great teachers are made, not born. (They avoid the genetic fallacy.) They see great lessons resulting from teacher effort in planning, conducting, and continual polishing and polishing lessons. Third, good teachers see their role as (a) planning and conducting coherent, well-orchestrated lessons (not giving lectures) and (b) serving as a knowledgeable guide, not a dispenser of information or an arbiter of correctness.

Carefully prepared and conducted lessons have a beginning, middle, and an end. Stevenson and Stigler call this "lesson coherence." To *begin* the lesson the teacher presents a practical, real-world problem or provocative issue that intellectually challenges students. Everything that follows is organized around solving the problem. (The problem is presented first. Then concepts and rules are presented second.) Teachers pose provocative questions and allow students adequate time for reflection.

The student is the protagonist who meets challenges and resolves problems during the lesson. As the protagonist, students, rather than the teacher, must construct knowledge. During the *middle* of the lesson teachers (a) lead students from what is known to what is unknown, (b) direct students' attention to the critical part of the problem, (c) provide variety by alternating whole-class work, small-group discussions, and individual application of what is being learned, and (d) have students present and defend the solutions and products they come up with. The emphasis is on students producing, explaining, and evaluating solutions to problems (not on rote mastery of facts and procedures). Teachers vary teaching procedures so that the procedures are responsive to differences in students' prior experiences. And teachers interweave instruction, practice, and evaluation into a coherent whole. Concrete representations are used to teach abstract concepts. The emphasis is on students constructing multiple solutions by generating ideas and evaluating their correctness. Student errors are used as an index of what still needs to be learned.

The lesson *ends* with (a) students' presenting what they have learned and defending their reasoning and (b) a review of what has been learned and how it relates to the problem or issue posed at the beginning of the lesson.

Such carefully prepared and conducted lessons require the integrated use of the three types of cooperative learning. Using a mixture of cooperative formal (whole-class, small-groups, pairs), informal (pairs, triads), and base groups in a lesson provides so many important aspects of good instruction that they cannot all be mentioned here. Using the three types of cooperative learning in an integrated way:

1. Helps teachers build more coherent lessons with a clear beginning, middle, and end.
2. Allows teachers to present more difficult problems, material, and intellectual challenges for students to solve.
3. Allows students to construct their own knowledge.
4. Provides variety, which engages and maintains students' interest and attention.
5. Allows many different learning modes (auditory, visual, kinesthetic) to be used within one lesson.
6. Requires students to actively explain and defend their reasoning and conclusions to groupmates.
7. Allows groupmates to assess the quality of a student's understanding and reasoning and provides immediate remediation if it is needed. Students use their own and their groupmates' errors as indications of what still needs to be learned.
8. Helps ensure that students are exposed to multiple strategies and procedures for solving problems and completing assignments.
9. Increases students' motivation to achieve as a result of the social support and group identification.

A typical lesson may be planned as follows. The teacher formally starts the class by welcoming the students and having them meet in their base groups to greet each other, review what has happened in previous class sessions, and focus students' attention on what is to be learned. The problem or issue to be studied is introduced, using informal cooperative learning groups. If direct teaching (such as a whole-class demonstration) is necessary, it is conducted with informal cooperative learning groups. Formal cooperative learning groups are then used to solve the problem presented or complete the assignment given. Members of different learning groups then meet and each student explains his or her group's reasoning and conclusions. Students may apply what they have learned by individually working on a set of similar problems or using the strategies to complete a similar assignment, and then meet in their formal cooperative learning group to assess their success and receive more help if it is needed. At the end of the class session students meet in their base groups to summarize and synthesize what they have learned.

An example of the integrated use of cooperative learning follows. Students arrive at school in the morning and meet in their base groups to welcome each other, complete a self-disclosure task (such as "What is each member's favorite television show?"), check each student's homework to make sure all members understand the academic material and are prepared for the day, and tell each other to have a great day. The teacher then begins a lesson on world interdependence. The teacher has a series of objects and wants the students to identify all the countries that are involved in creating those objects. To help students cognitively organize in advance what they know about the world economy, the teacher uses informal cooperative learning by asking students to turn to the person seated next to them and identify the seven continents and one product that is produced on each continent. They have four minutes to do so.

Formal cooperative learning is now used in the lesson. The objectives for the lesson are for students to learn about global economic interdependence and to improve their skill in encouraging each other's participation. The teacher has her thirty students count off from 1 to 10 to form triads randomly. They sit so they can either face each other or face the teacher. The teacher hands out the objects, which include a silk shirt with plastic buttons, a cup of tea (a saucer and a cup with a teabag and a lump of sugar in it), and a walkman and earphones (with a cassette tape of a Nashville star) made by Phillips (a European company). She assigns members of each triad the roles of hypothesizer (who hypothesizes about the number of products in each item and where they came from), a reference guide (who looks up each hypothesized country in the book to see what products it exports), and a recorder. After each item, the roles are rotated so that each student fulfills each role once.

The teacher introduces world economic interdependence by noting that:

1. A hand-held calculator most often consists of electronic chips from the United States, is assembled in Singapore or Indonesia, is placed in a steel housing from India, and is stamped with a label "Made in Japan" on arrival in Yokohama. (The trees and chemicals from which the paper and ink in the label are made and processed and the plastic in the keys and body are all made elsewhere.)
2. Modern hotels in Saudi Arabia are built with room modules made in Brazil, construction labor from South Korea, and management from the United States.
3. The global economic interdependence is almost beyond imagining.

The teacher then assigns the academic task of identifying how many countries contributed to the production of each object. She establishes positive goal interdependence by stating that it is a cooperative assignment and, therefore, all members of the group must agree on an answer before it is recorded and all members must be able to explain each of the group's answers. The criterion for success is to hand in a correctly completed report form and for each member to score 90 percent or better on a test to be given the next day on world economic interdependence. She establishes positive reward interdependence by stating that if the record sheet is accurate, each member will receive fifteen points and if all members of the group achieve 90 percent or better on the test, each member will receive five bonus points. Individual accountability is established by the roles assigned and the individual test. In addition, the teacher will observe each group to make sure all students are participating and learning. The teacher informs students that the expected social skill to be used by all students is encouraging each other's participation. She defines the skill and has each student practice it twice before the lesson begins.

While students work in their groups, the teacher monitors by systematically observing each group and intervening to provide academic assistance and help in using the interpersonal and small-group skills required to work together effectively. At the end of the lesson the groups hand in their report forms to be evaluated and process how well they worked together by identifying three things members did to help the group achieve and one thing that could be added to improve their group next time.

Next, the teacher then uses a generic cooperative lesson script to teach vocabulary. Studying vocabulary words is a routine that occurs every week in this class. The teacher instructs students to move into their vocabulary pairs, take the vocabulary words identified in the world interdependence lesson, and for each word (a) write down what they think the word means, (b) look it up in the text and write down its official definition, (c) write a sentence in which the word is used, and (d) learn how to spell the word. When they have done that for each word, the pair is to make up a story in which all of the words are used. Pairs then exchange stories and carefully determine whether all the words are used appropriately and are spelled correctly. If not, the two pairs discuss the word until everyone is clear about what it means and how it should be used.

The teacher uses informal cooperative learning to provide closure to the lesson by asking students to meet with a person from another group and write out four conclusions they derived from the lesson and circle the one they believe was the most important.

At the end of the school day the cooperative base groups meet (a) to review what students believe is the most important thing they have learned during the day, what homework has been assigned, what help each member needs to complete the homework, and (b) to tell each other to have a fun afternoon and evening.

SUMMARY

When direct teaching procedures such as lecturing are to be used, informal cooperative leaning groups are needed to focus student attention on the material to be learned, set a mood conducive to learning, help set expectations as to what will be covered in a class session, ensure that students cognitively process the material being taught, keep students' attention focused on the content, ensure that misconceptions, incorrect understanding, and gaps in understanding are corrected, provided an opportunity for discussion and elaboration which promote retention and transfer, make learning experiences personal and immediate, and provide closure to an instructional session. Students can summarize in three-to-five minute discussions what they know about a topic before and after a lecture. Short five minute discussions in cooperative pairs can be interspersed throughout a lecture.

Besides using a formal and informal cooperative learning, there is a need for a permanent base group that provides relatively long-term relationships among students. The primary responsibilities of a base group are for members to provide each other with support, encouragement, and assistance in completing assignments and to hold each other accountable for striving to learn. Base groups may be used in a class or in the school as a whole.

6

Structuring Individualistic Learning

NATURE AND APPROPRIATE USE OF INDIVIDUALISTIC LEARNING

Love many, trust few.
Learn to paddle your own canoe.

Stand on your own two feet.

> *Horatio Alger*

You have just handed out a four-page programmed booklet on how to use a microscope. You explain, "For some of the things we are going to be doing, each student will need to know how to use a microscope. I will give each of you a microscope and the other things you will need to work through this booklet. Take your time and work carefully until you have mastered the tasks outlined in the booklet. Let me know if you need help with anything." You then see that each student has a microscope and a set of materials, and you begin to move from student to student to see how they are progressing. The goal structure described in this learning situation is individualistic. In this chapter the conditions under which individualistic learning can be appropriately used are discussed, and the teacher's role in structuring individualistic learning activities is detailed. Finally, the skills students need to function effectively in an individualistic learning situation are discussed.

Interdependence

Individualistic learning exists when the achievement of one student is unrelated to and independent from the achievement of other students; whether or not a student achieves his or her goal has no bearing on whether other students achieve their goals (see Table 6.1). In other words, no interdependence results in a situation in which individuals work alone to reach a preset criterion of excellence. In such a situation, individuals

1. *Recognize that they have an individual fate* unrelated to the fates of their peers.
2. *Strive for self-benefit* to do the best they can irrespective of how their peers perform.
3. *Have a short-term time perspective* focused on maximizing their performance.
4. *Recognize that their identity depends on how their performance compares* with the preset criterion of excellence. Individuals expect to celebrate their individual success by themselves, with only their superiors (manager, teacher, or parent) emotionally involved in their performance. Individuals are basically indifferent to peers' successes or failures. Individuals do not cathect to their peers or the experience.
5. Recognize that their performance is *self-caused* by their own ability and effort. Individuals feel responsibility only to themselves and are invested in only their own success. They are obligated to the manager or teacher, but not to their peers.

TABLE 6.1 Appropriate Individualistic Learning

Interdependence	None
Instructional Tasks	Simple skill or knowledge acquisition; assignment is clear and behavior specified to avoid confusion and need for extra help
Perception of Goal Importance	Goal is perceived as important for each student; students see tasks as worthwhile and relevant, and each student expects eventually to achieve the goal.
Student Expectations	Each student expects to be left alone by other students; to work at own pace; to take a major part of the responsibility for completing the task; to take a major part in evaluating own progress and the quality of own efforts toward learning.
	Isolation, self-pacing, self-responsibility, self-evaluation.
Teacher–Student Interaction	Teacher is perceived to be the major source of assistance, feedback, reinforcement, and support.
Teacher Statements	"Do not bother David while he is working." "Raise your hand if you need help." "Let me know when you are finished."
Student–Student Interaction	None; students work on their own with little or no interaction with classmates.
Student–Materials Interaction	Complete set of materials and instructions for each student. Rules, procedures, answers are clear. Adequate space for each student.
Room Arrangement	Separate desks or carrels with as much space between students as can be provided.
Evaluation System	Criterion-referenced.

Individuals are not open to influence, are not *inducible* to their peers. Peers' actions do not substitute for individuals' actions.

Working alone does not marshal a number of motives into the service of productivity. Affiliation needs and the desire to be involved in relationships with others may operate directly against productivity in individualistic situations.

ESSENTIAL ELEMENTS OF INDIVIDUALISTIC SITUATIONS

God helps them that help themselves.
                                    Benjamin Franklin

Individuals are more effective when they can appropriately cooperate, compete, and work autonomously on their own. Being able to work individualistically on one's own when it is appropriate is an important competence. Individualistic efforts, however, must be appropriately structured to avoid a number of problems and barriers.

Appropriate Tasks

Individualistic situations are most appropriate when unitary, nondivisible, simple tasks need to be completed, such as the learning of specific facts or the acquisition or the performance of simple skills. The directions for completing the learning task need to be clear and specific so that students do not need further clarification on how to proceed and how to evaluate their work. It is important to avoid confusion as to how the students are to proceed and the need for extra help from the teacher. If several students need help or clarification at the same time, work grinds to a halt. Finally, the learning goal must be perceived as important, and students should expect to be successful in achieving those goals.

Importance of Goal: Relation to Cooperative Learning

Individualistically structured learning activities can supplement cooperative learning through a division of labor in which each student learns material or skills to be subsequently used in cooperative activities. Learning facts and simple skills to be used in subsequent cooperative learning projects increases the perceived relevance and importance of individualistic tasks. Within individualistic learning situations it is crucial that students perceive the task as relevant and worthwhile. Self-motivation is a key aspect of individualistic efforts. The more important and relevant students perceive the learning goal to be, the more motivated they will be to learn. Within classrooms, for example, students may individualistically learn facts and simple skills to be used subsequently in a cooperative project. Most divisions of labor are individualistic efforts within the context of an overall cooperative project. The goal

Be thou thine own home, and in thyself dwell. —*John Donne*

The man who goes alone can start today, but he who travels with another must wait till that other is ready. —*Henry David Thoreau*

"If everybody minded their own business," said the Duchess in a hoarse growl, "the world would go round a deal faster than it does." —*Lewis Carroll*

God helps them that help themselves. —*Benjamin Franklin*

If a man does not keep pace with his companions, perhaps it is because he hears a different drummer. Let him step to the music he hears however measured or far away. —*Henry David Thoreau*

How many a thing which we cast to the ground, when others pick it up becomes a gem! —*George Meredith*

Raphael paints wisdom, Handel sings it, Phidias carves it, Shakespeare writes it, Wren builds it, Columbus sails it, Luther preaches it, Washington arms it, Watt mechanizes it. —*Ralph Waldo Emerson*

must be perceived to be important enough so that concentrated effort is committed to achieving it. It is the overall cooperative effort that provides the meaning to individualistic work. It is contributing to the cooperative effort that makes individualistic goals important.

Teacher–Student Interaction

Within individualistic learning situations the teacher is the major source of assistance, feedback, reinforcement, and support. Students should expect periodic visits from the teacher, and a great deal of teacher time may be needed to monitor and assist the students.

Student–Materials Interaction

Each student needs a complete set of all necessary materials to complete the work individually. Each student has to be a separate, self-contained learner. Programmed materials, task cards, and demonstrations are among the techniques that can be used to facilitate the task. Provide separate desks or carrels, allowing as much space between students as possible.

Student–Student Interaction

No interaction should occur among students. Students should work on their own without paying attention to or interacting with classmates. Each student should have his or her own space and should be separated from other students. Since each student is working on the task at his or her own pace, student–student interaction is intrusive and is not helpful.

Student Role Expectations

Students expect to be left alone by their classmates in order to complete the assigned task, to work at their own pace in their own space, to take responsibility for completing the task, to take a major part in evaluating their own progress and the quality of their efforts, to be successful in achieving the learning goal, and to perceive the learning goal to be important.

Evaluation System

Evaluation should be conducted on a criterion-referenced basis. Students should work on their own toward a criterion that is set so that every student could conceivably be successful. There is an A for everyone if each student earns it individually.

ESTABLISHING AN INDIVIDUALISTIC STRUCTURE

The essence of an individualistic goal structure is giving students individual goals and using a criterion-referenced evaluation system to assign rewards. In a ninth-grade English class, the students have been reading a cluster of novels centering on the building of the railroads in the western United States. The teacher has taught a unit on character analysis covering the need to find out about the appearance, personality, and perspective of major characters in a story. The teacher now explains to the class that the names of several people from the novels are in a box and tells each student to draw a name. The assignment is for students to spend the next few days finding out as much as possible about their characters by reading appropriate passages in the novels and by using any other resources they can find. At the end of the week, there will be a number of discussions about the building of the railroad, and each student will be expected to introduce him- or herself and present the point of view of the selected character. Until the discussion, students are to work on their own, each one gathering the necessary information on the fictional character; if students need help, they are to come to the teacher so as not to intrude on the work of classmates. The teacher will work with each student through the next few days to see that each has all the materials needed and has mastered the perspective of the character he or she has drawn, so that all can contribute to the discussions. The specific procedures for teachers to structure such an individualistic learning situation are given in the following paragraphs.

Objectives

1. Specifying instructional objectives. The academic objective needs to be specified at the correct level for each student and matched to the right level of instruction according to a conceptual or task analysis. Often the objective will be to learn specific information or a simple skill to be subsequently used in a cooperative learning situation. Examples include learning the bones and muscles of the arm and shoulder in order to teach it to classmates who are studying other parts of the body, learning the meaning of vocabulary words in order to compose a group story with more understanding, and gathering information for a section of a group report.

Decisions

2. Arranging the classroom. Adequate space must be provided for each student so that he or she can work without being interrupted by others. Examples of isolating students from looking at and being disrupted by classmates include using the perimeter of the classroom by having students face the wall, having students sit back to back, and staggering rows of seats.

3. Planning the instructional materials to promote independence. Structuring the materials to be used in the lesson is especially important for individualistic learning. Each student needs a set of self-contained materials. And usually the materials need to contain a procedure for students to evaluate their own work. The programmed instruction format is often useful. The materials are the primary resource for learning in the individualistic situation.

Explaining the Task and Goal Structure

4. Explaining the academic task. The academic task needs to be explained in such a way that all students clearly understand what they are supposed to do, realize that they have all the materials they need, feel comfortable that they can do the task, and realize why they are doing the task. When assigning the academic task, teachers will:

   a. Set the task so that students are clear about the assignment. Instructions that are clear and specific are crucial in warding off student frustration.
   b. Explain the objectives of the lesson and relate the concepts and information to be studied to students' past experiences and learning to maximize transfer and

retention. Explaining the intended outcomes of the lesson increases the likelihood that students will focus on the relevant concepts and information throughout the lesson.

c. Define relevant concepts, explain procedures students should follow, and give examples to help students understand what they are to learn and to do in completing the assignment. To promote positive transfer of learning, point out the critical elements that separate this lesson from past learning.

d. Ask the class specific questions to check the students' understanding of the assignment. Such questioning ensures that thorough two-way communication exists, that the assignment has been given effectively, and that the students are ready to begin completing it.

Students must perceive the task as relevant and have some idea of how the information and skills they are learning are going to be useful in future learning situations.

5. Structuring goal independence. Communicate to students that they have individual goals and must work individualistically. The basic individualistic goal is for students to work by themselves, at their own pace, to master the material specifically assigned to them, up to the preset criteria of excellence adjusted for their previous performances. Students should work by themselves without interrupting and interfering with the work of classmates. Students are to ask for assistance from the teacher, not from other students. Students who finish quickly should go beyond the specific assignment and find ways to embellish it.

6. Structuring individual accountability. The purpose of the individualistic goal structure is for students to attend to a specific task and master it on their own. Individual accountability may be structured by the teacher circulating through the room and randomly asking individual students to explain their work.

7. Explaining criteria for success. A criterion for excellence is set to orient students toward the level of mastery required in the lesson. Students need to know specifically what is an acceptable performance on the task that signifies that they have completed the task successfully. Setting a criterion ensures that students are aware that everyone who achieves up to criterion gets an A and, therefore, students are not in competition with each other. Whether one student does or does not learn the material does not affect the success of other students. Each student is rewarded separately on the basis of his or her own work.

8. Specifying desired behaviors. The word *individualistic* has different connotations and uses. Teachers need to define *individualistic* operationally by specifying the behaviors that are appropriate and desirable within the learning situation, including the following:

a. Work alone without interacting with other students.

b. Focus on the task and tune out everything else.

c. Monitor your time and pace yourself accordingly.

d. Check with the teacher for help.

Students need to know what behaviors are appropriate and desirable within an individualistic learning situation.

Monitoring and Intervening

9. Monitoring students' behavior. Much of the teacher's time should be spent in observing students in order to see what problems they are having in completing the assignment and in working individualistically. The teacher should move throughout the room, checking students for understanding, answering questions, and checking for the expected student behaviors. The teacher needs to be active while students are working. Some teachers allow students to come to their desk for help, but students may have to wait in line for assistance. It is more efficient to have the teacher periodically circulate through the classroom to assess the students' progress on their assigned tasks, how much the students understand, and what help each student needs to complete the assignment. This method allows teachers to work with students who are not requesting help as well as those who are. The teacher may wish to (a) observe the class as a whole to determine the number of students on task and exerting effort to achieve or (b) observe a few students intensely to obtain the data necessary for individual feedback and constructive suggestions on how to work more efficiently. Systematic observing provides feedback on how well the task is suited for individualistic work and how well students are working individualistically.

10. Providing task assistance. In monitoring individual students as they work, teachers will wish to clarify instructions, review important procedures and strategies for completing the assignment, answer questions, and teach task skills as necessary. After the materials provided, the teacher is the major resource for student learning. In discussing the concepts and information to be learned, teachers should use the language or terms relevant to the learning. Instead of saying, "Yes, that is right," teachers may wish to say something more specific to the assignment, such as, "Yes, that is the suggested way to solve for the unknown in an equation." The use of specific statements reinforces the desired learning and promotes positive transfer. Typically, considerable task assistance is required within individualistic learning situations.

11. Intervening to teach individualistic skills. Although it is likely that students have experience in working alone, many students lack some of the basic skills necessary to work well individualistically. While monitoring the class, teachers sometimes find students without the necessary individualistic skills to work effectively on their own. These skills will need to be taught. Some of the basic skills needed in an individualistic learning situation are these:

a. Clarifying the need to learn the material and making a personal commitment to learning it.

    b. Tuning out extraneous noise and visual distractions and focusing in on the academic task.

    c. Monitoring own progress and pacing self through the material. Charts and records are often helpful in evaluating one's progress.

    d. Evaluating one's readiness to apply the material or skills being learned.

It is important that students learn to work autonomously on their own in the school setting. It strengthens cooperative learning when students can learn needed simple skills and factual information individualistically or participate successfully in a division of labor.

    In an individualistic situation teachers should intervene as quickly as possible. The amount of time in which students are struggling to work more efficiently should be minimized.

    12. Providing closure to the lesson. At the end of the lesson, students should be able to summarize what they have learned and to understand where they will use it in future lessons. To reinforce student learning, teachers may wish to summarize the major points in the lesson, ask students to recall ideas or give examples, and answer any final questions they may have.

Evaluation and Reinforcement

    13. Evaluating and reinforcing the quality and quantity of students' learning. Student learning needs to be evaluated by a criterion-referenced system. Each student will be evaluated independently of other students. The teacher sets a standard as to how many points a student will receive for mastering the assigned material at different levels of proficiency and gives each student the appropriate grade. Having students mark their progress on a chart is often helpful. Personal reinforcement needs to be given to each student. It is the teacher, not classmates, who gives praise for good work.

Teacher Role Checklist for Individualistic Instruction

1. What are the desired outcomes for the activity of learning specific knowledge and noncomplex skills?

2. Is the classroom arranged so that students
   _____ are isolated at separate desks or by a seating arrangement that separates them as much as possible?
   _____ are arranged to do their own work without approaching or talking with each other?
   _____ have individual sets of self-contained materials?

3. Have you effectively communicated to students that
   _____ the instructional goal is an individual goal (each student masters the material on his or her own)?
   _____ each student will be rewarded on the basis of how his or her work meets a fixed set of standards for quality and quantity?

4. Have you effectively communicated the expected patterns of student–student interaction? Do students know that they
   _____ should not interact with each other?
   _____ should work on the assignment alone, trying to completely ignore the other students?
   _____ should perceive teacher praise, support, or criticism of other students as irrelevant to their own mastery of the assigned materials?
   _____ should go to the teacher for all help and assistance needed?

5. Have you effectively communicated the expected patterns of teacher–student interaction? Do students know that the teacher
   _____ wants them to work by themselves and to master the assigned material without paying attention to other students, and will evaluate them on the basis of how their efforts match a fixed set of standards?
   _____ will interact with each student individually, setting up learning contracts, viewing student progress, providing assistance, giving emotional support for effort, and answering questions individually?
   _____ will praise and support students for working alone and ignoring other students?

INDIVIDUALISTIC SKILLS

Since there is no interaction with other students in an individualistic situation, learning under such a goal structure requires the fewest skills. Students need their own materials, enough space to be isolated from others, and a clear understanding of what they are supposed to do. The primary skill necessary is to be able to work on one's own, ignoring other students and not being distracted or interrupted by what other students are doing.

Besides being able to "tune out" noises, movement, and distractions, students need to clarify why they need to learn the information or skill, make a personal commitment to do so, and assume responsibility for task completion. Each student must be motivated to complete the task and learn the assigned material on his or her own. Completing a task on one's own depends on the importance one assigns to mastering the material. The importance will probably be greatest when the results of the individualistic efforts are to be contributed to a group project in which students collaborate with each other. Having one's classmates depend on one for certain skills or facts increases one's motivation to learn them.

Third, students must be able to monitor their own progress, pace themselves through the material, and evaluate their own progress. Charts and records often are used to help students evaluate themselves. Self-tests are commonly used. Students must also be able to evaluate their readiness to apply the material or skills being learned.

Finally, students must take a personal pride and satisfaction from successfully completing individualistic assignments. Although teachers can provide students some recognition, support, and reinforcement for individualistic success, the students must learn to give themselves needed "pats on the back" for a job well done.

Individualistic Efforts and Personal Autonomy

There is often a confusion between individualistic efforts and personal autonomy. The admiration given to individuals who have a strong sense of personal autonomy and who are able to resist social pressure and act independently is often directed toward individualistic efforts. As will be discussed in depth in Chapter 10, individualistic efforts do not build personal autonomy. It is social support and caring personal relationships that do so. Individualistic efforts and personal autonomy are quite distinct and separate.

Problems in Implementing Individualistic Efforts

In implementing individualistic efforts there are potential problems that have to be faced and dealt with:

1. *Talking and interacting with others.* The more socializing and discussions that take place within an individualistic situation, the lower the productivity.
2. *Competing with others.* In American society, persons working individualistically in the proximity of others doing similar work begin to compete.
3. *Complex or new tasks.* Individualistic work is most appropriate on simple skill- or knowledge-acquisition tasks. If the task is new or complex, individualistic efforts often are inadequate.
4. *Unimportant goal.* For many people it is hard to stay motivated while working alone. If the goal is perceived to be unimportant, attention will quickly wane, and effort will be small.
5. *Unclear rules and procedures.* Confusion leads to inaction. In individualistic situations clarification comes from authority figures who may or may not have time to explain the task and procedure again and again until it is understood.

6. *Lack of materials and resources.* In individualistic situations every person must be a self-contained unit. If needed materials and resources are lacking, then individualistic efforts grind to a halt.
7. *Lack of essential skills.*

SUMMARY

The basic elements of an individualistic goal structure include each student's working on his or her own toward a set criterion, having his or her own materials and space, perceiving the task as relevant and important, tuning out other students and distractions, and using the teacher as a resource. It is most appropriate to use the individualistic goal structure when the material to be learned is simple, straightforward, and needed for use in the near future. The jigsaw of materials in a cooperative group where each group member is to research a different part of the topic and then help the group synthesize the different aspects of the subject into one group report is an example of where students see a need to learn material on their own. The primary skill necessary is to be able to work on one's own, ignoring other students (that is, not being distracted or interrupted by what other students are doing).

The teacher's role in an individualistic learning situation is to arrange the room so that students will not be distracted by each other, give students their individual set of materials, explain that students are to work alone and check only with the teacher when they need help, set a clear criterion for success that everyone could conceivably reach, ask students to work on their own (clarifying the relevance of the assignment for themselves, tuning out distractions, and monitoring their own progress and pacing), circulating among the students and monitoring their work, intervening to teach skills or help students to refocus on their task, and giving students time to evaluate how well they have learned.

7

Structuring Competitive Learning

INTRODUCTION

After you have spent some time demonstrating how candles burn in jars under different conditions, bring in ten odd-sized and odd-shaped jars. Hold one up and ask, "Who can give me the best estimate of how long a candle will burn in this jar?" Then place the ten jars on tables around the room and assign three students to each jar. Assign the task of predicting how long a candle will burn in the jar, and structure the situation competitively by stating that the three students will be ranked from best to worst on the basis of the accuracy of their predictions. Do not make the reward for winning so important that students will lose the spirit of fun in the competition. Each student studies the jar, writes down the estimate on a slip of paper, and shares it with the two competitors. There is a feeling of excitement as you light each candle and place the jar over it. The students watch both the candle and the clock, timing the duration of the candle's burning. When the candle goes out, there is good-natured congratulating of the winners. In this chapter the conditions under which competitive learning can be appropriately used are discussed, and the teacher's role in structuring competitive learning activities is detailed. Finally, the skills students need to function effectively within a competitive learning situation are given. But first, because many educators have concerns about the instructional use of interpersonal competition, the common criticisms of interpersonal competition are reviewed.

CRITICISMS OF INTERPERSONAL COMPETITION IN SCHOOLS

Historical Roots

In the 1930s an organized advocacy of interpersonal competition in the schools was launched by a combination of various business interests. In 1934, in the midst of the depression, the Liberty League was formed; it united with other business organizations, such as the National Association of Manufacturers, to sell interpersonal competition to educators. Their efforts were so successful that the use of interpersonal competition gained steam in the 1940s and 1950s, and by the 1960s interpersonal competition was considered to be the "traditional" way of structuring student–student interaction. In the 1950s emphasis was placed on norm-referenced evaluation under the rationale that all nature could be fitted on a bell-shaped curve. Social Darwinism, expressed in the myth that it was a "dog-eat-dog" world in which only the fittest survive, became widespread. Observational studies have found that competition and individualistic learning are used 85 to 95 percent of the time in American schools. There is evidence, furthermore, that (1) most students perceive school as being competitive, (2) American children are more competitive than are children from other countries, (3) American children become more competitive the longer they are in school or the older they become, (4) Anglo-American children are more competitive than are other American children (for instance, Mexican-American and black American children), and (5) urban children are more competitive than are rural children (Johnson & Johnson, 1974, 1983a).

> Only a few children in school ever become good at learning in the way we try to make them learn. Most of them get humiliated, frightened, and discouraged. They use their minds, not to learn, but to get out of doing the things we tell them to do—to make them learn. In the short run, these strategies seem to work. They make it possible for many children to get through their schooling even though they learn very little. But in the long run these strategies are self-limiting and self-defeating, and destroy both character and intelligence. The children who use such strategies are prevented by them from growing into more than limited versions of the human beings they might have become. This is the real failure that takes place in school; hardly any children escape. —*John Holt,* How Children Fail *(1964)*

Early Critics

There have been a number of critics of an emphasis on interpersonal competition in the classroom. A large number of educators, psychologists, and popular writers in the 1960s challenged the notion that competition must be an inevitable part of

American education and that a large proportion of students experience failure (Glasser, 1969; Holt, 1964; Illich, 1971; Jackson, 1968; Johnson, 1970; Kagan, 1965; Kohl, 1969; Kohn, 1986; Nesbitt, 1967; Postman & Weingartner, 1969; Rathbone, 1970; Rogers, 1970; Silberman, 1971; Walberg & Thomas, 1971; Wilhelms, 1970). Their criticism of the use of interpersonal competition for instructional purposes included the subversion of intrinsic motivation for learning (in competition one learns to win, and knowledge that does not help one win is a waste of time); the valuing of "bettering" others; the joy taken in others' mistakes and failures (because they increase one's own chances for success); the viewing of life as a "rat race" aimed at outshining one's neighbors; the development of a contingent self-acceptance where one is of value only if one wins; feelings of guilt over winning and apprehension about being rejected by the individuals one has defeated; feelings of anger and hostility toward those who defeat one and toward the teacher, the school, and themselves; and in general feelings of anxiety, doubt, and self-orientation. Several of these criticisms are discussed in the following paragraphs.

> There is nothing new in all this. We have heard it before. During the latter half of the 19th century, and during the early part of the 20th century, this viewpoint formed the foundation for the doctrine of "Social Darwinism." It was implied in such ideas as "The Survival of the Fittest" and "The Struggle for Existence," and in such phrases as "The Weakest Go to the Wall," "Competition Is the Life-Blood of a Nation," and the like. Such ideas were not merely taken to explain, but were actually used to justify violence and war. —*Ashley Montagu (1965)*

Most Students Lose Most of the Time

John, a 34-year-old lawyer, was depressed. In trying to explain his depression to his psychotherapist, he stated, "All my life I've failed. I tried my best to be valedictorian of my high school class, and I finished second. I tried my best to be the top of my college class, and I finished third. I entered Harvard Law School and tried my best again to be the top of my class. I failed. I graduated seventh. Now my law firm has made me a partner a year later than I strived for. I've had failure after failure after failure. I'm having trouble sleeping. I'm depressed all the time. Often I feel that life isn't worth living."

Since there can be only one "winner" in a competitive situation, the vast majority of students will experience daily failure. Although there is limited evidence on the effects of prolonged failure, it seems reasonable to assume that a person's self-attitudes and feelings of competence will be affected. In the traditional competitive classroom, the purpose of classroom evaluation is to rank students from the "best" to the "worst" in order to separate the wheat from the chaff. In most classrooms, fairly stable patterns of achievement exist, so that the majority of students always lose and a few students always win. Thus a student may spend twelve years in public schools being confronted daily with the fact that he is a "loser." If the student desires to "win," the daily frustration of failing may be a concomitant of schooling. A sense of helplessness, worthlessness, and incompetence may result from such a situation. "Losers" in a competitive learning situation tend to perceive their learning experiences as boring, unfair, and not fun, and perceive themselves negatively (Crockenberg, Bryant, & Wilce, 1976). Atkinson (1965) predicted from his theory of achievement motivation that students who chronically experience failure will become primarily oriented toward avoiding failure (thus becoming non-achievement-oriented). Failure, furthermore, reduces the attraction students feel toward classmates (Ashmore, 1970; Blanchard, Adelman, & Cook, 1975).

Cheating

Rules, the way most coaches see it, are made to be winked at. Education can be sacrificed. Winning is everything, it is the only thing. Coaches' desire to win has no morality.

Anonymous college coach

In a serious competition, winning becomes so important that participants will break the rules to enhance their chances. Richard Turbo (in an article in the *Chicago Tribune Magazine* published on July 31, 1977) stated:

> Admission to the nation's 114 medical schools is so highly prized that the competition among premedical students has reached ruthless levels. Cheating, sabotage, forgery, and academic dishonesty are no longer uncommon among students seeking to enhance their chances. They steal critical books from the library and from each other. They sabotage one another's science experiments in an attempt to gain an advantage in the battle for grades. . . . If they were to help each other, students are afraid that they might give an important edge on exams to their peers. . . . several premedical students told of their malicious activities. "Yes, we cheat," they said. "We try to give the wrong information to other students. We take books from the medical library and destroy parts of them. We don't share information. We sabotage others' chemistry experiments. . . ."

High school students have declared that cheating is universal, necessary, and very easy. Whenever an answer is not known, the students cheat. A survey of students in sixty-one central Florida elementary schools, high schools, and colleges found that nine out of ten students have cheated on tests or have copied assignments or homework. Cheating has become a part of school experience, a part of the stress on grades, on passing, on good results at all costs. Competition is the reason for cheating, because "if you are not counted among the winners, you are not counted." The Girl Scouts of America conducted a nationwide survey of students in grades 4–12 from 233 public, private, and parochial schools from September 14 to October 30, 1989. Sixty-five percent of the 5,012 students interviewed stated that given the chance, they would cheat on an important examination.

And it is not just the students. A highly regarded school principal in Maryland was recently dismissed for giving his students extra time to finish segments of the Iowa Tests for Educational Development, thus artificially boosting their scores to make him look successful. The year before another Maryland principal had been forced to resign when it was learned that his students had earned dazzling scores on standardized tests because they had been pretested. Recently a study found that schools in almost all of the United States cheated to increase their students' scores on standardized tests. And it is not only schools. Insider stock trading scandals and fraud within the banking industry are additional examples.

Sport participants, as their competitive experience increases, become more committed to winning at any cost and less committed to values of fairness and justice (Kroll & Peterson, 1965; Loy, Birrell, & Rose, 1976; Webb, 1969). Competition has been found to inhibit empathic responses, and elite athletes, the ones who have weathered years of intense competition, have been found to be aloof and insensitive (Ogilvie & Tutko, 1971). Kleiber and Roberts (1981) found in a two-week study of soccer that crying occurred on three occasions as a result of perceived failure and injustice, and that quarreling took place at regular intervals, with a fistfight following one game. They also found that the participants with the most competitive experience were significantly less likely to behave altruistically and significantly more likely to behave in a rivalrous manner. The emphasis on winning in organized sport may lead children to become more rivalrous in social interactions with other children (Kagan & Madsen, 1972).

Overgeneralization of Results

Within competitions participants often overgeneralize the results. Winning seems to make a person more worthwhile, and losing seems to make a person less worthwhile. Brenda Bryant and her colleagues (Crockenberg, Bryant, & Wilce, 1976) found that children competing to write the best theme tended to see the winners as better students overall and more deserving people.

Interference with Adaptive Problem Solving

Competitive attitudes and behavioral patterns often interfere with individuals' capacity for adaptive problem solving. Nelson and Kagan found that American students so seldom cooperate spontaneously on the experimental tasks that it appeared that the environment provided for these children was barren of experiences that would sensitize them to the possibility of cooperation. Anglo-American children were found to engage in irrational and self-defeating competition by reducing their own rewards in order to reduce the rewards of peers even more. Nelson and Kagan (1972) stated:

Anglo-American children are not only irrationally competitive, they are almost sadistically rivalrous. Given a choice, Anglo-American children took toys away from their peers on 78 percent of the trials even when they could not keep the toys for themselves. Observing the success of their actions, some of the children gloated. "Ha! Ha! Now you won't get a toy." Rural Mexican children in the same situation were rivalrous only half as often as the Anglo-American child.

The socialization of American children into competitive attitudes and orientations is so pervasive that Staub (1971) found that American children often believe that helping a person in distress is inappropriate and is disapproved of by others.

High Anxiety Levels

Competition tends to increase anxiety and makes people feel less able to perform. Tseng (1969), for example, found that as rewards increase in value, so do the tension and frustration of failure; children who failed in competitive situations performed poorly in subsequent competitions.

Inappropriate Generalization to Other Areas of People's Lives

The germ that is going around the office does not remain confined to the office for long. Someone brings it home, and the whole family comes down with it. The disease that starts in school or the workplace is carried into living rooms and even bedrooms. The disease is a self centered, egocentric focus on gratifying one's own needs, even at the expense of others. The disease is a product of individualistic and competitive social structures. Its cure is learning how to cooperate with others.

No Contest

The most comprehensive critique of competition was written by Alfie Kohn (1986). He presents the thesis that gaining success by making others fail is an unproductive way of learning or working. In his book *No Contest*, Kohn summarizes data indicating that competition poisons relationships, causes anxiety, selfishness, self-doubt, poor communication, and aggression among individuals, and generally makes life unpleasant. He believes that the unfortunate consequences of competition are not restricted to "bad" or "excessive" competition; rather, they stem from the basic win–lose structure of competition. Kohn recommends that all competition be ended. Many students would agree. Despite the pervasive use of interpersonal competition there is solid evidence (see Johnson & Johnson, 1983b, 1989a) that students actually prefer to work cooperatively with their classmates.

ADVOCATES OF COMPETITION

Not everyone, however, is against competition. The famous coach of the Green Bay Packers, Vince Lombardi, once said, "Winning isn't everything. It's the only thing!" George Allen, the well-known coach of the Washington Redskins, said: "Every time you win, you are reborn. Every time you lose, you die a little." Bill Musselman, the renowned basketball coach, commented: "Defeat is worse than death because you have to live with defeat!" Frank McGuire stated, "In this country, when you finish second, no one knows your name." Leo Durocher offered this advice: "Nice guys finish last!" Finally, even an ex-president of the United States, Gerald Ford, stated, "It isn't enough to compete. Winning is very important. Maybe more important than ever. . . . If you don't win elections you don't play." The feelings of the advocates of competition are as strong as the feelings of the critics.

Despite the strong case against competition, and the strong feelings favoring competition, the proper scientific activity is to identify the conditions under which competition leads to (a) destructive and (b) constructive outcomes. Once the conditions have been identified, the guidelines for the instructional use of competition may be formulated (see Table 7.1)

NATURE AND APPROPRIATE
USE OF COMPETITIVE LEARNING

To say that "winning is everything" is ludicrous. I think it's good to lose every once in a while. I don't think there is anything wrong to having your backside handed to you every once in a while. Because you learn from it. You learn maybe you overlooked something, maybe you got carried away, maybe you were a little bit careless, maybe you did not make the commitment, or maybe someone is better than you. This is nothing wrong with that. In life you are going to find that some people are better than you.

Joe Paterno, Penn State football coach

In the classroom, competitively structured learning activities can supplement cooperation through entertaining drill-reviews in which a change of pace and a release of energy are desirable. Competition should be used when well-learned material needs to be reviewed. The emphasis should be placed on having an

TABLE 7.1 Appropriate Competitive Learning

Type of Instructional Activity	Skill practice, knowledge recall and review, assignment is clear with rules for competing specified.
Perception of Goal Importance	Goal is not perceived to be of large importance to the students, and they can accept either winning or losing.
Student Expectations	Each student expects to have an equal chance of winning; to enjoy the activity, win or lose; to monitor the progress of competitors; to compare ability, skills, or knowledge with peers.
Teacher–Student Interaction	Teacher is perceived to be the major source of assistance, feedback, reinforcement, and support. Teacher available for questions and clarification of the rules; teacher referees disputes and judges correctness of answers, rewards the winners.
Teacher Statements	"Who has the most so far?" "What do you need to do to win next time?"
Student–Materials Interaction	Set of materials for each triad or for each student.
Student–Student Interaction	Observing other students in one's triad. Some talking among students. Students grouped in homogeneous triads to ensure equal chance of winning.
Student Expectations	Review previously learned material. Have an equal chance of winning. Enjoy the activity, win or lose. Monitor the progress of competitors. Follow the rules. Be a good winner and loser.
Room Arrangement	Students placed in triads or small clusters.
Evaluation Procedures	Norm-referenced.

enjoyable drill-review rather than on winning. That the situation described at the beginning of this chapter is appropriately structured is evidenced in the enjoyment of the students as they compete with one another in a review of something they have already practiced, in the students' awareness that winning is secondary to having fun, and in the fact that all students believe they have a good chance of winning.

Intergroup Competition Versus Interpersonal Competition

There are two ways in which competition may be used for instructional purposes. Individuals can compete against each other to see who has learned the assigned material the best, or cooperative learning groups can compete to see which group has best mastered the assigned material. Although interpersonal competition has many instructional drawbacks, intergroup competition can be used effectively under certain conditions. *Whenever possible, make competition intergroup rather than interpersonal.*

Intergroup competition is a combination of intragroup cooperation and competition between groups. It is important for the teacher to ensure that the intergroup competition does not become so strong that it outweighs the intragroup cooperation. Once competition becomes too serious, all the destructive outcomes of competition will appear, and students resort to bickering, scapegoating, and negative interpersonal relationships. As the saying goes, "It's not whether you win or lose, it's how you play the game." The corollary in this situation would be, "It's not how fiercely you compete with the other groups, it's how comfortably you cooperate with your teammates."

What you lose in using intergroup competition is the flow of ideas and materials between groups and the overall class possibility of a division of labor. What you gain is a change of pace to provide some fun, energy, and variety within the classroom.

Interdependence

In an appropriate competition, clear negative interdependence exists. Formally, *competitive learning* exists when students' goal attainments are negatively correlated; when one student obtains his or her goal, all other students with whom he or she is competitively linked fail to obtain their goals (Deutsch, 1949a, 1962). Students work against each other to determine who can perform the highest. Competitive learning requires perceived scarcity of goals and winners. The incentive is to win by obtaining the highest score or grade. In their attempts to win, students

1. *Recognize their negatively linked fate.* When one wins, the others lose. Individuals perceive that their success creates failure for others and that obstructing competitors' achievement is beneficial to themselves.
2. *Strive for differential benefit* by trying to gain more than their classmates do. Students recognize that each is trying to defeat the others. Competitors typically attempt to obstruct each other's productivity. There is recognition that what helps a classmate to achieve hurts one's own chances of winning, and vice versa.
3. *Have a short-term time perspective* so that long-term joint productivity is perceived to be of less value than short-term personal advantage.
4. *Develop a relative identity* based on a performance ranking within the situation. One sees oneself as either a "winner" or a "loser" depending on how one compares with others. If one wins (and therefore celebrates), one's competitors lose (and therefore have no reason to celebrate). Winning is celebrated only by the winner. Losing results in feeling inadequate, jealous, and angry about one's failure.
5. *Recognize the relative causation of winning or losing.* In a competition, the outcomes one receives are caused by both one's own performance and the performance of competitors. No matter how well one performs, it is of no use if someone else performs even better. No matter how poorly one performs, it does not matter if all others perform even more poorly. The worse one's competitors perform, the greater one's chances of winning. Thus a person does not have control over his or her outcomes because the productivity of competitors negatively affects his or her chances of winning.

In competitive situations, students are closed to being influenced by each other (i.e., there is a lack of inducibility). The actions of competitors do not substitute for each other, so if one member of the group has taken the action, all others still have to engage in the action even though it may be futile to do so. Once one person has won, for example, all others may have to complete the task knowing that they have lost and that their efforts will not benefit them. Competing, furthermore, creates motives that are contradictory and operate against each other. Affiliation needs and the desire to be involved in relationships with others may operate directly against productivity in competitive situations because someone who makes good grades may not be popular with his or her peers.

To structure lessons competitively, teachers need to make the negative interdependence among groups clear.

Appropriate Tasks

Competition should be used when well-learned skills need to be practiced; when well-learned material needs to be reviewed; or when simple, unitary or nondivisible (i.e., unable to be divided into subtasks), overlearned tasks need to be performed (Johnson & Johnson, 1974, 1989a; Miller & Hamblin, 1963). Competition is frequently used when speed on a very simple task or sheer quantity of performance (i.e., maximizing task) is required. Working in the presence of competitors improves performance on a variety of tasks such as fishing-reel winding (Triplett, 1898), dressing in familiar clothes (Markus, 1978), recognition of salient stimuli (Cottrell, Wack, Sekerak, & Rittle, 1968), negotiating simple mazes (Hunt & Hillery, 1973), and copying simple material (Sanders & Baron, 1975).

When tasks are new or complex, competition is inappropriate. Researchers have found that working in the presence of competitors hampers performance on such tasks as solving difficult anagrams (Green, 1977), dressing in unfamiliar clothes, recognizing novel stimuli, negotiating difficult mazes, and copying difficult material. The underlying reason that has been offered to explain why competition enhances performance on simple overlearned tasks only is that competition increases anxiety, evaluation apprehension, and drive, which in turn increases the likelihood that the dominant or most probable response will occur. If the dominant response includes behaviors that lead to successful performance (as in the case of simple tasks), then people do better when in a high drive state. If the dominant response primarily includes behaviors that lead to poor performance (as in the case of difficult tasks), then people do worse when in a high drive state (Zajonc, 1965).

Relation to Cooperative Learning

Competition is first and foremost a cooperative activity. Appropriate competition takes place within a context of cooperation. Competitors have to cooperate to decide: the nature of the contest, the determination of who wins and who loses, the rules governing their behavior during the competition, where the competition occurs, and when it begins and ends. This underlying cooperative foundation keeps the competition in perspective and allows participants to enjoy it, win or lose. The stronger the cooperative foundation, the more constructive the competition. When it does not matter who wins or who loses, such as when playing tennis with a friend, the cooperative goal of enjoying each other's company while obtaining exercise dominates. The shared cooperative experience then dominates. Constructive competition thus provides an enjoyable and exciting change of pace within ongoing cooperative relationships to demonstrate mastery of the skills and knowledge required for the cooperative efforts. Intergroup competition is often more constructive than interpersonal competition because teams tend to handle winning and losing more constructively than do individuals.

Teacher–Student Interaction

The teacher is perceived to be the major source of assistance, feedback, reinforcement, and support. The teacher needs to be available for questions and clarifications of the rules, to referee disputes, to judge the correctness of answers, and to reward the winners. Common teacher statements are, "Who has the most so far?" "What do you need to do to win next time?"

Student–Materials Interaction

In order to ensure that all students have appropriate access to the curriculum materials, a set of materials needs to be provided for each triad or for each student. Clear and specific rules, procedures, and answers are an absolute necessity. Ambiguity ruins competition because too much time is spent worrying about what is fair and unfair, what the procedures actually are, and whether or not the answers are correct.

Student–Student Interaction

Student–student interaction within competitive situations is controlled by clustering students homogeneously, maximizing the number of winners, structuring clear rules and procedures, ensuring that students do not take winning or losing too seriously, and providing an opportunity to monitor the progress of others.

Homogeneous grouping to motivate competitive efforts.   For competition to be constructive, all participants must be motivated to win. Motivation to strive to win depends on being evenly matched with competitors. In order for competition to be an exciting challenge, all participants must believe that they have a good chance to win. Accordingly, competitors should be evenly matched. For a competition, therefore, teachers should group students homogeneously. Who wins and who

All of us are the inheritors of a tradition of thought, relating to the nature of life, which has been handed down to us from the nineteenth century. Life, this view holds, is struggle, competition, the survival of the fittest. In the jungle, a fight with "Nature, red in tooth and claw"; in society, the claw is perhaps gloved, and the fight is called a "struggle" in which "the race is to the swiftest," in which "the strongest survive and the weakest go to the wall." —*Ashley Montagu (1966)*

All plants and animals are bound together by sharing the same earth, air, and water. They are also linked by a competition for solar energy, on which their lives depend. Once believed to be a ruthless and unbridled battle, more recent study of this struggle for existence suggests that cooperation and interdependence may be more important for the survival of a species than a no-quarter war. —*Peter Farb (1963)*

loses should vary. If individuals believe they have little chance of winning, they will not be motivated.

Younger brothers rarely are able to beat older brothers and, therefore, lose all interest in competing. A barrier to constructive competition is having individuals matched against others who are far better or worse than they. In a competition, participants are ranked from best to worst. After a while, fairly stable patterns of achievement often exist, so that the majority of participants lose over and over again and a few individuals always win. *Constant winners tend to work only hard enough to win, and constant losers tend to be unmotivated.* Hurlock (1927) found in an experiment with children that members of a group that was defeated on the first of four days of competition never overcame their initial failure and attained inferior scores for the entire duration of the experiment, even though the groups had been matched on the basis of ability. Matthews (1979) concluded that losers tend to give up and withdraw from the contest. Halisch and Heckhausen (1977) found that children who believed they had a chance of winning increased their speed of response on a simple task when they became aware of being slightly behind a competitor, but children who believed that they had no chance of winning decreased their speed of response in similar circumstances. Finally, Lepley (1937), in a study on whether or not competition enhances speed of performance, placed two rats in a runway and rewarded the faster runner. The slower runner quickly quit running at all, whereas the faster runner maintained the speed that led to reward.

In compulsory situations, such as school, students may spend up to twelve years being confronted every day with the fact that they are "losers." Whereas winners are almost unanimously fully satisfied with their experiences and themselves, "losers" tend to perceive (1) their learning experiences as boring, unfair, and not fun, and (2) themselves negatively (Crockenberg, Bryant, & Wilce, 1976). If students aspire to be "winners," the daily frustration of failing tends to produce a sense of helplessness, worthlessness, and incompetence. Any stable pattern of winning or losing developed over time among competitors will tend to decrease the performance of all concerned. (Losers will give up and withdraw from the contest, and winners will work only as hard as needed to win as their less effortful performances will continue to be reinforced.)

Atkinson (1965) predicted from his theory of achievement motivation that students who chronically experience failure will become primarily oriented toward avoiding failure (thus becoming nonachievement-oriented). The tendency to avoid failure inhibits the student from attempting a task on which he or she is to be evaluated, especially when the probability of success is intermediate. If forced into achievement-oriented situations, individuals who are dominated by a tendency to avoid failure are likely to choose tasks with a very high or a very low chance of success. Doing so minimizes their anxiety about failure, for if the chance of success is very high they are almost sure not to fail, and when the chance for success is very low no one can blame them for failure. Failure, furthermore, reduces the attraction individuals feel toward peers (Ashmore, 1970; Blanchard, Adelman, & Cook, 1975).

Two ways for teachers to maintain student motivation in competitive situations are to (a) use competition only as an entertaining change of pace and (b) reformulate homogeneous competitive clusters each time competition is used so that students always face new competitors.

Maximizing the number of winners. By arranging a class into small clusters of evenly matched students, teachers can provide a challenging and realistic competition among students and maximize the number of winners in the class at the same time. In a class of thirty, for example, there is only one winner if the class participates as a whole in a competition. If the class is divided into triads, there are ten winners in a class of thirty. This method increases the likelihood of any one student's believing that he or she can win, especially when students are assigned to homogeneous triads.

Even when students are placed in a triad with classmates who achieve at the same level, if a stable pattern of who wins and who loses develops, the perceived likelihood of winning will decrease drastically for the "losers." Teachers, therefore, will wish to change the membership in each triad each time a competition is held. A procedure for doing so is called bumping (see Figure 7.1). Bumping involves (a) ranking the competitive triads from the highest (the three highest achievers are members) to the lowest (the three lowest achievers are members), (b) moving the winner in each triad up to the next highest triad, and (c) moving the loser down

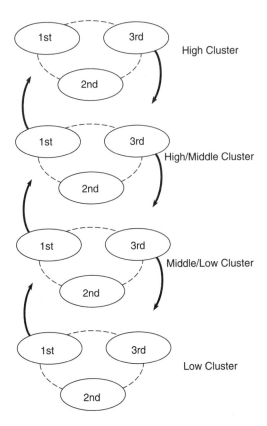

FIGURE 7.1 Bumping process

to the next lowest triad. In this way, students will always face new competitors and believe that they have a chance to win.

Ability to monitor progress of competitors. Participants in an appropriate competition need to be able to audit and monitor the relative progress of competitors in order to know whether they are ahead or behind. In competition, the only way individuals can judge their progress is by comparing themselves with their competitors. In athletic events there is a scoreboard to keep players posted. Successful competition in schools requires the same sort of ongoing feedback. Such auditing or monitoring may facilitate performance on simple, unitary, nondivisible, over-learned tasks but may hinder performance on complex tasks (Bond & Titus, 1983).

Unimportance of who wins or loses. Competition is most appropriate when it is viewed not as a crucial test, but as an interlude—fun, a change of pace—as students collaborate to complete an assignment or master a body of knowledge. A group relay race is an example; students race up and down the playground for the fun of it rather than to win at all costs. In the example at the beginning of this chapter, students engage in temporary competition while completing a cooperative unit on burning candles. If students can compete for fun and enjoyment, win or lose, competitive drills are an effective change of pace in the classroom as a low-key test of the success of cooperative learning groups in ensuring that all members have mastered the material being studied.

In an appropriate competition, it should be relatively unimportant whether one wins or loses. Winning cannot be a life-or-death matter if it is to be enjoyed. While competing, students should view their learning goal as being relatively unimportant so that they can accept either winning or losing. The focus should be on learning rather than winning. High levels of anxiety appear when winning becomes too important, along with all the destructive consequences of competition noted by the research. Healthy competition creates a relatively low level of anxiety by focusing on having fun. It should always be more fun to win than to not win, but in school winning is not an end in itself. Students should focus first on learning, second on having fun, and last on winning.

Clear boundaries and criteria.   In a competition, interaction among students is strictly controlled through the rules and procedures. Although the students are encouraged to share their progress, they are not expected to share ideas or solutions. Some talking may be necessary. In general, however, there is little discussion allowed except where it deals with challenging the correctness of each other's answers.

In order for competition to be constructive, the procedures, rules, and boundaries of the competition must be clear. Competitions need to have a clear beginning, a clear ending, clear criteria for selecting winners, and a clear set of rules and procedures that control interaction. The period of competition (when it starts and ends) must be clearly specified. This can be done in terms of (a) the time or number of attempts allowed to make the response (as in races where competitors are ranked on time taken to travel a certain distance or golf where competitors are ranked on number of strokes required) or (b) the response criteria that must be met for the contest to be concluded (games such as table tennis, where the first person to obtain 21 points wins).

Many competitions are poorly defined, with no clear starting line, no clear criteria for determining winners or losers, no clear finish line, vagueness about rules, and ambiguity about where and when competition does and does not exist. Most teachers do not structure specific competitive conditions except during examinations; at other times a diffuse and ambiguous competitive climate exists. This ambiguous competitive climate (where students are unsure of whether they are ahead or behind, unclear as to what the rules are, and unclear as to what they must do to win) has several destructive consequences. Students become insecure, hostile toward classmates, and fearful about being defeated. As a consequence, they may behave inappropriately and feel unhappy. Ambiguity ruins competition, because too much time is spent worrying about what is fair and unfair, what the procedures actually are, and whether or not one's responses are better than those of others.

Student Role Expectations

The basic role expectations for students within competitive learning situations are to expect to review previously learned material, to have an equal chance of winning, to enjoy the activity (win or lose), to monitor the progress of competitors, and to compare their abilities, skills, or knowledge with those of similar peers. In a competitive learning situation, students are to (a) interact in planned and informal ways to keep track of each other's progress, (b) look less to the teacher for judgment of progress and more to other students to compare their progress, (c) have a set of materials either individually or in common with a triad of students, according to the demands of the situation, (d) follow the rules (i.e., play fair), (e) have fun, and (f) be good winners and losers. Fair play is embodied in modesty in victory, in graciousness in defeat, and in that generosity of outlook that creates warm and lasting human relationships.

Evaluation System

Within competitive learning situations a norm-referenced evaluation system is used, such as grading on the normal curve and having students ranked from best to worst. In a competition, it is imperative that participants can be clearly ranked from best to worse in performance. When competition is based on a period of time, quantity or quality of the competitive response is used to rank competitors. If the contest ends when response criteria are met, ranking is based on time or the number of attempts required to reach criteria. Since in a competition rewards are received by only one or a few of the participants, and the reward one receives depends on how highly one's response is ranked on a specified criterion, the criterion and the procedure for ranking must be clear, objective, and unbiased for competition to work.

ESTABLISHING A COMPETITIVE STRUCTURE

A science class has been working on a unit involving things that sink and float. The class was divided into cooperative learning groups, and the groups experimented with a variety of materials. One of the materials was clay. Each group was given the same weight of clay and instructed to build a clay boat. As the groups experimented with different designs, the teacher decided to have an entertaining change of pace by structuring a class competition to see which group could design and build the boat that would hold the most weight. Each cooperative group was told to build a boat and ensure that all group members understood the design. The group members were then assigned to competition triads consisting of members of three different groups who were at the same achievement level. Each member was given a new lump of clay and was told to build a boat according to his or her group's design and explain its design to the other two competitors. The boats were then

Be content with your lot; one cannot be first in everything. —*Aesop*

No man lives without jostling and being jostled; in all ways he has to elbow himself through the world, giving and receiving offence. —*Thomas Carlyle*

You can't make the world all planned and soft. The strongest and best survive—that's the law of nature after all—always has been and always will be. —*Businessman in* Middletown, *Lynd and Lynd*

There's no gap so large as the gap between being "first" and being "second" —*Anonymous second-place finisher*

It's not whether you win or lose, it's how you play the game. —*Unknown*

The enjoyment of competing, win or lose, encourages competition; having to win each time discourages it. —*Anonymous competitor*

A good answer may not be good enough. It has to be better than someone else's. —*R. Dreeben in* On What Is Learned in School *(1968)*

placed in water, and weights were placed inside each boat until it sank. The boat that supported the most weight before sinking won. The winning boat was worth 6 points, the second-place boat was awarded 4 points, and the last-place boat was awarded 2 points. After the competition students returned to their cooperative groups and added up their points for a total group score. The winning group was announced. The class then studied the winning design and determined why it was better than the others. Each group then built a replica of the winning boat.

The essence of a competitive goal structure is to give students individual goals and use a norm-referenced evaluation system in rewarding them. Assigning the individual goal of being the best speller in the class, giving a test, ranking students from best to worst on spelling, and distributing rewards accordingly would be an example. The teacher's role in using competition appropriately is explained in the following paragraphs. The procedures described are indebted to the Teams-Games-Tournament (TGT) procedure pioneered by David DeVries and Keith Edwards at Johns Hopkins University (DeVries & Edwards, 1974). Inspired by the implications of James Coleman's research on adolescents, DeVries and Edwards developed TGT as a classroom procedure combining cooperative learning, inter-group competition, and a game format. Their work at the Center for Social Organization of Schools at Johns Hopkins University in developing, evaluating, and implementing TGT is a landmark in the development of cooperative learning procedures. Their pioneering work was continued by one of David DeVries' doctoral students, Robert Slavin.

The teacher's role in conducting competitive lessons consists of the following sixteen steps.

Objectives

1. Specifying instructional objectives. The academic objective needs to be specified at the correct level for each student and matched to the right level of instruction according to a conceptual or task analysis. Often the objective will be to review previously learned material.

Decisions

2. Assigning students to heterogeneous cooperative learning groups. Students are assigned to cooperative learning groups of four members so that each group is a cross section of the class in academic performance (one high, one low, and two middle achievers) and various other individual characteristics such as sex and ethnic background. The groups should be balanced so that the average academic performance levels of all the groups are about equal. The cooperative learning group prepares its members to do well in the academic competitions. The groups periodically compete with each other to be the best group in the class. Cooperative groups are given time to study together so that students can help and encourage each other to learn, and group membership is held stable for a period of time so that group cohesion and commitment can be built. An intergroup competition takes place once a week or so as a change of pace. Most of the time intergroup cooperation is structured.

3. Planning the competition. The competition is conducted as follows:

a. Students are assigned to competition triads so that each student is placed in competition with two other students, each of whom represents a different cooperative learning group. In order to create equitable competition, each triad consists of students of comparable academic achievement (as determined by prior performance).

b. The competition lasts for thirty to fifty minutes. At the end of a competition the students in each triad compare their scores to determine the top scorer, the middle scorer, and the low scorer. The ranks are converted into points, with a fixed number of points assigned to the top scorer (6 points), middle scorer (4 points), and low scorer (2 points) in each triad. If two students tie for first place, each receives 5 points. If two students tie for second place, each receives 3 points. In a three-way tie, each student receives 4 points.

c. A cooperative learning group score is derived by adding the scores of all the individual members. Group scores are then ranked and listed. Care should be taken to ensure that having fun is more important than winning.

4. Assigning students to competitive triads. A class competition is structured so that each student competes as a representative of his or her cooperative learning group with students of equal aptitude from other groups. When students compete, they should be placed in homogeneous triads based on ability or previous achievement. Groups of three maximize the number of winners in the class (pairs tend to make the competition too personal). Rank the students in each cooperative learning group from highest to lowest on the basis of their previous achievement. Given that only one student from a group can be in a competitive triad, assign the three highest-achieving students in the class to Table 1, the next three to Table 2, and so on until the three lowest-achievement students in the class are in the bottom triad. This system creates equal competition within each triad and makes it possible for students of all achievement levels to contribute maximally to their group scores if they do their best. Figure 7.2 illustrates the relationship between the cooperative learning groups and the competitive triads.

5. Preparing instructional materials. Make a question sheet consisting of about thirty items, an answer sheet, a copy of the rules, and a set of cards numbered from 1 to 30. On each card write one question from the question sheet. The questions can be either recognition or recall questions. Each competitive triad should receive one set of cards and one answer sheet. An example of the cards and answer sheet are given in Table 7.2. The rules appear in Table 7.3.

6. Arranging the classroom. The room should be arranged so that the triads are separated from each other and students within each triad sit close to each other.

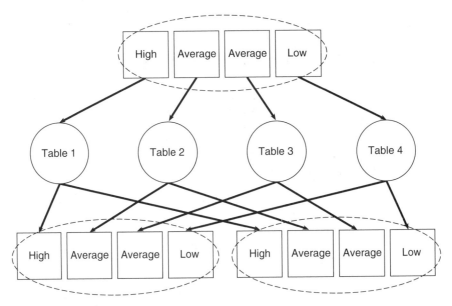

FIGURE 7.2 Assignment to tournament tables

TABLE 7.2   Sample Game

Background of the game: The students in a seventh-grade English class were studying sentences. In the game they were asked to identify the item as either a complete or an incomplete sentence. If the item was an incomplete sentence the player had to tell why it was incomplete. A sentence was incomplete because either the verb or the subject was missing.

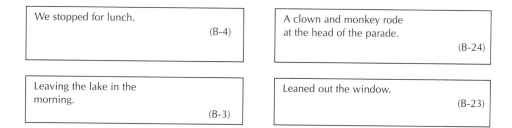

We stopped for lunch.	A clown and monkey rode
(B-4)	at the head of the parade.
	(B-24)

Leaving the lake in the morning.	Leaned out the window.
(B-3)	(B-23)

Sentences Game II: Answer Sheet B

B-1	Complete sentence		B-13	Complete sentence
B-2	Complete sentence		B-14	Complete sentence
B-3	Incomplete sentence; no subject		B-15	Incomplete sentence; no subject
B-4	Complete sentence		B-16	Complete sentence
B-5	Incomplete sentence; no verb		B-17	Complete sentence
B-6	Incomplete sentence; no verb		B-18	Incomplete sentence; no verb
B-7	Complete sentence		B-19	Incomplete sentence; no subject
B-8	Complete sentence		B-20	Complete sentence
B-9	Incomplete sentence; no verb		B-21	Incomplete sentence; no verb
B-10	Incomplete sentence; no verb		B-22	Incomplete sentence; no subject
B-11	Incomplete sentence; no verb		B-23	Incomplete sentence; no subject
B-12	Incomplete sentence; no subject		B-24	Complete sentence

This game was developed by David DeVries, Keith Edwards, and Gail Fennessey in cooperation with Carol Hopkins, a teacher at Northern Parkway Junior High School, Baltimore, MD.

Explaining the Task and Goal Structure

7. Explaining the academic task. The task is to learn and demonstrate mastery of the assigned material.

8. Structuring negative goal interdependence. Explain to students that their goal is to answer more questions correctly than the other two members of the triad in order to maximize the number of points they take back to their cooperative learning group so that their group can win by having more overall points than any other group in the class. Make sure the procedures, rules, criteria for winning, and the definition of what is and is not a correct answer are clearly understood by all students. Competition bogs down if there are disputes or misunderstandings over such matters.

9. Explaining criteria for success. Within each triad, the student who answers the most questions correctly receives 6 points, the second-place student receives 4

TABLE 7.3 Rules of Play

I. To start the game, shuffle the cards and place them face down on the table. Play is in a clockwise rotation.

II. To play, each player in turn takes the top card from the deck, reads it aloud, and does one of two things:

   A. Says he or she does not know or is not sure of the answer and asks if another player wants to answer. If no one wants to answer, the card is placed on the bottom of the deck. If a player answers, the following procedure is followed.

   B. Answers the question immediately and asks if anyone wants to challenge the answer. The player to his or her right has the first chance to challenge. If this player does not wish to challenge, then the next player to the right may challenge.

      1. If there is no challenge, another player should check the answer:

         a. If correct, the player keeps the card.

         b. If incorrect, the player must place the card on the bottom of the deck.

      2. If there is a challenge and the challenger decides not to answer, the answer is checked. If the original answer is wrong, the player must place the card on the bottom of the deck.

      3. If there is a challenge and the challenger gives an answer, the answer is checked:

         a. If the challenger is correct, he or she receives the card.

         b. If the challenger is incorrect, and the original answer is correct, the challenger must give up one of the cards he or she has already won (if any) and place it on the bottom of the deck.

         c. If both answers are incorrect, the card is placed on the bottom of the deck.

III. The game ends when there are no more cards in the deck. The player who has the most cards is the winner.

This game was developed by David DeVries, Keith Edwards, and Gail Fennessey in cooperation with Carol Hopkins.

points, and the last-place student receives 2 points to take back to his or her cooperative learning group. If two students tie for first place, each receives 5 points. If two students tie for second place, each receives 3 points. In a three-way tie, each student receives 4 points. In a cooperative learning group of four members, the group could have between 8 and 24 points total. The group that has the most points wins.

10. Specifying desired behaviors. Each student should try to win in his or her triad. Students are to work alone answering each of their questions without consultation with other group members. If they need help or clarification, they are to ask the teacher. They should keep track of where they stand in the competition and make adjustments in their strategy accordingly. In addition, they should

    a. Seek fun and enjoyment.

    b. Win with humility and pleasure.

    c. Lose with dignity.

    d. Recognize and deal with inappropriate anxiety.

    e. Monitor progress of competitors.

    f. Form realistic perceptions of own skills.

Students need to know what behaviors are appropriate and desirable within a competitive learning situation.

Monitoring and Intervening

11. Monitoring students' behavior. After explaining the rules, procedures, and expected behaviors to students, teachers must observe to see that they are being followed. Much of the teacher's time should be spent in observing students in order to see what problems they are having in completing the assignment and in working competitively. The teacher should move throughout the room, checking triads for understanding, answering questions, settling disputes over answers, and checking for the expected student behaviors. Some systematic and anecdotal record keeping will enhance the processing at the end of the lesson and is easily done by tallying on an observation sheet the number of times the teacher sees targeted desired behaviors and jotting down specific instances of appropriate behavior.

12. Providing task assistance. In monitoring the triads, teachers will wish to clarify instructions, review important procedures and rules, and teach task-competitive skills as necessary. The teacher is the major resource for student learning and is also the judge and jury in settling disputes over which answer is correct. The major focus of the competitive triads should be on reviewing the previously learned material and not arguing over answers. The teacher's task assistance should focus attention on the learning and minimize the importance of winning. Make sure that rules are followed, no one cheats, and disputes are settled quickly.

13. Intervening to teach competitive skill. Students will have experience in competing but will often lack the skills to compete appropriately. Students may take the competition too seriously or feel so anxious that they do not enjoy it. Intervene to encourage the fun of competing or to deemphasize the importance of winning when it seems necessary. It is important that students learn to compete appropriately for fun and enjoyment. It strengthens cooperative learning when students can review previously learned material in a gamelike situation.

14. Providing closure to the lesson. At the end of the lesson, students should have adequately reviewed previously learned material so that they can easily contribute their learning to future collaborative efforts.

Evaluation and Reinforcement

15. Evaluating and reinforcing the quality and quantity of students' learning. Within the competitive triads, students' performance needs to be evaluated by a norm-referenced procedure. Similarly, groups are then evaluated by a norm-referenced procedure.

16. Processing the competition. It is important that competitions be discussed afterward to allow students to evaluate their skills, discuss their feelings, and realize

In a large city high school, a teacher had just finished chatting with two students and moved to the front of the class, the signal that class was about to begin. "You've spent the last few weeks doing projects that relate to the fifteenth, sixteenth, and seventeenth centuries," she began. "Now, we'll give you a chance to see what you know about some of the people you've met in your reading." She explained that they were going to play a game called *Contemporaries,* in which one student would name a famous person and describe that person's contribution to the times; the next student would then name a contemporary person and that person's contribution, and so on. Any student who was stuck without a name to contribute, or suggested a name that was challenged and found not to be contemporary, would drop out until a new game was started. Meanwhile, the game would continue until one student was the winner.

The teacher divided the class into groups of five, using a list that grouped students in such a way that each student in a cluster had a reasonable chance to win. The students jumped into the game with great enthusiasm and obvious enjoyment. Occasionally there was a burst of laughter when a name came up that was obviously not contemporary or when a challenged student was proven correct and the challenger had to drop out. Near the end of the period the teacher stopped the game and gave the winners from each group a chance to try their skill against each other, temporarily establishing a class champion. The last few minutes before the bell were spent discussing the several instances in which many in the class didn't realize that two famous people were contemporaries, and what it would take to be able to win next time. After class, the teacher jotted down a few notes about things she had noticed or overheard, observing especially where students seemed to have difficulty with the competition.

How appropriate is this instance of competition? Check it out with the summarized criteria.

how to behave even more appropriately next time. Processing may be done individually with students' completing a questionnaire on their reactions and behavior, may be done in their competitive triads or cooperative learning groups, or may be done as a whole class. A combination of individual and small-group processing is usually effective. During their monitoring, teachers may observe students engaging in inappropriate actions and plan to provide personal feedback later. Most feedback, however, should be positive. An open and frank discussion of the competition can defuse hurt feelings and ensure increased constructiveness of future competitions.

COMPETITIVE SKILLS

Students in Midwest Middle School are learning how to build paper airplanes as part of a physics unit. Different designs are built and demonstrated in order for students to learn the principles of flight. As an entertaining change of pace, the teacher decides to have a competition to see which cooperative group can design the plane that flies the farthest, stays in the air the longest, is the most acrobatic,

and is the most accurate. (Teachers who conduct such competitions may wish to add another category that brings elements of luck and humor into the competition.) The class then studies the winning designs and determines why the planes were so effective. Finally, each group has to build replicas of the winning designs.

Competition, when it is appropriate, is fun and adds spice to classroom life.* Competition involves much less interaction among students and less coordination of behavior than cooperation, and there are fewer skills essential to competing than to cooperating. Appropriate competition, however, does require several skills.

The first competitive skill is playing fair. Students must understand and obey the rules. Rules should be clarified before the competition begins so that students know what is and is not fair. In some competitions, for example, students are allowed to enhance their chances of winning by obstructing their opponents' progress (e.g., "sending" another player's ball away from the wicket in croquet), whereas in other competitions such disruption of opponents' progress would be declared unfair (e.g., cutting in too soon in a track race). If the rules are clear in the beginning, students' actions will usually be appropriate. If any student feels it is necessary to break the rules, the situation is probably inappropriate for competition (e.g., the student perceives that the goal is too important and the situation is too serious).

A second skill is being a good winner and a good loser. This means winning with humility, pleasure, and modesty, and being gracious when you lose. Any student should be able to win or lose gracefully. The third skill is enjoying the competition, win or lose. The purpose of competition is to have an enjoyable experience drilling on previously learned material. The fourth skill is monitoring the progress of competitors to know how one stands in the competition. Since

---

*The two authors once decided that they had a reasonable chance to win a footrace with their dad. At the time the two authors were four and five years old, and their father was twenty-seven. We decided that an old man of twenty-seven would not be very much competition! So we refused to come home for dinner, thinking he could never catch us. A short race and some swiftly administered physical aversive stimuli ended all motivation to race our father again in the future.

Teacher Role Checklist for Competitive Learning

1. What are the desired outcomes for the drill activity?

2. Is the classroom arranged so that students
   _____ Are clustered together, working on their own, but able to monitor the progress of their competitors?
   _____ Have access to each other only (a) if it is required by the nature of the competition or (b) to know whether they are ahead or behind the others?
   _____ Have an individual set of self-contained materials?

3. Have you effectively communicated to students that
   _____ The instructional goal is relative (to win more points for one's group than competitors win for theirs)?
   _____ Each student will be rewarded on the basis of how his or her work compares to the work of the other students in the competition triad?

4. Have you effectively communicated the expected patterns of student–student interaction? Do students know that they should
   _____ Interact only to check the progress of other students and to abide by the rules of the competition?
   _____ Work on the assignment by trying to do the task better, faster, and more completely than competitors?
   _____ Perceive teacher praise or support of a competitor's work as an indication that their own work is inferior and teacher criticism of a competitor's work as an indication that their own work is superior?
   _____ Ignore comments from other students?
   _____ Go to the teacher for all help and assistance needed?

5. Have you effectively communicated the expected pattern of teacher–student interaction? Do students know that the teacher
   _____ Wants each student to try to do better on the assignment than the other students and will evaluate students' work on the basis of how it compares with the work of other students?
   _____ Will interact with each triad of students to clarify rules and the task without giving one student more help than another, and often making clarifications to the entire class?
   _____ Will praise and support students working alone and trying to do better, faster, and more work than any other student in the triad or classroom?

---

winning is the goal of competition, the only way to know where one stands is to know where the others are. Teachers can promote the development and use of monitoring skills by

1. Making clear that monitoring is part of the competition and that students can watch each other's progress.

2. Setting up several methods of monitoring including charting students' progress on the board, checking periodically to bring everyone up to date, and modifying the triads in which students compete.

The fifth skill is *not* to overgeneralize the results of the competition. Winning does not make a student a more worthwhile person, and losing does not make a student less worthwhile. Being defeated in a spelling contest does not make a student a "loser." The results of any one competition provide very limited information about a student's personal worth. Clearly separating the results of competitions from one's view of oneself is an important competitive skill.

SUMMARY

To be most effective, individuals should be able to cooperate, compete, and work autonomously on their own appropriately Johnson & Johnson, 1989a). Being able to compete for fun and enjoyment is an important competence. The major concern with the instructional use of competition is that students bring more to the competition than is intended by the teacher. Students may begin a competition with the attitude that they would "prefer to die" rather than be defeated. The anxiety produced in such students and the students around them is counterproductive. Competitions need to be kept light and fun, emphasizing review or drill, probably in a game format. Students should be homogeneously grouped so that they perceive themselves as having a chance to win, probably in threesomes to maximize the number of winners. The instructions, rules, procedures, and materials need to be clear and specific. The teacher needs to be the major resource for all students and the arbitrator of disputes. The major teacher role is to keep students focused on learning and not getting sidetracked by arguments or hurt feelings. Processing afterward is a vital part of teaching students to handle competition appropriately and enjoy it. Students need to learn how to win with enjoyment and lose with dignity. Students can be defeated, but are never "losers."

The importance of spreading an umbrella of cooperation over the class before competition is initiated cannot be overemphasized. Having students work together, get to know each other, cheer for shared successes, and develop collaborative skills is the best foundation for making competition appropriate. In one of our teacher-training sessions, a coach announced that he was not excited about cooperation. He preferred competition, believed in it, and liked to stress it with his teams. After several cooperative experiences we structured a competition involving vocabulary words, and the coach lost badly. After quiet reflection, he concluded, "I learned something about myself today. I have always hated to lose, but I found that I do not mind losing nearly as much when I lose to people I like." Building a strong cooperative learning environment may be the best way to provide a setting in which students can learn how to compete appropriately.

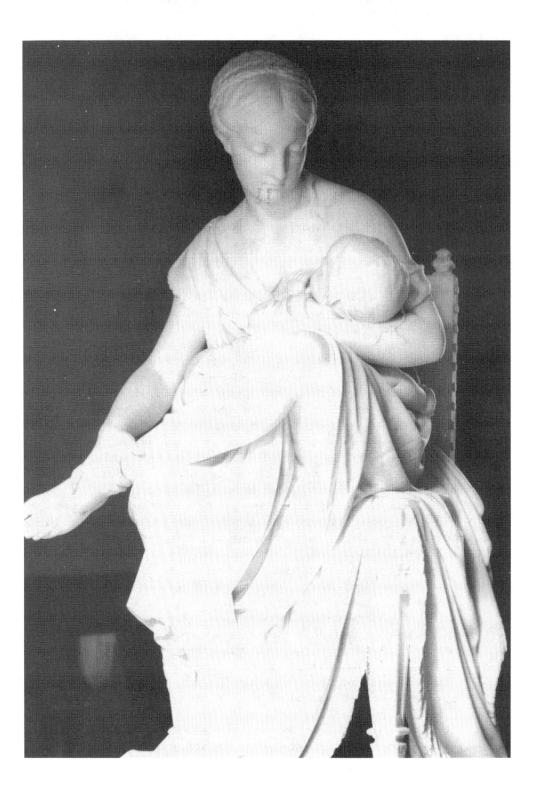

8

Student Acquisition of Cooperative Skills

INTRODUCTION

Once upon a time there were three students named Shadrach, Meshach, and Abednego. Shadrach was very concerned with being better than Meshach and Abednego. Whenever the teacher asked the three to work together, Shadrach would hide his own ideas and draw out the ideas of Meshach and Abednego. Shadrach would then secretly write his own report, taking pride that it was "better than" the group's report. This did not make Meshach and Abednego very happy. In fact, they began to refuse to work with Shadrach. Whenever the teacher said, "Would you three please work on this project together," Meshach and Abednego would say, "NO!" This did not make the teacher happy. Shadrach would just sit and smile and say, "I'm best!" After failing many times to get Shadrach to cooperate with Meshach and Abednego, the teacher sought the advice of two wise educators. They suggested that perhaps Shadrach had never learned the skills needed to cooperate. "Teach Shadrach to be cooperative," they suggested, "and his behavior will change." So the teacher did. And, not only did Shadrach's behavior change, but Meshach and Abednego also learned how to cooperate more successfully.

This story illustrates an important point in using goal structures in your classroom. You now know how to structure instruction so that cooperative, competitive, or individualistic behavior by students is appropriate, but it does not follow that students will *engage* in cooperative, competitive, or individualistic behavior. The students must have the appropriate skills in order to respond to the goal structure implemented by the teacher. With each type of goal structure comes a set of skills that each student needs to have mastered. Teachers often assume that students have the skills necessary to cooperate or compete with other students, or to work productively by themselves. This is often not the case, even when students are in high school or college. Family background and the nature of a student's peer groups influence the development of such skills. Many students come to school unable to work alone, to cooperate with others, or to compete successfully. To use all three types of goal structures successfully, teachers should deliberately teach the skills students need in order to engage in behavior appropriate to each type of goal structure, and they should make sure that students perceive the goal structures correctly. They should also establish classroom norms and climate that support the use of the skills.

TEACHING STUDENTS COOPERATIVE SKILLS

Students who have never been taught how to work effectively with others cannot be expected to do so. Thus the first experience of many teachers who structure cooperative learning is that their students cannot collaborate with each other. Yet it is within cooperative situations, where there is a task to complete, that social skills become most relevant and should ideally be taught. All students need to become skillful in communicating, building and maintaining trust, providing leadership, and managing conflicts (Johnson, 1991, 1993; Johnson & F. Johnson, 1991). Teaching collaborative skills becomes an important prerequisite for academic learning, since achievement will improve as students become more effective in working with each other.

There are two reasons that collaborative skills are directly taught in classrooms where teachers are serious about using cooperative learning. The first is that interpersonal and small-group skills are the engine that powers cooperative learning groups. For cooperative learning groups to be productive, students must be able to engage in the needed collaborative skills. Without good leadership, effective communication, the building and maintenance of trust, and the constructive resolution of conflicts, cooperative learning groups will not maximize their productivity and effectiveness.

Second, collaborative skills in and of themselves are important instructional outcomes that relate to future career and life success. Most people realize that a college education or vocational training improves their career opportunities. Many people are less aware that interpersonal skills may be the most important set of skills to their employability, productivity, and career success. Employers typically value verbal-communication, responsibility, interpersonal, initiative, and decision-making skills. A question all employers have in mind when they interview a job applicant is: Can this person get along with other people? Having a high degree of technical competence is not enough to ensure a successful career. A person also has to have a high degree of interpersonal competence.

In 1982, for example, the Center for Public Resources published *Basic Skills in the U.S. Workforce,* a nationwide survey of businesses, labor unions, and educational institutions. The center found that 90 percent of the people fired from their jobs were fired for poor job attitudes, poor interpersonal relationships, and inappropriate behavior. Being fired for lack of basic and technical skills was infrequent. Even in high-tech careers, the ability to work effectively with other high-tech personnel is essential, and so is the ability to communicate and work with people from other professions to solve interdisciplinary problems.

In the real world of work, the heart of most jobs, especially the higher-paying, more interesting jobs, is getting others to cooperate, leading others, coping with complex problems of power and influence, and helping solve people's problems in working together. Millions of technical, professional, and managerial jobs today require much more than technical competence and professional expertise. They also require leadership. Employees are increasingly asked to get things done by influencing a large and diverse group of people (bosses, subordinates, peers, customers, and others), despite lacking much or any formal control over them, and despite their general lack of interest in cooperating. They are expected to motivate others to achieve goals, negotiate and mediate, get decisions implemented, exercise authority, and develop credibility. The interpersonal and small-group skills developed within cooperative efforts are important contributors to personal employability and career success.

In addition to career success, social skills are directly related to building and maintaining positive relationships and to psychological health. Maintaining a set of good friends your whole life long, being a caring parent, maintaining a loving relationship with your spouse—all directly relate to how interpersonally skilled you are. Quality of life as an adult largely depends on social skills. The more socially skilled a person is, furthermore, the healthier he or she tends to be psychologically. For these and many other reasons, it is important that students learn the interpersonal and small-group skills necessary to build and maintain cooperative relationships with others.

In this chapter we shall first discuss how students learn skills. We shall then discuss the skills a student needs in order to cooperate, compete, or function individualistically. Ensuring that students have the needed skills is an important first step in using goal structures in your classroom.*

HOW DO YOU TEACH SKILLS?

What is your role in teaching students skills? As Chapter 4 indicates, one of the major reasons for monitoring students' behavior is to be able to identify the students who are having difficulties owing to missing or underdeveloped skills.

---

*Students may at times overestimate their skill level and attempt behavior of which they are not really capable. Once the younger of the two authors decided that he had the skills needed to beat up the older of the two authors. (He was at the young and foolish age of three.) He proceeded to demonstrate his skills the first time the older of the two authors made a face at him. Besides being cruelly humiliated, the younger of the two authors has had to look at his brother making faces at him for the past fifty years without being able to do anything about it.

Periodically you will want to review crucial skills with all your students. What are the steps you go through to ensure that students learn cooperative, competitive, and indivualistic skills?

Step 1: Ask the students what skills they think they will need in order to cooperate (compete, work individually) successfully. To be motivated to learn a skill, the students must see the need for the skill. If students do not suggest the needed skills, you will, of course, have to. But it is important to help students understand why they need the skill.

Step 2: Help the students get a clear understanding of what the skill is, conceptually and behaviorally. In order to learn a skill, the student must have a conception of what the skill is and how the behaviors are executed. First, the behaviors have to be identified and placed in proper sequence and in close succession. It is often helpful to demonstrate the skill, describe it step by step, and then demonstrate it again. Therefore, you need to be able to describe and do the skills being taught. Pointing out good models in other students is also useful. You might ask your students to identify someone in the class who has mastered that particular skill and can be used as a model. (See Table 8.1 for an activity example.)

Step 3: Set up practice situations. Once the skill is properly understood, the behavioral patterns need to be practiced until they are firmly learned.

Step 4: Ensure that each student receives feedback on how well he or she is performing the skill. Receiving feedback on performance is necessary in order to correct errors, identify problems in learning the skill, identify progress in skill mastery, and compare actual performance with the desired standard of performance. Feedback may be the single most important factor affecting the acquisition of skills. The more immediate, specific, and descriptive (as opposed to evaluative) the feedback, the more it will help skill development. (See Johnson, 1993, for a full discussion of

TABLE 8.1   Constructing a T-Chart

1. Write the name of the skill to be learned and practiced and draw a large T underneath.
2. Title the left side of the T "Looks Like" and the right side of the T "Sounds Like."
3. On the left side write a number of behaviors that operationalize the skill. On the right side write a number of phrases that operationalize the skill.
4. Have all students practice "Looks Like" and "Sounds Like" several times before the lesson is conducted.

ENCOURAGING PARTICIPATION

Looks Like	Sounds Like
Thumbs Up	"What is your idea?"
Smiles	"Good idea!"
Eye Contact	"Awesome!"
Pat on the Back	"That's interesting."

Source: D. W. Johnson, R. Johnson & E. Holubec: *Circles of learning: Cooperation in the classroom* (4th ed). Edina, MN. Interaction, 1993. Reprinted with permission of the authors.

feedback.) The better the advance conceptualization or understanding of the skill, the more helpful the feedback will be concerning the enactment of the behaviors involved in the skill. Feedback is often quite interesting to students and increases their motivation to learn the skill. An important aspect of feedback is captured in rewarding students who successfully master the skill being taught. When students have been rewarded for skill mastery, they will tend to use the skills, and other students will imitate the behavior of those rewarded. It is not necessary to provide feedback for every student. Dividing the students into cooperative groups in which they give each other feedback on skill performance often is just as effective.

Step 5: Encourage students to persevere in practicing the skill. In learning skills, students will need to persevere. The process of learning most skills involves a period of slow beginning, followed by a period of rapid gain, followed by a plateau in which performance does not increase, followed by another spurt of learning, followed by another plateau, and so on. Plateaus are quite common in skill learning, and perseverance is necessary to keep one practicing until the next period of rapid gain begins.

After a series of classroom observations, anthropologist Jules Henry (1963) suggested that teachers encourage competition and criticism among students by modeling competitive behavior and rewarding it when it occurs—an observation that is consistent with existing research results (Bandura, Ross, & Ross, 1963). Because there is evidence that students are most likely to imitate the person with the greatest power and control over the distribution of rewards, the teacher's behavior will have a powerful influence on student behavior. In addition, a study by Masters (1972) indicates that if teachers offer an inequitable distribution of valued rewards to students, low-rewarded students are unlikely to be imitated. Thus, if a teacher models competitive behaviors and rewards students for engaging in competitive behaviors, the effect will be a great deal of competitive behavior on the part of most students.

Step 6: Set up situations in which the skiffs can be used successfully. Students need to experience success in skill development. It is their increasing sense of mastery that motivates further efforts to learn complex skills. If the skills are as necessary as the authors believe they are (and as research indicates), students will receive some reinforcement naturally as they begin to function more effectively within the goal structures.

Step 7: Require the skills to be used often enough to become integrated into the students' behavioral repertoires. A new skill must be integrated into a student's behavioral repertoire. It is at this stage that the performance of the skill becomes involuntary, automatic, and, finally, natural. After students have engaged in cooperative, competitive, and individualistic skills for a sufficiently long period, they will believe that the behavior is a natural response to the goal structure and will use the skills with little conscious awareness of doing so.

Step 8: Set classroom norms to support the use of the skills. Even if students master needed skills, they will not use them unless they believe that they are appropriate and supported. Johnson (1970) has a detailed discussion of how to establish classroom norms. Teacher modeling of the skills, the rewarding of students who appropriately engage in the skills, and the explicit statement of how you expect students to behave will influence the degree to which students engage in behavior appropriate to the goal structures.

Teacher Checklist for Student Skill Development

1. Do students believe the skill is needed and useful?

2. Do students understand what the skill is, what the behaviors are, what the sequence of behaviors is, and how it looks when it is all put together?

3. Have students had an opportunity to practice the skill?

4. Have students received feedback on how well they perform the skill? Was the feedback immediate, descriptive, and specific?

5. Have students persevered in practicing the skill?

6. Have students had the opportunity to use the skill successfully?

7. Have students used the skill frequently enough so that they have integrated the skill into their natural behavior?

8. Do the classroom norms support the use of the skill?

COOPERATIVE SKILLS

No skills are more important to a human being than the skills of cooperative interaction. Cooperation is the most important and basic form of human interaction, and the skills of cooperating successfully are the most important skills anyone needs to master. There is no way to overstate this point. Competitive and individualistic behavior cannot take place unless persons are interacting within a broad cooperative framework. As stated previously, cooperation is the forest; competition and individualized effort are but trees.

Because almost all human behavior is cooperative, all interpersonal, group, and organizational skills can be identified as cooperative skills. It is impossible to list all such skills in this section, so we shall concentrate upon the more important and basic ones. Readers interested in a more thorough coverage of interpersonal and group skills are referred to Johnson (1993) and Johnson and F. Johnson (1991). The skills especially important for cooperation are communication skills, skills in building and maintaining trust, and controversy skills.

The Importance of Peer Tutoring

In most classrooms the resources of the students are seriously underutilized under a rigid competitive or individualistic goal structure in which the teacher is supposed to teach each student. The opportunities for students to teach other students are lost. Yet considerable research indicates that many students may learn better from their peers than from adults and that many students benefit greatly from teaching other students. Learning is apparently inhibited for some children when they are taught by what to them are giants and representatives of an alien adult world. Some children learn considerably better if they have the opportunity to learn from their peers. Communication may be more effective, amount of reinforcement may increase, and peer group encouragement may be more motivating when students teach each other. Although some students may be clumsy teachers at first, the research indicates that with practice and reinforcement for effective tutoring, most children can become rather good teachers.

1. Peer tutors are often effective in teaching children who do not respond well to adults.

2. Peer tutoring can develop a deep bond of friendship between the tutor and the person being helped, the result of which is very important for integrating slow learners into the group.

3. Peer tutoring takes pressure off the teacher, who can then teach a large group of students; at the same time, it allows the slow learners the individual attention they need.

4. The tutors benefit by learning to teach, a general skill that can be very useful in an adult society.

5. Peer tutoring happens spontaneously under cooperative conditions, so the teacher does not have to organize and manage it in a formal, continuing way.

COMMUNICATION SKILLS*

Communicating is the first step in cooperating. Unless people can communicate with each other, they cannot cooperate. Although it is very difficult to find a definition of communication with which everyone will agree, it is clear that *communication* is the exchange or sharing of thoughts and feelings through symbols that represent approximately the same conceptual experience for everyone involved.

*For a more complete discussion of communication and a series of exercises to increase communication skills, see Johnson (1993) and Johnson and F. Johnson (1994). Many of the misunderstandings between the authors when they were young stemmed from poor communication. Because the younger author didn't talk at all until about age four and then not so well, the older author needed to communicate in a more or less nonverbal manner.

In emphasizing communication skills to students, it is possible to divide these skills into two categories—sending and receiving. Each student must be able to send messages that correctly represent her ideas, beliefs, feelings, opinions, reactions, needs, goals, interests, resources, and a host of other things; the skills needed to send these messages we will lump under "sending skills." Each student must also be able to receive messages accurately so that he can understand the other person's ideas, beliefs, feelings, and so on; the skills needed to receive these messages we will lump under "receiving skills." Through sending and receiving, two students can clarify their mutual goals, plan how they are going to proceed to accomplish their goals, provide relevant information and intuitions to each other, reason together, coordinate their behavior, share their resources, give help and assistance to each other, and spark each other's creativity. Thus it is upon sending and receiving skills that we shall focus in this section. What are important sending skills? The following are some of the most crucial (Johnson, 1973):

1. Clearly and unambiguously communicate your ideas and feelings. Clearly "own" your message by (a) using personal pronouns such as "I" and "my" and (b) letting others know what your thoughts and feelings are. Students "disown" their messages when they use expressions such as "most people," "some people," "our group," making it difficult to tell whether they really think and feel what they are saying or are simply repeating the thoughts and feelings of others.

2. Make your message complete and specific. Include clear statements of all necessary information that the receiver needs in order to comprehend the message. Being complete and specific seems obvious, but often people will not communicate the frame of reference they are using, the assumptions they are making, their intentions in communicating, or the leaps in thinking they are making. Thus, although listeners may hear the words, they will not comprehend the "meaning" of the message.

3. Make your verbal and nonverbal messages congruent with each other. Every face-to-face communication involves both verbal and nonverbal messages. Usually these messages are congruent, so by smiling and expressing warmth nonverbally, a person can be saying that he or she has appreciated your help. Communication problems arise when a person's verbal and nonverbal messages are contradictory; if a person says, "Here is some information that may be of help to you" with a sneer and in a mocking tone of voice, the meaning you receive is confused by the two different messages being simultaneously sent.

4. Ask for feedback concerning the way in which your messages are being received. In order to communicate effectively, you must be aware of how the receiver is interpreting and processing your messages. The only way to be sure is to seek feedback continually as to what meanings the receiver is attaching to your messages.

Being skilled in sending messages is only half of what is needed to communicate effectively; one must also have receiving skills. Receiving skills include providing feedback concerning the reception of another person's message; this feedback facilitates clarification and continued discussion. The major purpose for providing such feedback is to communicate one's desire to understand completely the ideas

General Guidelines for Paraphrasing

1. Restate the sender's expressed ideas and feelings in your own words rather than mimicking or parroting his or her exact words.

2. Preface paraphrased remarks with, "You think . . . ," "Your position is . . . ," "It seems to you that . . . ," "You feel that . . . ," and so on.

3. Avoid any indication of approval or disapproval.

4. Make your nonverbal messages congruent with your verbal paraphrasing; look attentive, interested, and open to the sender's ideas and feelings, and show that your are concentrating upon what the sender is trying to communicate.

5. State as accurately as possible what you heard the sender say and describe the feelings and attitudes involved.

6. Do not add to or subtract from the sender's message.

7. Put yourself in the sender's shoes, and try to understand what he or she is feeling and what the message means.

and feelings of the sender. The major barrier to effective communication is the tendency most people have to judge, evaluate, approve, or disapprove of the messages they are receiving. For instance, the receiver may respond nonverbally or openly with, "I think you're wrong," "I don't like what you said," "I think you're right," or "That is the greatest (or worst) idea I have ever heard!" Such evaluative receiving will make the sender defensive and cautious, thereby decreasing the openness of the communication. Thus it is highly important for the receiver to indicate that he or she wants to understand the sender and will not evaluate the sender's messages until full understanding is reached. The specific receiving skills are paraphrasing, perception checking for feelings, and negotiating for meaning.

5. Paraphrase accurately and nonevaluatively the content of the message and the feelings of the sender. The most basic and important skill involved in receiving messages is paraphrasing. To *paraphrase* is to restate the words of the sender, and it should be done in a way that indicates an understanding of the sender's frame of reference. The basic rule to follow in paraphrasing is: You can speak up for yourself only after you have first restated the ideas and feelings of the sender accurately and to the sender's satisfaction.

6. Describe what you perceive to be the sender's feelings. Sometimes it is difficult to paraphrase the feelings of the sender if they are not described in words in the message. Thus a second receiving skill is the perception check for the sender's feelings. This check is made simply by describing what you perceive to be the sender's feelings. This description should tentatively identify the sender's feelings without expressing approval or disapproval and without attempting to interpret or explain the causes of the feelings. It is simply saying, "Here is what I understand your feelings to be. Am I accurate?"

7. State your interpretation of the sender's message, and negotiate with the sender until there is agreement on the message's meaning. Often the words contained in a message do not carry the actual meaning. A person may ask, "Is it safe to drive this fast?" and mean, "Please slow down." A person may say, "That's a good suggestion," and mean, "I will ignore what you are saying and get rid of you by giving a superficial response." Sometimes paraphrasing the content of a message will do little to communicate your understanding of the message. In such a case, you negotiate the meaning of the message. You may wish to preface your response to the sender with, "What I think you mean is . . ." If you are accurate, you then continue the discussion; if you are inaccurate, the sender restates the message until you can state what the essential meaning of the message is. Keep in mind that it is the process that is important in negotiating meaning, not the actual phrasing you use. After the process becomes natural, a variety of introductory phrases will be used. Be tolerant of others who are using the same phrases over and over as they are developing this skill.

The sending and receiving skills described here seem very simple to most people. Yet they are very difficult to master fully and are indispensable when interacting with others. You should practice them consciously until they are as automatic as saying good morning.

Another element that has a great influence upon both communication and cooperation is the trust level within a relationship. It is to this issue that we now turn.

BUILDING AND MAINTAINING A TRUSTING CLIMATE

Why is trust important? Trust is a necessary condition for stable cooperation and effective communication. The higher the trust, the more stable the cooperation and the more effective the communication. Students will more openly express their thoughts, feelings, reactions, opinions, information, and ideas when the trust level is high. When the trust level is low, students will be evasive, dishonest, and inconsiderate in their communications. Students will more honestly and frequently declare their cooperative intentions and make contributions to a cooperative effort when they believe they are dealing with highly trustworthy individuals. Cooperation rests upon everyone's sharing resources, giving and receiving help, dividing the work, and contributing to the accomplishment of mutual goals. Such behaviors will occur when there is trust that all are contributing to the group's progress and are using their openness and resources for group rather than personal gain. The development and maintenance of trust are discussed at length in Johnson (1993); if possible, you should review the chapters on trust, self-disclosure, and acceptance before going ahead with this chapter.

What is trust? Making a choice to *trust* another person requires the perception that the choice can lead to gains or losses, that whether you will gain or lose depends upon the behavior of the other person, that the loss will be greater than the gain, and that the person will likely behave so that you will gain rather than

lose. Sounds complicated, doesn't it? There is nothing simple about trust; it is a complex concept and is difficult to explain. Examples may help.

Trust is lending your older brother your bicycle; you may either gain his appreciation or lose your bike—which one happens depends upon him. You will suffer more if your bike is wrecked than you will gain by his appreciation, and you really expect him to take care of your bike! (Sad experience has led the younger of the two authors to recommend that you never lend your bike to your older brother.) For another example, consider this situation: A student is in a small group that is supposed to complete a report on the play *Macbeth*. The student begins to contribute to the discussion knowing that she will gain if she contributes good ideas that others accept and will lose if her ideas are laughed at and belittled. Whether she gains or loses depends upon the behavior of the other members of her group. She knows she will feel more hurt if she is laughed at than satisfaction if her ideas are appreciated. Her expectation is that the other group members will consider her ideas and accept them. The issue of trust is expressed in the question every student asks: "If I openly express myself, will what I say be held against me?"

When student groups work on problem-solving tasks, what are the crucial elements of trust? Student cooperation requires openness and sharing, which are determined by the expression of acceptance, support, and cooperative intentions. *Openness* is the sharing of information, ideas, thoughts, feelings, and reactions to the issue the group is pursuing. *Sharing* is the offering of one's materials and resources to others in order to help them move the group toward goal accomplishment. *Acceptance* is the communication of high regard for another person and his contributions and behavior. *Support* is the communicating to another person that you recognize his strengths and believe he has the capabilities needed to productively manage the situation he is in. *Cooperative intentions* are the expectation that you are going to behave cooperatively and that everyone else will also. From these definitions, *trusting behavior* may be defined as openness and sharing, and *trustwor-*

thy behavior may be defined as expressing acceptance, support, and cooperative intentions. In assessing a student's trustworthy behavior, it is important to remember that accepting and supporting the contributions of other group members does not mean that one will agree with everything they have to say. A person can express acceptance and support the openness and sharing of others while at the same time expressing different ideas and opposing points of view. This is an important point in building and maintaining trust.

What is the teacher's role in initiating and encouraging trust among students during periods of cooperative activities? The following are some suggestions:

1. Encourage students to openly contribute their information, ideas, thoughts, feelings, intuitions, hunches, and reactions to the group's discussion and work.
2. Encourage students to share materials and resources.
3. Ensure that the students have the skills to express acceptance, support, and desire to cooperate.
4. Encourage students to express cooperative intentions, acceptance, and support toward each other during their cooperative interactions.
5. Point out rejecting and nonsupportive behaviors that shut off future cooperation, such as silence, ridicule, and superficial acknowledgment of an idea.
6. Periodically, have groups that are cooperating fill out the questionnaire on trusting and trustworthy behavior and discuss the results to see how their cooperation could be improved in the future.

Productive cooperation will exist within a group when members are both trusting and trustworthy; nonproductive cooperation will take place when group members are distrustful and untrustworthy. It is also possible for members of a group to be trusting but not trustworthy or to be trustworthy but not trusting. This pattern is represented as follows:

	High Acceptance and Support	*Low Acceptance and Support*
High Openness and Sharing	Trusting and trustworthy	Trusting, but untrustworthy
Low Openness and Sharing	Distrustful, but trustworthy	Distrustful and untrustworthy

EXAMINATION OF TRUST BEHAVIOR

In order to help you assess the level of trust within groups of students working cooperatively, a questionnaire is provided. This questionnaire may be reproduced and given to classes old enough to read or may be used as a guide to interview students who cannot read at the necessary level. The procedure for using the questionnaire is as follows:

1. Have the students complete the questionnaire.
2. Have the students score the questionnaire.
3. Have the students discuss in their cooperative groups the way in which each member completed the questionnaire. Group members are to share their impressions of each other's trusting and trustworthy behavior. If such a discussion cannot take place, the students are to discuss the level of trust in the group indicated by such a lack of openness and feedback.
4. Instruct the students as to how they can skillfully build and maintain trust in their cooperative groups.

Remember that trust is appropriate only when individuals are cooperating. When they are competing, other skills are appropriate. The emphasis, therefore, should be placed on trust within a specific cooperative situation, not upon trust relationships in a wide variety of situations. The questionnaire is given in the next section. It is followed by instructions on scoring.

Your Behavior

Following are a series of questions about your behavior in the cooperative situation you have now completed (or are involved with). Answer each question as honestly as you can. There are no right or wrong answers. It is important for each student to describe his or her behavior as accurately as possible.

1. I offer facts, give my opinions and ideas, provide suggestions and relevant information to help the group discussion.
Never   Seldom   Frequently   Always

2. I express my willingness to cooperate with other group members and my expectations that they also will be cooperative.
Never   Seldom   Frequently   Always

3. I am open and candid in my dealings with the entire group.
Never   Seldom   Frequently   Always

4. I give support to group members who are on the spot and struggling to express themselves intellectually or emotionally.
Never   Seldom   Frequently   Always

5. I keep my thoughts, ideas, feelings, and reactions to myself during group discussions.
Never   Seldom   Frequently   Always

6. I evaluate the contributions of other group members in terms of whether their contributions are useful to me and whether the other group members are right or wrong.
Never   Seldom   Frequently   Always

7. I take risks in expressing new ideas and my current feelings during a group discussion.

    Never   Seldom   Frequently   Always

8. I communicate to other group members that I am aware of, and appreciate, their abilities, talents, capabilities, skills, and resources.

    Never   Seldom   Frequently   Always

9. I offer help and assistance to anyone in the group in order to bring up the performance of everyone.

    Never   Seldom   Frequently   Always

10. I accept and support the openness of other group members, supporting them for taking risks and encouraging individuality in group members.

    Never   Seldom   Frequently   Always

11. I share any materials, books, sources of information, or other resources I have with the other group members in order to promote the success of all members and the group as a whole.

    Never   Seldom   Frequently   Always

12. I often paraphrase or summarize what other members have said before I respond or comment.

    Never   Seldom   Frequently   Always

13. I level with other group members.

    Never   Seldom   Frequently   Always

14. I warmly encourage all members to participate, giving them recognition for their contributions, demonstrating acceptance of and openness to their ideas, and generally being friendly and responsive to them.

    Never   Seldom   Frequently   Always

To score this questionnaire, count "Never" as 1, "Seldom" as 2, "Frequently" as 3, and "Always" as 4. √ Reverse the scoring on questions 5 and 6. Then add the scores in the following way:

Openness and Sharing	*Acceptance and Support*
1. _____	2. _____
3. _____	4. _____
√ 5. _____	√ 6. _____
7. _____	8. _____
9. _____	10. _____
11. _____	12. _____
13. _____	14. _____
Total _____	Total _____

If a student has a score of 21 or more, classify him or her as trusting or trustworthy, whichever the case might be. If a student has a score of less than 21, classify him or her as distrustful or untrustworthy, whichever the case might be.

> **Tutoring Skills**
>
> In order to provide help and assistance to fellow cooperators, a student needs to learn
>
> 1. How to recognize that he or she needs help.
>
> 2. How to ask others for help.
>
> 3. How to search for others who may need assistance.
>
> 4. How to provide instruction, feedback, and reinforcement for other students.
>
> Such skills can be easily learned through a series of role-playing situations developed by the teacher.

LEADERSHIP SKILLS

Perhaps Benjamin Franklin became a renowned leader because he was able to vary his behavior systematically from situation to situation so as to provide the appropriate leadership actions at the appropriate time. There currently is a consensus among social scientists that leadership skills and competencies are not inherited from one's ancestors, that they do not magically appear when a person is assigned to a leadership position, and that the same set of competencies will not provide adequate leadership in every situation. Different situations require different approaches to leadership.

Groups have at least two basic objectives: to complete a task and to maintain effective collaborative relationships among the members. The *distributed-actions theory of leadership* emphasizes that certain functions need to be filled if a group is to meet these two objectives. It defines *leadership* as the performance of acts that help the group to complete its task successfully and maintain effective working relationships among its members. For a group to complete its task successfully, group members must obtain, organize, and use information to make a decision. In doing so they require certain task-leadership actions. Members have to contribute, ask for, summarize, and coordinate the information. They have to structure and give direction to the group's efforts and provide the energy to motivate decision making. For any group to be successful, such task-leadership actions have to be provided.

But it does no good to complete a task if the manner of doing so alienates several group members. If a number of group members refuse to come to the next meeting, the group has not been successful. Thus members must pay attention to maintaining good working relationships while working on the task. The task must be completed in a way that increases the ability of group members to work together effectively in the future. For these things to happen, certain maintenance-leadership actions are needed. Members have to encourage one another to participate. They have to relieve tension when it gets too high, facilitate communication among themselves, and evaluate the emotional climate of the group. They have to discuss how the group's work can be improved, and they have to listen carefully and respectfully to one another. These leadership actions are necessary for the maintenance of friendly relationships among members and, indeed, for the success of the group.

The distributed-actions theory of leadership includes two basic ideas: (1) Any member of a group may become a leader by taking actions that help the group complete its task and maintain effective collaborative relationships; (2) any leadership function may be fulfilled by different members performing a variety of relevant behaviors. Leadership, therefore, is specific to a particular group in a particular situation. Under specific circumstances any given behavior may or may not serve a group function. Under one set of conditions a particular behavior may be helpful; under another set it may impair the effectiveness of the group. For example, when a group is trying to define a problem, suggesting a possible solution may not be helpful; however, when the group is offering various solutions to a defined problem, suggesting a possible solution may indeed be helpful.

From the perspective of this theory, leadership is a learned set of skills that anyone with certain minimal requirements can acquire. Responsible group membership and leadership both depend on flexible behavior, the ability to diagnose what behaviors are needed at a particular time in order for the group to function most efficiently, and the ability to fulfill these behaviors or to get other members to fulfill them. A skilled member or leader, therefore, has to have diagnostic skills in order to be aware that a given function is needed in the group and must be sufficiently adaptive to provide the diverse types of behaviors needed for different conditions. In addition, an effective group member or leader must be able to utilize the abilities of other group members in providing the actions needed by the group.

For at least three reasons, it is usually considered necessary for the behaviors that fulfill group functions to be distributed among group members. First, if members do not participate, then their ideas, skills, and information are not being contributed. This hurts the group's effectiveness. The second reason is that members are committed to what they help build. Members who participate become more committed to the group and what the group has done. Members who remain silent tend not to care about the group and its effectiveness. The more members feel they have influenced the group and contributed to its work, the more committed they will be to the group. The third reason is that active members often become worried or annoyed about the silent members and view them as unconcerned about task completion. Unequal patterns of participation can create maintenance problems within the group.

Sometimes actions within a group not only help it to operate but serve the individual as well. Such individually oriented behavior sometimes involves issues or personal identity (Who am I in this group? Where do I fit in?); personal goals and needs (What do I want from this group? Are the group's goals consistent with my personal goals?); power and control (Who will control what we do? How much power and influence do I have?); and intimacy (How close will we get to each other? How much can I trust the other group members?).

The distributed-actions theory of leadership is one of the most concrete and direct approaches available for improving a person's leadership skills and for improving the effectiveness of a group. People can be taught the diagnostic skills and behaviors that help a group accomplish its task and maintain effective collaborative relationships among its members. There is, however, some criticism of the approach. Members can take so many different actions to help in task achievement and group maintenance that specific ones are hard to pin down. What constitutes leadership then depends on the view of the person who is listing the leadership behaviors.

UTILIZING CREATIVE CONTROVERSY

Have you learned lessons only of
those who admired you, and were tender
with you, and stood aside for you?
Have you not learned great lessons
from those who braced themselves
against you, and disputed the passage
with you?

Walt Whitman, Leaves of Grass

Involved participation in cooperative groups will inevitably produce conflicts among ideas, opinions, conclusions, theories, and information of members. Such controversies are an important aspect of cooperative learning. *Controversy* exists when one person's ideas, information, conclusions, theories, and opinions are incompatible with those of another, and the two seek to reach an agreement. When teachers structure an academic controversy, they assign students to cooperative groups of four, divide the group into two pairs, and assign a "pro" position to one pair and a "con" position to another pair. Teachers carefully establish (1) positive goal interdependence by stating that the goal of the controversy is to write a group report that represents the best thinking of all members, (2) positive resource interdependence by dividing the materials into pro and con positions, and (3) individual accountability by announcing that a test will be given to each student on both positions. Teachers then require the pairs of students to do the following things (Johnson & Johnson, 1992a):

1. Prepare the best case for their assigned position.
2. Present and advocate their assigned position to the opposing pair.
3. Refute the opposing pair's position and reasoning while rebutting attacks on their own position and reasoning.
4. Reverse perspectives by presenting the opposing position as sincerely and forcefully as they can.
5. Reach a decision based on a synthesis of the best ideas and thinking from both sides.

In effect, students are required to orally rehearse the relevant information; advocate a position; teach their knowledge to peers; analyze, critically evaluate, and rebut information; reason both deductively and inductively; and synthesize and integrate information into factual and judgmental conclusions that are summarized into a joint position to which all sides can agree. Controversy enhances individual achievement, higher-level reasoning, and long-term retention, as well as the quality of relationships among group members. In order to function effectively within a cooperative learning group, students will have to have the skills required for promoting and managing controversies constructively. These skills are as follows:

1. Define controversies as problem-solving situations in which differences need to be clarified, rather than as "win–lose" conflicts in which one person's ideas have to dominate. Destructive controversies are characterized by an orientation on the part of students to "win" at the expense of other group members whose ideas are defeated. In a "win–lose" situation, every action is seen in terms of who is going to dominate whom. Such a competitive orientation within a cooperative situation will seriously undermine cooperation. When controversy is approached from a problem-solving point of view, students tend to recognize the legitimacy of each other's ideas and contributions and search for a solution accommodating the needs of all group members.

2. Be critical of ideas, not persons. *Ideas* are discussed, not personalities, and nothing personal is meant in disagreement. It is possible to express disagreement without personally rejecting, and students should be encouraged to do so. This is an important skill for cooperators to learn.

3. Appropriately pace the differentiation phase (bringing out differences) and the integration phase (putting the different ideas together) of the problem-solving process.

Many of the controversy skills are promoted by inquiry learning situations. There is a strong relationship between inquiry teaching and cooperation; inquiry tasks are problem-solving situations, and a cooperative goal structure generally is the most appropriate one to use. The question-asking strategies, brainstorming of alternatives, open discussion of ideas, and other aspects of inquiry teaching will all help in resolving controversies. Other suggestions for inquiry teaching are these:

1. Initiate controversy in order to increase student interest and motivation. Sharpening up students' ideas, opening up new possibilities, and deepening the level of analysis and insight can all be accomplished by teachers when they initiate controversies.

2. Reward the posing of alternatives (which will increase controversy) by students.

3. Reward students for changing their minds when confronted with evidence. (This is an important behavior for teachers to model.)

4. Encourage students to consider alternatives from different points of view. (The story of the three blind men and an elephant is always a good example of the value of perspective taking.)

First, all different points of view are brought out and explored. Second, creative syntheses to arrive at the best solution are sought. It is a serious mistake to look for ways to integrate ideas before all the differences have been explored. The potential for integration is never greater than the adequacy of the differentiation already achieved.

   4. Take the point of view or perspective of other students so that you understand what they are saying from their frame of reference. This procedure, sometimes called *role reversal,* is a skill that everyone must master. It is the ability to understand how a situation appears to other students and how they are reacting cognitively and emotionally to the situation. It is crucial for integrating different perspectives into a more complete and higher-quality solution to the problem being worked upon. The opposite of such perspective taking, *egocentrism,* is the inability to take another person's perspective.

   In addition to promoting constructive controversy within cooperative learning groups, there are other conflict procedures and skills that teachers will wish students to develop. Much of teachers' time is spent dealing with conflict among students, between students and staff, between staff and parents, or even among staff members. Conflicts are inevitable whenever committed people work together to achieve mutual goals. Conflicts are constructively managed through a five-step procedure (Johnson & Johnson, 1991b). The first step is creating a cooperative context. In order for long-term mutual interests to be recognized and valued, individuals have to perceive their interdependence and be invested in each other's well being. The second step is structuring academic controversies. In order to maximize student achievement, critical thinking, and higher-level reasoning, students need to engage in intellectual conflicts. Within structured controversies, students work with a learning partner in examining an academic issue, preparing a pro or con position, advocating their position to an opposing pair, criticizing the opposing position, reversing perspectives, and synthesizing the best arguments on both sides to derive a conclusion. The use of academic controversy is a very

powerful instructional procedure that will move cooperative learning groups to new heights of productivity and higher-level learning.

The third step is teaching students how to negotiate, and the fourth step is teaching students how to mediate. Students may be taught the basic steps and skills of negotiating an agreement with an opponent. They may then be trained as mediators to help their classmates successfully negotiate resolutions to their conflicts. Students first try to negotiate their conflicts and, if negotiation fails, ask a peer mediator for help. Finally, when mediation fails, the teacher or principal arbitrates the conflict (step 5). This is a last resort because it typically involves deciding who is right and wrong, leaving at least one student angry toward the arbitrator. The procedures for using this five-step process of utilizing constructive conflict to improve instruction may be found in *Teaching Students to Be Peacemakers* by Johnson and Johnson (1991b).

USING BONUS POINTS TO TEACH SOCIAL SKILLS

Many teachers may want to use a structured program to teach students the interpersonal and small-group skills they need to cooperate effectively with classmates. Such a program will provide students with the opportunity to help their groups earn bonus points using targeted cooperative skills. These points can be accumulated for academic credit or for special rewards such as free time or minutes listening to one's own choice of music. The procedure for doing so is as follows:

1. Identify, define, and teach a social skill you want students to use in working cooperatively with each other. This skill becomes a target for mastery.
2. Use group points and group rewards to increase the use of the cooperative skill:
   a. Each time a student engages in the targeted skill, the student's group receives a point.
   b. Points may only be awarded for positive behavior.
   c. Points are added and never taken away. All points are permanently earned.
3. Summarize total points daily. Emphasize daily progress toward the goal. Use a visual display such as a graph or chart.
4. Develop an observational system that samples each group an equal amount of time. In addition, utilize student observers to record the frequency of students using the targeted skills.
5. Set a reasonable number of points for earning the reward. Rewards are both social and tangible. The social reward is having the teacher say, "That shows thought"; "I like the way you explained it"; "That's a good way of putting it"; "Remarkably well done." The tangible reward is the points earned, which may be traded in for free time, computer time, library time, time to play a game, extra recess time, and any other activity that students value.
6. In addition to group points, class points may be awarded. The teacher, for example, might say, "Eighteen people are ready to begin and help the class earn a reward," or, "I noticed twelve people worked the last 25 minutes." Class points may be recorded with a number line, beans in a jar, or checks on the chalkboard.

7. In addition to social skills, potential target behaviors include following directions, completing assigned tasks, handing in homework, behaving appropriately in out-of-class settings such as lunch or assemblies, or helping substitute teachers.

Processing Checklist

_____ 1. Teacher selects two or three skills to observe for.

_____ 2. Teacher appoints observers and prepares observation form.

_____ 3. Teacher observes and intervenes when necessary.

_____ 4. Student observers assess how well collaborative skills have been performed.

_____ 5. Groups process by using student observers as a source of feedback.

_____ 6. Whole class processes, summarizing the feedback from each group and the teacher's observation.

_____ 7. Group members set goals for performing collaborative skills in the next group session.

SUMMARY

If the potential of cooperative learning is to be realized, students must have the prerequisite interpersonal and small-group skills and be motivated to use them. These skills need to be taught just as systematically as math and social studies. Doing so involves communicating to students the need for the social skills, defining and modeling the skills, having students practice the skills over and over again, processing how effectively the students are performing the skills, and ensuring that students persevere until the skills are fully integrated into the students' behavioral repertoire. Doing so will not only increase student achievement, but will also increase students' future employability, career success, quality of relationships, and psychological health.

Nothing we learn is more important than the skills required to work cooperatively with other people. Most human interaction is cooperative. Without some skill in cooperating effectively, it is difficult (if not impossible) to maintain a marriage, hold a job, or be part of a community, society, and world. In this chapter we have discussed only a few of the interpersonal and small-group skills needed for effective cooperation. For a more thorough and extensive coverage of these skills see _Reaching Out_ (Johnson, 1993), _Joining Together_ (Johnson & F. Johnson, 1991), _Human Relations and Your Career_ (Johnson, 1991), _Circles of Learning_ (Johnson, Johnson, & Holubec, 1984/1993), and _Teaching Students to Be Peacemakers_ (Johnson & Johnson, 1991b).

Assessment, Evaluation, and Group Processing

INTRODUCTION

Sophocles (496–406 B.C.), a Greek playwright, believed, "Look and you will find it . . . what is unsought will go undetected." To implement cooperative learning effectively, teachers and students must look to see what is going well and what could be improved. Assessment, evaluation, and group processing are necessities if students are to learn, grow, and develop intellectually and socially. The final phase in the teacher's role is to evaluate student learning and structure student processing of their collaborative efforts. Data may be also gathered to evaluate the quality of the instructional program. In examining evaluation and processing, it is helpful to discuss the changing nature of assessment, the new assessment and evaluation formats, the assessment of academic efforts in cooperative learning groups, and the assessment of the teamwork among group members in cooperative learning situations.

CHANGING ASSESSMENT PRACTICES

Assessment practices in schools are changing in at least five ways. First, *schools are under increasing accountability pressures that require them to prove they are doing a good job.* Schools have to prove that they are doing more than presenting educational opportunities. They must prove that they are achieving outcomes. Outcomes-based education has become the order of the day.

Second, *schools are reexamining the outcomes they are trying to achieve*. There are four sources of pressure on educators to reexamine the outcomes of schooling. The first is that definitions of achievement are being expanded. Initially, as a reaction to increased accountability, teachers and administrators focused their planning and instructional efforts on preparing students to do well on standardized tests. Because standardized tests have many shortcomings, educators have become interested in assessing other educational outcomes, such as actual performances and procedures and skills that relate to "real-world" activities. Many of the most valued educational outcomes cannot be translated into objective paper-and-pencil test items. Assessments of achievement, for example, must measure (a) achievement-related behaviors (ability to communicate, cooperate, perform certain motor activities, and solve complex problems), (b) achievement-related products (writing themes or project reports, art products, craft products), or (c) achievement-related attitudes and dispositions (locus of control, self-concept).

The second pressure on educators to reexamine educational outcomes is the changing organizational structure of the school. With the change to a team-based, high-performance organizational structure (that emphasizes cooperative learning in the classroom and colleagial teaching teams in the building), the assessment of teamwork becomes just as important for quality education as the assessment of taskwork. In the new organizational structure, outcomes such as the quality of the instructional program being delivered by teacher teams become just as important as the students' achievement.

The third pressure on educators to reexamine their outcomes is the awareness that high school graduates and even college graduates lack the competencies necessary to be citizens in our society and live a high-quality life. High school graduates and even college graduates often are unemployable. These graduates often do not vote or inform themselves on the issues. They fail to build and maintain stable friendships and family relationships. Schools have focused on preparing students for the next level of education without focusing on preparing them for employment, citizenship, and quality of life. A fourth-grade teacher may think primarily in terms of getting students ready for the fifth grade, and a high school teacher may think primarily in terms of getting students ready for college. The competencies needed for the next level of education may be quite different from the competencies needed later in life. Schools are being held accountable to teach successfully what students need to advance educationally, get and hold a job, be a citizen, and have a high quality of life.

A fourth pressure on schools is the need to compete with schools in other countries. The internationalization of the economy has resulted in an internationalization of schools. It is no longer enough to be one of the best schools in a local area; it is no longer enough to be one of the best schools in the state; it is no longer enough to be one of the best schools in the nation. The quality of a school in America has to be compared with the quality of schools in Japan, Germany, Finland, Thailand, and every other country in the world. Schools in America have to be educating "world-class workers" and individuals who are able to work for and be successful in international companies that have branches and employees from all over the world.

Third, *more assessment options are required.* With increased accountability and a reexamination of the outcomes, educators have become interested in more varied assessment formats and procedures. Assessment options include (a) paper-and-pencil-assessments (teacher-made tests and quizzes, textbook tests and quizzes, standardized tests, homework and seatwork assignments), (b) performance assessments (measures based on observation and judgments of individual products), (c) authentic assessments (role playing and simulations), and (d) quality charts. One of the new rules is, "Make your assessment processes fit the target." If English teachers want to assess students' writing ability, for example, they should have students write, not answer multiple-choice questions about sentence structure and grammar.

Fourth, *teachers are becoming more directly involved in assessment and evaluation.* After decades of leaving assessment to the professionals, teachers are having to reenter the assessment process by using formats other than the traditional paper-and-pencil achievement test. In order to use the new assessment formats, teachers have to conduct the assessments themselves for a number of reasons. One is that many assessment procedures have to be used daily on an ongoing basis (rather than once or twice a year). It is not feasible to employ assessment experts to implement a wide variety of assessment options continually in every classroom in a school or district. Another reason is that experts are not available for many of the new assessment formats. Valid and reliable standardized tests may be easier to develop than valid and reliable performance measures. Finally, teachers are being encouraged to become directly involved in assessment through action research. In action research projects, teachers are expected to systematically collect, analyze, and interpret data about the cognitive and social growth and development of their students.

Fifth, *students are becoming more directly involved in assessment and evaluation.* The new assessment formats are often labor-intensive. It takes a lot of work and a lot of time to gather and analyze the data. Teachers simply do not have the time to do it without help and assistance. The most natural source of help for teachers is students. Students also have to be involved because they are the ones who have to implement and use the results of the assessment. Student commitment to implement the results of an evaluation are greater when they collect, analyze, and interpret the data themselves. An additional reason for student involvement in assessment is that continuous improvement requires continuous self-assessment by teams and individual members. If students are to improve continuously, an assessment and evaluation procedure must be instituted within the ongoing life of cooperative learning groups.

In summary, the demand for accountability has led to a reexamination of the outcomes of schooling which, in turn, has led to an interest in a wider variety of assessment options. Many of the most valued and needed outcomes cannot be assessed by standardized tests or other paper-and-pencil measures. The challenge is to find assessment options that can be used to measure a broad array of valued outcomes. The more assessment options available, the easier it is to get a more complete picture of instructional quality. Assessment formats should fit the targeted outcome. These assessment options require that both teachers and students become directly involved in gathering, analyzing, and interpreting data about the instructional process in the classroom.

THE NEW ASSESSMENT FORMATS

Assessment and evaluation are inseparable. *Assessment* is the collection of data on the basis of which a judgment is to be made. *Evaluation* is the rendering of a judgment on the merits of a performance. Evaluation may be based on the traditional paper-and-pencil tests that measure what students know, performance assessments, authentic assessments, and quality school procedures. The use of cooperative learning increases the ease with which the new assessment formats may be used.

Performance-based assessment requires students to demonstrate what they can do with what they know by performing a procedure or skill. In a performance assessment, the student completes or demonstrates the same behavior that the assessor desires to measure. If the behavior to be measured is writing, for example, the student should write, not complete multiple-choice questions about sentence structure or grammar. The performance is evaluated on the basis of the professional judgment of the assessor. Thus, teachers need (a) an appropriate method of sampling the desired performances and (b) a clearly articulated set of criteria to serve as the basis for evaluative judgments. They will also need to put students in cooperative learning groups most of the time. Most important procedures and skills cannot be demonstrated by an isolated individual.

Authentic assessment is requiring students to demonstrate the desired procedure or skill in a "real-life" context. Students solve simulated real-life problems or complete simulated real-life tasks. An authentic assessment of writing, for example, may involve students role playing that they are newspaper reporters who have to research and write an article of a prescribed number of words on an assigned topic to meet a fixed deadline (in order for the paper to go to press) under the direction of an editor. Or students may be assigned to research teams working on a cure for cancer; who have to conduct an experiment, write a lab report summarizing their results, write a journal article, and make an oral presentation at a simulated convention. Authentic assessment generally requires the use of cooperative learning groups; in the real world, most procedures and skills are used in interpersonal, group, and organizational contexts.

Performance assessment refers to the kind of student response to be examined, and authentic assessment refers to the context in which that response is performed. Although not all performance assessments are authentic, it is difficult to imagine an authentic assessment that is not also a performance assessment. In both performance and authentic assessment, furthermore, cooperative learning becomes a necessity. Most important procedures and skills cannot be demonstrated by an isolated individual, and in the real world procedures and skills are used in interpersonal, group, and organizational contexts.

In assessing students' ability to perform procedures and skills in real-life contexts, there is some disagreement as to whether educators should focus on (a) only assessing and evaluating the outcomes of instruction or (b) primarily assessing and evaluating the educational process. Traditionally, it is the outcomes of instruction that have been the focus of attention. W. Edwards Deming and other advocates of *total quality management* in business and industry, however, stress that instead of measuring outcomes (inspecting quality in), the emphasis should be on improving the process by which the work is done in order to achieve zero defects or a "perfect product every time." In order to promote total quality in a school, both students (cooperative learning groups) and teachers (colleagial teaching teams) have to be assigned to teams. The teams are placed in charge of the quality of the work of its members. Team members, therefore, have to be trained to organize their work, assess its quality daily, and place the results on a quality chart to help them evaluate their effectiveness.

Total quality learning is the continuous improvement of the process of students' helping teammates learn. To do quality work, students have to be placed in cooperative learning groups. The groups are heterogeneous to ensure that members see the whole picture of educating all class members. Then an eight-step process of total quality learning is implemented. These steps are based on Deming's fourteen recommendations for improving the quality of work within business and industrial organizations. First, the teacher establishes strong positive goal interdependence to create a constancy of purpose among group members and in the classroom as a whole. Second, students adopt the new philosophies of total quality learning (each group member hands in perfectly done assignments every time) and continuous improvement (each day students know more than they did and are more capable than they were the day before). Third, the teacher drives out fear by eliminating all competition and other factors that lead to student humiliation or self-defense. Fourth, caring and committed relationships among students are emphasized to ensure that group members provide each other with the ongoing academic and personal social support that total quality learning requires. Fifth, students promote each other's academic success by helping, sharing, assisting, and encouraging efforts to learn and be a contributing team member. Sixth, students use a variety of tools to assess daily the quality of teamwork and the quality of members' academic learning. Seventh, the assessment results are plotted on a quality chart that provides an ongoing record of the group's progress in ensuring that all members learn. Eighth, the quality chart and other assessment results are used to refine and improve continuously team effectiveness in maximizing the learning of all members. Deming believes that if teachers concentrate on this eight-step process, the quality of students' learning will take care of itself.

HOW IT ALL FITS TOGETHER

The demand for accountability has led to a reexamination of the outcomes of schooling. A wider variety of assessment options is necessary to determine whether or not schools are being successful in achieving these new and broader outcomes. The more assessment options available, the easier it is to get a more complete picture of instructional quality. The assessment options include the traditional paper-and-pencil format, performance assessments, authentic assessments, and assessing the quality of learning. These assessment options require that both teachers and students become directly involved in gathering, analyzing, and interpreting data about the instructional process in the classroom. The use of cooperative learning increases the ease with which the new assessment formats may be used.

The accountability pressures, the reformulated outcomes, and the assessment formats are used for two major purposes: to evaluate the quality of students' academic efforts and to evaluate the quality of students' teamwork.

EVALUATING QUALITY OF ACADEMIC EFFORTS

Assessment and cooperative learning are closely tied together. In every cooperative learning lesson, teachers are responsible for ensuring that assessment and evaluation take place. The use of the new assessment procedures, furthermore, can best take place in cooperative learning groups. Teachers have a number of responsibilities in evaluating students' academic efforts in cooperative lessons. The steps in doing so include specifying academic objectives, translating into an academic assignment, determining the criteria for success, communicating the task and the criteria to students, monitoring the academic efforts of the cooperative groups and intervening when necessary, and evaluating the resulting learning. These steps are discussed in the following sections.

Structuring the Lesson

The teacher specifies the academic objectives of the lesson. In order to achieve those objectives, the teacher designs an instructional task. After the task is defined, the teacher determines the criteria for success. The teacher establishes evaluation criteria, involving students in developing criteria when it is appropriate. The teacher then communicates both the task and the criteria for success to students.

Conducting the Lesson

After the students begin working, the teacher systematically monitors each learning group and intervenes when necessary to ensure that students correctly understand the academic content of the assignment. The monitoring and interventions provide opportunities for gathering observation data about the quality of the explanations and intellectual interchange among group members, and for conducting individual oral examinations to ensure that all group members are learning the assigned material.

Observational procedures   While the students work together in cooperative learning groups, teachers systematically gather observation data about the quality of the explanations and intellectual interchange occurring among group members. Observation data may be gathered by the use of formal observation schedules on which the frequency of behaviors are tallied, checklists, rating scales, or anecdotal impressions. These data are available for formative evaluation and for indices of such outcomes as effort and higher level reasoning.

Observational procedures are aimed at describing and recording behavior as it occurs. From observing students' behaviors, teachers gain the information needed to make judgments about the current competence of the students and the success of the instructional program. To observe students engaging in such outcomes of science instruction as scientific reasoning, scientific problem solving, and metacognitive thinking, students must be observed "thinking out loud" in cooperative learning groups. In essence, cooperative learning groups are "windows into students' minds." Teachers assign students to small cooperative groups and give them an assignment. As the groups work, the teacher moves from group to group listening to the students interact with each other. From listening to students explain how to complete the assignment, the teacher can assess what students understand and what they do not understand, the level of cognitive reasoning they are using, and the strategies they are using to approach the assignment. In addition, the teacher can assess how frequently metacognitive strategies are being used. A variety of observation sheets are given in Johnson, Johnson, and Holubec (1993).

Many times students know what the "correct" answer to a question is without understanding the scientific principles and theories on which the answer is based. Correct answers on a test and completed homework assignments tell teachers very little about students' reasoning processes and understanding of science. The only way teachers can be sure that students really understand the subject being studied is by listening to students explain what they know to each other step by step. To do so, students must be working in cooperative (not competitive or individualistic) learning groups.

Student involvement in evaluation may be facilitated by teaching students how to observe and gather information useful data on the interaction among group members. One observer may be appointed. Cooperative learning groups offer a unique opportunity for immediate diagnosis of level of understanding, immediate feedback from peers, and immediate remediation to correct misunderstandings and fill in gaps in students' understanding. Training students to observe each other's cognitive reasoning and strategies for solving problems and completing assignments will facilitate the cycle of immediate diagnosis-feedback-remediation.

Interview procedures   In addition to observing students work, teachers will wish to interview students systematically to determine the level of cognitive reasoning, problem solving, and metacognitive thinking. Assign students to cooperative learning groups. The groups should be heterogeneous in terms of math and reading ability. Give a set of questions to the groups on Monday. Instruct the students to prepare all group members to respond to the questions. Give time during each class period for the groups to practice their responses to the questions. On Thursday and Friday conduct an oral examination with the students, using the following procedure.

Meet with a group and randomly select one member to explain the answer to a randomly selected question. When that member finishes responding to the question, other group members can add to the answer. Judge the answer to be "adequate" or "inadequate." Then ask another member a different question. Repeat this procedure until all questions have been answered or until the teacher judges the group to be inadequately prepared. In this case, the group has to return to the assignments and practice until they are better prepared. Give some guidance by identifying particular weaknesses and strengths in the member's answers. All group members are given equal credit for successfully passing the test.

Assessing and Evaluating Student Learning

After the lesson or unit is completed, the teacher assesses and evaluates individual student learning and group products. This is accomplished by checking students' homework daily, giving paper-and-pencil achievement tests, evaluating performance measures (such as presentations, compositions, and videos), self and peer ratings, group projects, and scientific projects.

Individual assessment is more frequent than is group assessment. The purpose of cooperative learning groups is to make each member a stronger individual in his or her own right. This creates a pattern to classroom learning—students learn in a group and then demonstrate what they know and can do alone.

There are two levels of assessment and evaluation—the individual and the group. At either the individual or the group level, assessments can focus on homework, paper-and-pencil tests, individual logs or journals, portfolios of products (exhibits, stories, songs, drawings, paintings, videos), presentations or performances, participation in class, the use of social skills, or actions in simulations. Assessments can be conducted by the teacher, groupmates, or oneself. Assessments can take place during or after the lesson, in structured or in unstructured situations. In an unstructured situation, students are given an open-ended, ambiguous situation in which they are to select and use important concepts, skills, and habits of mind. Students must define the problem, plan and carry out a strategy, discover and defend a solution, and communicate the solution to a specific audience. Some of the specific ways that assessments can be conducted in cooperative learning groups follow.

Checking homework   In order to assess the quality of students' homework daily, a procedure can be implemented to check homework quickly at the beginning of each class period. Students are requested to bring their completed homework to class and demonstrate that they understand how to do it correctly.

The cooperative procedure is as follows. Students enter the classroom and meet in their cooperative learning groups. The groups should be heterogeneous in terms of math and reading ability. One member (the *runner*) goes to the teacher's desk, picks up the group's folder, and hands out materials in the folder to the appropriate members. Members compare answers and quiz each other on the homework assignment. The cooperative goal is to ensure that all group members bring their completed homework to class and understand how to do it correctly. Two roles are assigned: *explainer* (explains how to complete the homework correctly) and *accuracy checker* (verifies that the explanation is accurate, encourages others, and provides coaching if needed). The explainer reads the first part of the assignment and explains step by step how to complete it correctly. The other group members check for accuracy. The roles are rotated clockwise around the group so that each member does an equal amount of explaining. The group should concentrate on the parts of the assignments that members did not understand. Any questions members have about completing the assignment correctly are answered. The runner records how much of the assignment each member completed. At the end of the assigned review time, the members' homework is placed in the group's folder and the runner returns it to the teacher's desk.

There is an alternative to this procedure. Students are assigned to pairs. The teacher randomly picks questions from the homework assignment. One student explains the correct answer step by step. The other student listens, checks for accuracy, and prompts the explainer if he or she does not know the answer. Roles are switched for each question.

Paper-and-pencil achievement tests   Tests may be given both to assess and to increase student learning. The first sequence of testing is review of the material to be covered in the test in a cooperative learning group, taking the test individually, and then retaking the test in the cooperative learning group (group review, individual test, group test). Students are assigned to cooperative learning groups that are heterogeneous in terms of reading and math ability. The groups study together all week. On Thursday, the groups meet to ensure that all group members know and understand the material on which they will be tested. On Friday, an examination is given. The students take the test individually, making two copies of their answers. One answer sheet they hand in to the teacher (who then scores the answers). They keep the second answer sheet. After all members have finished the test, the group meets to take the test again. Their task is to answer each question correctly. The cooperative goal is for all group members to understand the material covered by the test. For any answer that they are in disagreement over or are unsure of, they are required to find the page and paragraph in the text that contains the answer. The teacher randomly observes the groups to check that they are following the procedure. If all members of the group score above a present criterion (such as 90 percent correct) on the individual tests, then each member receives a designated number (such as 5) of bonus points. The bonus points are added to their individual score to determine their individual grade for the test.

The second sequence of testing is to give weekly group tests and an individual final exam. Each cooperative group is divided into two pairs. Each pair takes the weekly exam, conferring on the answer to each question. The task is to correctly answer each question. The cooperative goal is to have one answer for each question that both agree upon and both can explain. They cannot proceed until they agree on the answer. Once the two pairs are finished, the cooperative group of four meets and retakes the test. Their task is to answer each question correctly. The cooperative goal is for all group members to understand the material covered by the test. Group members confer on each question. On any question to which the two pairs have different answers or members are unsure of the answer, they find the page number and paragraph in the textbook where the answer is explained. Each group is responsible for ensuring that all members understand the material they missed on the test. If necessary, group members assign review homework to each other. The teacher randomly observes each group to check that they are answering the questions correctly. Each cooperative group then hands in one answer sheet with a list of all members. Each member signs the answer sheet to verify that (a) he or

she understands the content and (b) all other group members understand the content covered by the test. All group members are given equal credit for successfully passing the test.

At the end of the grading period, each student takes an individual final examination. If any student scores below a preset criterion (such as 80 percent), then the cooperative group meets and reviews the content with the student until he or she can successfully pass the test. This rarely happens, as the group members have verified each week that they all are learning the assigned content.

Performance measures   In addition to paper-and-pencil tests, teachers may wish to examine actual performances of students. Students, for example, may present for assessment samples of their work in a portfolio, compositions, exhibitions, demonstrations, video projects, science projects, surveys, and even actual job performances.

Cooperative learning groups are essential for performance assessments. First, they prepare students to give the performance. Second, they assess the performances of members of other groups in order to provide immediate feedback to help the students improve. Third, they provide the setting in which group members analyze their feedback and plan how to improve their performances.

Peer editing: cooperative learning in composition   Students are assigned to cooperative groups and are assigned the task of writing a composition or report. Each student writes his or her own composition. The assignment is structured cooperatively by informing students that all group members must sign a statement verifying that each member's composition is perfect according to the criteria set by the teacher. Each group member will receive two scores for the composition. The first is based on the quality of his or her composition. The second is based on the total number of errors made by the group (the number of errors in their composition plus the number of errors in their groupmates' compositions).

A typical procedure follows (Johnson, Johnson, & Holubec, 1993). First, the teacher assigns students to cooperative learning pairs with at least one good reader in each pair. The task of writing individual compositions is given. Students are informed that the criterion for success is a well-written composition by each student. Depending on the instructional objectives, the compositions may be evaluated for grammar, punctuation, organization, content, or other criteria set by the teacher.

Second, Student A describes to Student B what he or she is planning to write. Student B listens carefully, probes with a set of questions, and outlines Student A's composition. The written outline is given to Student A. This procedure is then reversed with Student B describing what he or she is going to write and Student A listening and completing an outline of Student B's composition, which is then given to Student B.

Third, each student researches the material he or she needs to write the compositions, keeping an eye out for material useful to his or her partner. If one student does not have the skills required to use reference materials and the library effectively, the partner teaches him or her how to do so.

Fourth, the two students work together to write the first paragraph of each composition to ensure that they both have a clear start on their compositions. Each student then writes his or her composition individualistically. When completed, the students proofread each other's compositions, making corrections in capitalization, punctuation, spelling, language usage, topic sentence usage, and other aspects of writing specified by the teacher. Suggestions for revision are explained. Each student then revises his or her composition, making the suggested revisions. The two students then re-read each other's compositions and sign their names (indicating that they personally guarantee that no errors exist in the composition).

While the students work, the teacher monitors the pairs, intervening where appropriate to help students master the needed writing and cooperative skills. When the composition is completed, the students discuss how effectively they worked together (listing the specific actions they engaged in to help each other), plan what behaviors they are going to emphasize in the next writing pair, and thank each other for the help and assistance received.

Class presentations and peer assessment   When students are required to give class presentations, the task is to prepare and conduct a presentation on an assigned topic. The cooperative goal is for all members to learn the material being presented and gain experience in making presentations. First, the teacher assigns students to groups of four, gives each group a topic, and requires them to prepare one presentation that each group member can give in its entirety. The presentation should be given within a certain time frame and should be supported with visuals or active participation by the audience. Second, the groups are given time to prepare and rehearse. All group members should be able to give the presentation. Third, the class is divided into four sections (one in each corner of the classroom). One member of each group goes to each section. Each student makes a presentation to his or her section. The audience rates the performance on a reaction form provided by the teacher. A presentation is evaluated on the basis of the degree to which it was (a) scholarly and informative, (b) interesting, concise, and easy to follow, (c) involving (audience active, not passive), (d) intriguing (audience interest in finding out more on their own), and (e) organized (has introduction, body, and conclusion). In addition, the teacher adds criteria uniquely aimed at the purposes of the presentation. At the end of the presentation, one copy of the rating form is given to the teacher and one copy is given to the presenter. The teacher systematically observes part of all presentations. Finally, the groups meet to evaluate how effectively each member made the presentation. Remedial help is given to any member who had problems presenting.

Any performance given by a student, whether it is a speech, a musical performance, a science demonstration, a dramatic presentation, or a videotape project, can be evaluated by peers as well as a teacher.

Self and other rating   Thomas Mann (1875–1955), a German writer, once said, "No one remains quite what he was when he recognizes himself." Having students rate themselves and their groupmates is an important addition to most lessons. First, students rate the quality and quantity of their learning. Second, students rate the

report
card

To Parent:

This is a report of work and progress.
Our schools wish to develop each pupil
to the limit of his capacity
that he may make the most of himself
and contribute the greatest good to society.
Citizenship, character, service, and loyalty—
knowledge, skills, attitudes, and appreciation
are our goals.
Home and school must work together.
We are here to serve you and yours.

Sincerely yours,

Superintendent

quality and quantity of the learning of each of their groupmates. Third, students discuss and reflect on their learning experiences (under the guidance of an observant teacher), comparing their self-ratings with the ratings they receive from groupmates.

There are a number of factors that teachers need to assess besides test scores. Students need arrive at class on time and be prepared to learn (have the essential materials, resources, and attitudes). Students need to provide academic help and assistance to groupmates and ask groupmates for help when they need it. In using a rating form, students need to clearly understand the purpose of the form and how it will be used, the number of points (if any) the form will count in evaluating students, and the questions on the form.

Student Self and Peer Evaluation Form

This form will be used to assess the members of your learning group. Fill out form one on yourself. Fill out form one on each member of your group. During the group discussion, give each member the form you have filled out on him or her. Compare the way you rated yourself with the ways your groupmates have rated you. Ask for clarification when your rating differs from the ratings given you by your groupmates. Each member should set a goal for increasing his or her contribution to the academic learning of all group members.

Person being rated: _____

Circle the number of points earned by each group member (4 = Excellent, 3 = Good, 2 = Poor, 1 = Inadequate)

4   3   2   1   On time for class.

4   3   2   1   Arrives prepared for class.

4   3   2   1   Reliably completes all assigned work on time.

4   3   2   1   Work is of high quality.

4   3   2   1   Contributes to groupmates' learning daily.

4   3   2   1   Asks for academic help and assistance when he or she needs it.

4   3   2   1   Gave careful step-by-step explanations of how to do the assignment (did not just tell correct answers).

4   3   2   1   Related what is being learned to previous knowledge.

4   3   2   1   Helped draw a visual representation of the cognitive structure of what is being learned.

Group products   The usual rule for cooperative learning groups is that students learn how to do something in a group and then perform it alone. Thus, in schools individual assessment is more common than group assessment. In real life it may be just the opposite. In most organizations the success of the organization as a whole, divisions in the organization, and teams in the division are focused on more frequently than is the success of each individual employee. Authentic assessment, therefore, most often means group assessment. Thus, there are times when a classroom assignment may be given requiring a group report, exhibit, performance, video, or presentation.

Scientific project   In a scientific project students are given the task of conducting an inquiry using the scientific method. The cooperative goal is for group members to complete one project in which everyone has contributed a share of the work, everyone can explain its content and how it was conducted, and everyone can present to the class. The procedure is as follows. Students are assigned an initial project and are placed in cooperative learning groups to complete it. The required materials are provided. Second, the group completes the project, ensuring that all members contributed and agree on and can explain the results. The teacher systematically observes each group and provides feedback and coaching. Third, the group hands in their report to the teacher; each member can present the results to a section of the class, and a test may be given on the scientific method and the content of the project. Fourth, the assignment can be extended by the teacher's presenting the relevant algorithm, procedure, concept, or theory required to complete the project. Students are then given a more complex project that requires them to apply what they have just learned.

Group celebration   The end of all assessment and evaluation of academic learning by group members is a celebration of members' hard work and success.

EVALUATING QUALITY OF SOCIAL SKILLS

In addition to evaluating efforts to achieve academically, teachers need to assess and evaluate students' efforts to work together cooperatively. In real job situations, most people are evaluated on how effectively they work with others. Schools need

to catch up. There are ten places in a cooperative lesson that teachers are involved in evaluating students use of social skills.

1. The teacher must decide which social skill is going to be emphasized in the lesson and make practicing it one of the objectives of the lesson. Every cooperative lesson is a lesson on social skills and teamwork as well as academics.

2. The teacher operationally defines the social skill with a T-Chart. It is often helpful to have the class generate the list of nonverbal actions and verbal phrases that make up the skill.

3. The teacher teaches the social skill to the students. The skill may be modeled, explained step by step, and practiced by the students before the lesson begins. Inform students that use of the skrill during the lesson is expected.

4. The teacher prepares the observation form, appoints observers, and explains the observation form to the observers. There are three sources of observers: the teacher, students, and visitors. The teacher is always an observer. Students may regularly be used as observers—either a few roving student observers to monitor all groups or, preferably, one observer for each group. Visitors should not be allowed to sit and watch a lesson passively. Teachers should give them an observation sheet and ask them to help collect data on each group's effectiveness.

5. The observers use the observation form to monitor the interactions among group members while they work on the academic lesson, paying special attention to the targeted social skill. *Observation* is aimed at recording and describing members' behavior as it occurs in the group, that is, to provide objective data about the interaction among group members. The behavior of group members is observed so that students may be given feedback about their participation in the group and so that inferences can be made about the ways in which the group is functioning. Observation procedures may be structured or unstructured. The teacher moves from group to group in a systematic way, recording frequencies of targeted behaviors and intervening to help the group work better when it is necessary. Students assess each other's use of the targeted social skill and provide immediate remediation to help each other master it.

6. The group members assess how often and how well they individually performed the targeted social skill and other expected behaviors. Group members may fill out a checklist or questionnaire about their actions in the group.

7. The observer reports to the group the information gathered, and group members report their impressions as to how they behaved. The observer summarizes his or her observations in a clear and useful manner and describes them to the group as feedback. The observer then helps group members make inferences from the observations about how well the group functioned, how frequently and well each member engaged in the targeted skill, and how the interaction among group members could be modified to make it more effective. The observer ensures that all group members receive positive feedback about their actions in the group.

8. The group members reflect on and analyze the effectiveness of their use of social skills. Reflection is needed in order to discover what helped and hindered them in completing the academic assignment and whether specific actions had a positive or negative effect. After small-group processing, there is whole-class processing.

9. The group members set goals for improving their social skills competence during the next group meeting. *Goal setting* is the link between how students did today and how

they will do tomorrow. Members discuss the goals and publicly commit to achieving them.

10. The group members celebrate their hard work in mastering social skills.

QUALITY OF IMPLEMENTATION OF INSTRUCTION PROCEDURES

In order for teachers' expertise in implementing cooperative learning to improve continuously, they must assess the quality of their efforts (Johnson & Johnson, 1989b). The procedure for such assessment is to establish a set of criteria and rate the extent to which each member of the teaching team is meeting the criteria. The results are then charted each week to help the group (a) determine the frequency and fidelity with which each group member is implementing cooperative learning and (b) set goals for implementation efforts for the coming week. An example of a quality chart follows. During the colleagial support group meeting:

1. Each member shows his or her implementation log and reports the degree to which he or she:
   a. Taught at least one cooperative learning lesson per day.
   b. Planned a classroom routine to be done cooperatively.
   c. Taught at least one social skill.
   d. Assisted colleagues in using cooperative learning.
   e. Co-taught a lesson with a colleague.
   f. Visited the classrooms of all other group members and noted something positive that was taking place.

   These criteria may be changed to make them more challenging according to the experience and competence level of group members. More advanced criteria include using four types of positive interdependence in each lesson, conducting sequences of cooperative strategies within one lesson, and reading an article or chapter on cooperative learning.

2. Group members receive points according to the extent to which they reached each criterion (0 = Did not do, 1 = Half did, 2 = Did). Thus, a group member could earn between 0 and 12 points for the week.

3. The points earned by group members are added together and divided by the number of members. The result is the group score.

4. The score is plotted on the group's quality chart.

5. The group (a) discuss the results and the long-term trend and (b) plan either how to improve their implementation efforts during the coming week or how to maintain their high level of implementation.

6. Group members celebrate how hard they are working and how successful they are.

The procedure by which the criteria are created for the implementation of cooperative learning is benchmarking (Johnson & Johnson, 1989b). *Benchmarking* is establishing operating targets based on best-known practices. Given next is a description of the benchmarking procedure. Working with a partner, plan how to

FIGURE 9.1 Data summary chart

	DAVID	ROGER	EDYTHE	DALE	TOTAL
Daily CL Lesson					
Coop. Routine					
Daily Social Skill					
Helped Colleague					
Cotaught					
Walked Throughs					
Total					

(0 Points = Did not do, 1 Point = Half did, 2 Points = Did)

apply it in your school for the use of cooperative learning, colleagial support groups, and peer mediation.

1. Identify the "best of the best" in instructional procedures in the world. Two of the criteria for identifying are (a) surveying the research to see what is proven to be effective and (b) locating the schools where it is most successfully implemented. If you can, visit the school. Take careful notes and photographs to help you identify all the subtle nuances that make the program work. The procedures and strategies identified have to fit together logically. (You have to conceptually understand what you are observing.)
2. Set a goal to achieve that level of performance in your classroom and school as a minimum.
3. Plan the methods you will use to achieve the goals. Do not mimic the past. A cooperative (not mass-production) process is required to change your school. Coop-

FIGURE 9.2 Quality chart

12										
11										
10										
9										
8										
7										
6										
5										
4										
3										
2										
1										
0	1	2	3	4	5	6	7	8	9	10

erative learning, colleagial support groups, peer mediation, and other new methods, processes, and practices must be adopted.

4. Develop performance measures to evaluate every procedure's contribution toward reaching goals. Assess the effectiveness of what you are doing and adapt the procedures and strategies to your specific situation.

5. Continue to move your benchmark higher as you reach your initial goals.

Assessing the quality and quantity of the use of cooperative learning by team members provides a colleagial teaching team with the data required for continuous improvement. The use of colleagial teaching teams, quality charts, and the benchmarking process is discussed in more depth in Johnson and Johnson (1989b) and Johnson, Johnson, and Holubec (1993).

SUMMARY

The demand for accountability has led to a reexamination of the outcomes of schooling. A wider variety of assessment options is necessary to determine whether or not schools are being successful in achieving these new and broader outcomes. The more assessment options available, the easier it is to get a more complete picture of instructional quality. The assessment options include the traditional paper-and-pencil format, performance assessments, authentic assessments, and assessing the quality of learning. These assessment options require that both teachers and students become directly involved in gathering, analyzing, and interpreting data about the instructional process in the classroom. The use of cooperative learning increases the ease with which the new assessment formats may be used.

The accountability pressures, the reformulated outcomes, and the assessment formats are used for two major purposes: to evaluate the quality of students' academic efforts and to evaluate the quality of students' teamwork. The quality of academic efforts is assessed by structuring the lesson (specifying the academic objectives, designing a task, establishing evaluation criteria), conducting the lesson (communicating task and criteria to students, monitoring and observing to measure quality of intellectual exchange, interviews and oral examinations to measure learning, and intervening to improve the learning process), and assessing and evaluating student learning (checking homework, achievement tests, performance measures such as compositions and presentations, self and peer relating, group products, and scientific projects), and group celebration.

The quality of teamwork is assessed by setting a social skills objective, operationally defining them with T-Charts, teaching the skills to students, observing the use of the social skills, having students assess the quality of their use of social skills, giving feedback to the students and groups, having students set growth goals for improving team work, and celebrating the group's hard work. Finally, the quality of the instructional program is assessed through the use of quality charts and benchmarking.

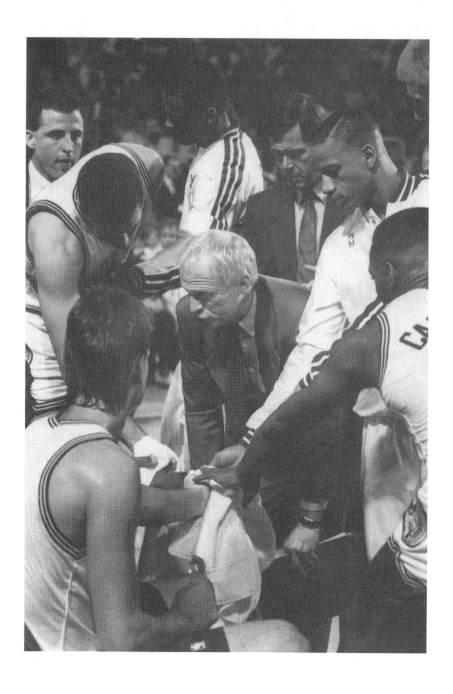

10

Cooperation and Conflict

INTRODUCTION

Frank Koch, in *Proceedings,* the magazine of the Naval Institute, reported the following:

> Two battleships assigned to the training squadron had been at sea on maneuvers in heavy weather for several days. I was serving on the lead battleship and was on watch on the bridge as night fell. The visibility was poor with patchy fog, so the captain remained on the bridge keeping an eye on all activities. Shortly after dark, the lookout on the wing of the bridge reported, "Light, bearing on the starboard bow." "Is it steady or moving astern?" the captain called out. Lookout replied, "Steady, captain," which meant we were on a dangerous collision course with that ship. The captain then called to the signalman, "Signal that ship: We are on a collision course, advise you change course 20 degrees." Back came a signal, "Advisable for you to change course 20 degrees." The captain said, "Send, I'm a captain, change course 20 degrees." "I'm a seaman, second class," came the reply, "You had better change course 20 degrees." By that time the captain was furious. He spat out, "Send, I'm a battleship. Change course 20 degrees." Back came the flashing light, "I'm a lighthouse." We changed course.

Cooperative relationships are like that. Members of a cooperative group may feel like a captain of a battleship, too powerful to be challenged as it cruises through the seas. When faced with the realities of working together to get the job done, however, they may find it is they who have to change course.

Cooperation and conflict go hand in hand. Once cooperative learning is established in the classroom and faculty colleagial support groups have been established in the school, conflicts among group members are inevitable. The more group members care about achieving the group's goals and the more they care about each other, the more likely they are to have conflicts with each other. The absence of conflict often is a sign of apathy and indifference, not harmony. If the conflicts are managed constructively, they are an essential and valuable source of creativity, fun, higher-level reasoning, and effective decision making. When they are managed destructively, they are the source of divisiveness, anger, frustration, and failure. In order to manage conflicts constructively, students and faculty need to learn the procedures for doing so and must become skillful in their use.

Students do have procedures for managing conflicts, but often the procedures are not constructive and are not shared among all classmates. One student may use physical violence, another may use verbal violence, another may withdraw,

M
A
N
A
G
I
N
G

C
O
N
F
L
I
C
T

Create a Cooperative Environment

Structure Academic Controversies.
Teach Procedure
and Skills.

Structure Peacemaking Program.
Teach Negotiation and Mediation
Procedures and Skills.
Arbitrate as a Last Resort.

FIGURE 10.1   (*Source:* © Johnson & Johnson)

and a fourth may try to persuade. The multiple procedures for managing conflicts within classrooms create some chaos in how conflicts are managed. This is especially true when students are from different cultural, ethnic, social-class, and language backgrounds. Life in schools gets easier when all students (and staff members) are taught to use the same set of procedures in managing conflicts. The three steps in doing so are to create a cooperative context, teach students how to engage in academic controversies constructively, and establish a peer-mediation program in the classroom and school (see Johnson & Johnson, 1989, 1991b, 1992a).

ESTABLISHING A COOPERATIVE CONTEXT

The best way I know how to defeat an enemy is to make him a friend.

Abraham Lincoln

In order for conflicts to be resolved constructively, a cooperative context must be established. The more participants in a conflict recognize and value their long-term mutual interests, perceive their interdependence, and are invested in each other's well-being, the easier it is to resolve conflicts constructively. The best way to establish a cooperative classroom environment is for teachers to use cooperative learning the majority of the day.

ENGAGING IN ACADEMIC CONTROVERSY

It's best that we should not all think alike. It's difference of opinion that makes horse races.

Mark Twain

In a social studies class students are considering the issue of civil disobedience. They learn that in the civil rights movement, individuals broke the law to gain equal rights for minorities. In numerous instances, such as in the civil rights and antiwar movements, individuals wrestle with the issue of breaking the law to redress a social injustice. In the past few years, however, prominent public figures from Wall Street to the White House have felt justified in breaking laws for personal or political gain. In order to study the role of civil disobedience in a democracy, students are placed in a cooperative learning group of four members. The group is then divided into two pairs. One pair is given the assignment of making the best case possible for the constructiveness of civil disobedience in a democracy. The other pair is given the assignment of making the best case possible for the destructiveness of civil disobedience in a democracy. In the resulting conflict, students draw from such sources as the Declaration of Independence by Thomas Jefferson, *Civil Disobedience* by Henry David Thoreau, *Speech at Cooper Union, New York* by Abraham Lincoln, and *Letter from Birmingham Jail* by Martin Luther King, Jr. to challenge each other's reasoning and analyses concerning when civil disobedience is, or is not, constructive.

Controversy exists when one student's ideas, information, conclusions, theories, and opinions are incompatible with those of another, and the two seek to reach an agreement. Controversies are resolved by engaging in what Aristotle called *deliberate discourse* (i.e., the discussion of the advantages and disadvantages of proposed actions) aimed at synthesizing novel solutions (i.e., creative problem solving). In an academic controversy students engage in the following steps (Johnson & Johnson, 1977, 1992a):

1. *Research and Prepare a Position:* Each pair develops the position assigned, learns the relevant information, and plans how to present the best case possible to the other pair. Near the end of the period, pairs are encouraged to compare notes with pairs from other groups who represent the same position.

2. *Present and Advocate Their Position:* Each pair makes it's presentation to the opposing pair. Each member of the pair has to participate in the presentation. Students are to be as persuasive and convincing as possible. Members of the opposing pair are encouraged to take notes, listen carefully to learn the information being presented, and clarify anything they do not understand.

3. *Refute Opposing Position and Rebut Attacks on Their Own:* Students argue forcefully and persuasively for their position, presenting as many facts as they can to support their point of view. The group members analyze and critically evaluate the information, rationale, and inductive and deductive reasoning of the opposing pair, asking them

for the facts that support their point of view. They refute the arguments of the opposing pair and rebut attacks on their position. They discuss the issue following a set of rules to help them criticize ideas without criticizing people, differentiate the two positions, and assess the degree of evidence and logic supporting each position. They keep in mind that the issues is complex and they need to know both sides to write a good report.

4. *Reverse Perspectives:* The pairs reverse perspectives and present each other's positions. In arguing for the opposing position, students are forceful and persuasive. They add any new information that the opposing pair did not think to present. They strive to see the issue from both perspectives simultaneously.

5. *Synthesize and Integrate the Best Evidence and Reasoning into a Joint Position:* The four members of the group drop all advocacy and synthesize and integrate what they know into factual and judgmental conclusions that are summarized into a joint position on which all sides can agree. They (a) finalize the report (the teacher evaluates reports on the quality of the writing, the logical presentation of evidence, and the oral presentation of the report to the class); (b) present their conclusions to the class (all four members of the group are required to participate orally in the presentation); (c) individually take the test covering both sides of the issue (if every member of the group achieves up to a certain criterion, they all receive bonus points); and (d) process how well they worked together and how they could be even more effective next time.

As Thomas Jefferson noted, "Difference of opinion leads to inquiry, and inquiry to truth." Such intellectual "disputed passages" create higher achievement (characterized by critical thinking, higher-level reasoning, and metacognitive thought) when they (a) occur within cooperative learning groups and (b) are carefully structured to ensure that students manage them constructively (Johnson & Johnson, 1977, 1979, 1992a). Students who participated in an academic controversy recalled more correct information, were better able to transfer learning to new situations, used more complex and higher-level reasoning strategies in recalling and transferring information learned, and were better able to generalize the principles they learned to a wider variety of situations. In problem-solving situations, controversy tended to increase the number and quality of ideas, the creation of original ideas, the use of a wider range of ideas and originality, the use of more varied strategies, and the number of creative, imaginative, and novel solutions. Controversy also tended to result in greater liking and social support among students, greater ability to accurately take the perspectives of others, and higher academic self-esteem. Engaging in a controversy can also be enjoyable and exciting. Samuel Johnson once stated, "I dogmatize and am contradicted, and in this conflict of opinions and sentiments I find delight."

John Milton, in *Doctrine and Discipline,* stated: "Where there is much desire to learn, there of necessity will be much arguing, much writing, many opinions; for opinion in good men is but knowledge in the making." The process through which academic controversies result in the above outcomes is posited to be as follows

(Johnson & Johnson, 1979, 1992a): First, when students are presented with an issue or problem, they have an initial conclusion based on categorizing and organizing their current information and experiences and their specific perspective. Second, when asked to present their conclusion and its rationale to others, they engage in cognitive rehearsal, conceptually reorganize the rationale for their position as they present it, deepen their understanding of their position, and find themselves using higher-level reasoning strategies. Third, classmates present opposing positions (based on their information, experiences, and perspectives). This intellectual "disputed passage" causes students to become uncertain as to the correctness of their views. A state of conceptual conflict or disequilibrium is aroused. Fourth, the more uncertain students become, the more motivated they are to search actively for more information, new experiences, a more adequate perspective. Berlyne calls this active search epistemic curiosity. Like Macbeth (who said, "Stay, you imperfect speakers, tell me more"), students want more information. In their search, divergent attention and thought are stimulated and a higher-level reasoning process is sought in hopes of resolving their uncertainty. Fifth, students resolve their uncertainty by accommodating the perspective and reasoning of others and developing a new, reconceptualized, and reorganized conclusion. As Andre Gide said, "One completely overcomes only what one assimilates." Novel solutions and decisions are detected that are, on balance, qualitatively better. Finally, the process can then be repeated to promote even greater learning and understanding. There are hundreds of studies that validate this posited process (Johnson & Johnson, 1989a). Perhaps it is this process that Edmund Burke had in mind when he said, "He that wrestles with us strengthens our nerves, and sharpens our skill. Our antagonist is our helper."

TEACHING STUDENTS TO BE PEACEMAKERS

In cooperative teams, whether they involve students or faculty, members differ in terms of their individual wants, needs, values, and goals. Two students may both want to use a book or a computer. Two individuals may both want to be first in line. One teacher may wish to use phonics in a reading program; another teacher may wish to use a whole language approach. When such conflicts of interests (conflicts between two individuals' wants, needs, values, and goals) occur, settlements must be negotiated. To teach students the procedures and skills they need to manage conflicts of interests constructively, a three-step peacemaking program is needed.

The first step in the peacemaker program is to teach all students to negotiate constructive resolutions to their conflicts. Students need to both understand the negotiation procedure and have the skills required to use it. The negotiation procedure and skills need to be overlearned so that they are available for use when emotions run high and feelings such as fear and anger are intense.

To negotiate to solve the problem, students need to define their conflict, exchange positions and proposals, view the situation from both perspectives, invent options for mutual gain, and reach a wise agreement. Students are taught the following procedure (Johnson & Johnson, 1991b, 1991c):

1. State what you want. ("I want to use the book now.")
2. State how you feel. ("I'm frustrated.")
3. State the reasons for your wants and feelings. ("You have been using the book for the past hour. If I don't get to use the book soon, my report will not be done on time. It's frustrating to have to wait so long.")
4. Summarize your understanding of what the other person wants, how the other person feels, and the reasons underlying both.
5. Invent three optional plans to resolve the conflict.
6. Choose one and shake hands.

The second step is to teach all students how to mediate constructive resolutions of their classmates' conflicts. When students cannot successfully negotiate a constructive resolution to their conflicts, peer mediators should be available to help them do so (Johnson & Johnson, 1991b). *Mediation* is the utilization of the services of another person to help settle a dispute. The purpose of mediation is to help classmates negotiate a constructive resolution to their conflicts. All students should be taught how to mediate constructive resolutions of their classmates' conflicts by introducing the mediation process, presenting the guidelines and the rules for mediation, assisting the participants through the negotiation sequence, and finalizing the agreement. The mediation procedure the students are taught to use is as follows (Johnson & Johnson, 1987, 1991b, 1991c).

First, the mediator introduces him- or herself and the process of mediation. The mediator asks the students if they want to solve the problem and does not proceed until both answer "yes." The mediator explains the guidelines by stating: (a) "Mediation is voluntary. My role is to help you find a solution to your conflict that is acceptable to both of you"; (b) "I am neutral. I will not take sides or attempt to decide who is right or wrong. I will help you decide how to solve the conflict"; and (c) "Each person will have the chance to state his or her view of the conflict without interruption." The mediator explains the rules—*"The rules— you must agree to are (a) agree to solve the problem, (b) no name calling, (c) do not interrupt, (d) be as honest as you can, (e) if you agree to a solution, you must abide by it (You must do what you have agreed to do), and (f) anything said in mediation is confidential (I, the mediator, will not tell anyone what is said)."* Second, the mediator takes the two participants through the steps of negotiation—what each person wants, how both feel, their reasons are explained, they reverse perspectives, they generate three optional agreements, and they finally reach an agreement. Third, the mediator becomes the keeper of the agreement and checks the next day to see if the agreement is working. If it is not, the mediation process is repeated.

The third step is for the teacher to implement the peacemaker program. Students received thirty minutes of training per day for thirty days. The curriculum is *Teaching Students to Be Peacemakers* (Johnson & Johnson, 1991b, 1991d). Students role-play and practice the procedures and skills involved in negotiating and mediating until they can negotiate and mediate at a routine-use level. Once the initial training is complete, the program is implemented. Each day the teacher selects two class members to serve as official mediators. They are responsible for helping classmates resolve any conflicts for which they cannot negotiate a wise agreement. The mediators wear official T-shirts, patrol the playground and lunchroom, and are available to mediate any conflicts that occur in the classroom or school. The role of class mediator is rotated throughout the class so that each student serves as class mediator an equal amount of time. Refresher lessons are taught once or twice a week to refine students' negotiation and mediation skills.

THE LAST RESORT

If the students cannot negotiate a constructive resolution to their conflict, if the peer mediators cannot promote an agreement, and if the teacher cannot mediate a resolution to the conflict, then the teacher arbitrates. *Arbitration* is the submission of a dispute to a disinterested third party (such as a teacher or principal) who makes a final and binding judgment as to how the conflict will be resolved. Negotiation and mediation are self-empowering—they enable students to make decisions about issues and conflicts that affect their own lives rather than having a decision imposed on them by teachers and administrators. This does not mean, however, that students will always be able to resolve their conflicts constructively. When negotiation and mediation fail, the arbitrator's judgment is final and binding.

PEACEMAKING AND DISCIPLINE PROBLEMS

Discipline problems plague classrooms and schools. Students bicker, threaten, tease, and harass each other. Conflicts involving racial and cultural differences are increasing. Truancy is epidemic. Violence is escalating. Generally, conflicts among students and between students and staff occur with frequency and consume considerable teacher and administrator time.

Classroom and school discipline programs may be classified on a dimension from being based on external rewards and punishments that control and manage student behavior to being based on teaching students the competencies and skills required to resolve their interpersonal conflicts constructively, cope with stress and adversity, and behave in appropriate and constructive ways. At one end of the continuum, the focus is on the faculty and staff controlling and managing student behavior. At the other end of the continuum, the focus is on students regulating their own and their peers actions.

External Rewards or Punishments 1—2—3—4—5—6—7 Competencies for Self-Regulation

Most discipline programs are clustered at the adult administering external rewards and punishment end of the continuum. Thus, it is up to the staff to monitor student behavior, determine whether it is within the bounds of acceptability, and force students to terminate inappropriate actions. When the infractions are minor, the staff often arbitrate ("The pencil belongs to Mary; Jane be quiet and

sit down.") or cajole students to end hostilities ("Let's forgive and forget. Shake hands and be friends."). If that does not work, students may be sent to the principal's office for a stern but cursory lecture about the value of getting along, a threat that if the conflict continues more drastic action will ensue, and a final admonition to "Go and fight no more." If that does not work, time-out rooms may be used. Eventually, some students are expelled from school. Such programs teach students that adults or authority figures are needed to resolve conflicts. The programs cost a great deal in instructional and administrative time and work only as long as students are under surveillance. This approach does not empower students. Adults may become more skillful in how to control students, but students do not learn the procedures, skills, and attitudes required to resolve conflicts constructively in their personal lives at home, in school, at work, and in the community.

At the other end of the continuum are programs aimed at teaching students self-responsibility and self-regulation. *Self-regulation* is the ability to act in socially approved ways in the absence of external monitors. It is the ability to initiate and cease activities according to situational demands. Self-regulation is a central and significant hallmark of cognitive and social development. To regulate their behavior, students must monitor their own behavior, assess situations and take other people's perspectives to make judgments as to which behaviors are appropriate, and master the procedures and skills required to engage in the desired behavior. In interaction with other people, students have to monitor, modify, refine, and change how they behave in order to act appropriately and competently.

If students are to learn how to regulate their behavior, they must have opportunities to (a) make decisions regarding how to behave and (b) follow through on the decisions made. Allowing students to be joint architects in matters affecting them promotes feelings of control and autonomy. Students who know how to manage their conflicts constructively and regulate their own behavior have a developmental advantage over those who do not. Ideally, students will be given the responsibility of regulating their own and their classmates' behavior so that teachers can concentrate on instruction rather than control. The peer-mediation program teaches all students the joint problem-solving and decision-making competencies and skills they need to regulate their own and their classmates' behavior.

SUMMARY

With cooperation comes conflict. How conflict is managed largely determines how successful cooperative efforts tend to be. In order to ensure that conflicts are managed constructively, a cooperative classroom and school must be established, students must be directly taught how to manage intellectual conflicts inherent in learning groups, and students must be directly taught to negotiate constructive resolutions of their conflicts and to help their classmates do likewise through the peer-mediation process. By ensuring that students manage their conflicts constructively, their learning is enhanced, the quality of life within the school is increased, and students learn the procedures and skills they need to regulate their own behavior and deal with adversity in their lives.

11

The Cooperative School

INTRODUCTION

Nothing new that is really interesting comes without collaboration.

James Watson, Nobel Prize winner
(co-discoverer of the double helix)

Ford Motor Company knew it had to do something different, dramatically different, to gain back market share from imports. A new mid-sized car was conceived to be Ford's best chance to do so. For years Ford had operated within a mass-manufacturing structure whose motto was "any color as long as it is black." Designers etched out sketches and gave them to Manufacturing with the order, "Build it!" Sales inherited the car and had to figure out how to sell it. That was the way Ford had always built cars. But not this time. An interdisciplinary team was created made up of designers, engineers, manufacturing and financial executives, and sales and marketing people. Together they created the Taurus, a car whose sales neared 1 million units in its first four production years and which has consistently won praise from both auto experts and consumers.

Ford is not the only company to switch to cooperative teams. Whereas there is an American myth of progress being spurred on by Lone Rangers, in today's corporations that image is about as current as bustles and spats. From Motorola to AT&T Credit Corporation, self-managing, multidisciplinary teams are in charge of keeping the company profitable. And they are succeeding. Teams get things done.

Team development is at the core of the changes necessary to alter the way faculty and students think and work. It is the best way of educating students the right way the first time. That does not mean that reorganizing students and faculty into teams will be easy. Changing the school culture while getting all faculty working together to educate students right the first time may be the biggest challenge facing any school.

There are two steps in moving from a competitive–individualistic mass-manufacturing organizational structure to a high-performance cooperative-team structure. The first step is using cooperative learning procedures the majority of the time. The second step is organizing faculty into colleagial support groups that focus on the continuous improvement of the use of cooperative learning and instruction in general. These steps are taken not because they are popular, but because it is rational to do so. Currently available data indicates that a cooperative team-based organizational structure is more desirable for many reasons (see Chapter 2) than is a competitive–individualistic mass-manufacturing organizational structure.

The team-based organizational structure is known as the *cooperative school.* The change is reflected in the use of cooperative learning in the classroom, faculty colleagial teaching teams in the school, a school-based decision-making structure, and faculty meetings that predominantly use cooperative procedures. The heart of the cooperative school is the colleagial teaching team. The focus of the colleagial teaching team is the continuous improvement of teacher expertise in using cooperative learning. That expertise is enhanced by using quality charts and the benchmarking procedure. In order for the cooperative school to be implemented and successful, leadership must be provided that helps teachers do a better job each day.

THE COOPERATIVE SCHOOL

For nearly a century, schools have functioned as "mass production" organizations that divided work into small component parts performed by individuals who worked separately from and, in many cases, in competition with peers. Teachers have worked alone, in their own room, with their own set of students, and with their own set of curriculum materials. Both teachers and students have been considered to be interchangeable parts in the organizational machine. Students can be assigned to any teacher because teachers are all equivalent and, conversely, teachers can be given any student to teach because all students are considered to be the same.

W. Edwards Deming and others have suggested that more than 85 percent of all the things that go wrong in any organization are directly attributable to the organization's structure, not the nature of the individuals involved. Retraining teachers to use cooperative learning while organizing teachers to mass-produce educated students is self-defeating. Changing methods of teaching is much easier when the changes are congruent with (not in opposition to) the organizational structure of the school. In order for schools to focus on the quality of instruction, they need to change from a mass production, competitive–individualistic organizational structure to a high-performance, cooperative team-based organizational structure (see Johnson & Johnson, 1989b). This new organizational structure is generally known as the cooperative school.

In a cooperative school, students work primarily in cooperative learning groups, teachers and building staff work in cooperative teams, and district administrators work in cooperative teams (Johnson & Johnson, 1989b) (see Figure 11.1). The organizational structure of the classroom, school, and district are then congruent. Each level of cooperative teams supports and enhances the other levels. Structuring cooperative teams is the heart of improving schools and must precede

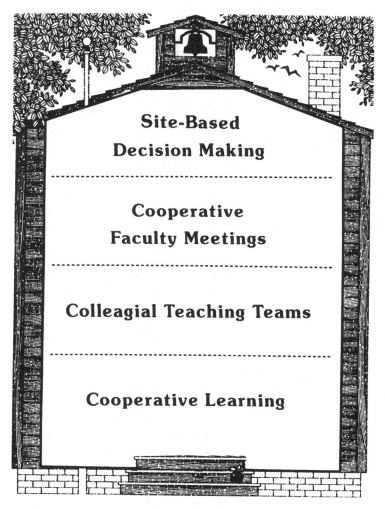

Site-Based

Decision Making

Cooperative

Faculty Meetings

Colleagial Teaching Teams

Cooperative Learning

FIGURE 11.1 The cooperative school

all other improvement initiatives. Effective teamwork is the very center of improving the quality of instruction and education. It forms the hub around which all other elements of school improvement revolves. The primary units of performance in schools need to be teams. Teams are, beyond all doubt, the most direct sources of continuous improvement of instruction and education.

A cooperative school structure begins in the classroom with the use of cooperative learning the majority of the time (Johnson & Johnson, 1989b). Cooperative learning groups are the primary work team, and work teams are the heart of the team-based organizational structure. Quality learning does not take place in isolation; it results from a team effort to challenge each other's reasoning and maximize each other's learning. Cooperative learning is used to increase student achievement, create more positive relationships among students, and generally improve students' psychological well-being. Cooperative learning is also the prerequisite and foundation for most other instructional innovations, including thematic curriculum, whole language, critical thinking, active reading, process writing, materials-based (problem-solving) mathematics, and learning communities. A secondary effect of using cooperative learning is that it affects teachers' attitudes and competencies toward working collaboratively with colleagues. What is promoted in instructional situations tends to dominate relationships among staff members.

The second level in creating a cooperative school is to form colleagial teaching teams, task forces, and ad hoc decision-making groups within the school (Johnson & Johnson, 1989b). The use of cooperation to structure faculty and staff work involves (a) colleagial teaching teams, (b) school-based decision making, and (c) faculty meetings.

Just as the heart of the classroom is cooperative learning, the heart of the school is the colleagial teaching team. *Colleagial teaching teams* are small cooperative groups (from two to five faculty members) whose purpose is to increase teachers' instructional expertise and success (Johnson & Johnson, 1989b). The focus is on generally improving instruction and specifically increasing members' expertise in using cooperative learning. These teams are first and foremost safe places where (a) members like to be, (b) there is support, caring, concern, laughter, camaraderie, and celebration, and (c) the primary goal of continually improving each other's competence in using cooperative learning is never obscured.

School-based decision-making is created through the use of two types of cooperative teams (Johnson & Johnson, 1989b). First, a task force considers a school problem and proposes a solution to the faculty as a whole. Second, the faculty is divided into ad hoc decision-making groups and considers whether to accept or modify the proposal. Third, the decisions made by the ad hoc groups are summarized, and the entire faculty then decides on the action to be taken to solve the problem. More specifically, task forces plan and implement solutions to schoolwide issues and problems such as adopting a curriculum or behavior in the lunchroom. Task forces diagnose a problem, gather data about the causes and extent of the problem, consider a variety of alternative solutions, make conclusions, and present a recommendation to the faculty as a whole. Ad hoc decision-making groups are used during faculty meetings to involve all staff members in important school decisions. These groups are part of a small-group/large-group procedure in which staff members listen to a recommendation, are assigned to small groups, meet to consider the recommendation, report to the entire faculty their decision, and then participate in a whole-faculty decision as to what the course of action should be. The use of these three types of faculty cooperative teams tends to increase teacher productivity, morale, and professional self-esteem.

Faculty meetings represent a microcosm of what administrators think the school should be. If administrators use a competitive–individualistic format of lecture, whole-class discussion, and individual worksheets in faculty meetings, they have made a powerful statement about the way they want their faculty to teach. The clearest modeling of cooperative procedures in the school may be in faculty meetings and other meetings structured by the school administration. Formal and informal cooperative groups, cooperative base groups, and repetitive structures can be used within faculty meetings just as they can be used within the classroom. In this way, faculty meetings become staff development and training as well as business meetings.

The third level in creating a cooperative school is to implement administrative cooperative teams within the district (Johnson & Johnson, 1989b). Administrators organized into teams (to increase their administrative expertise and success), task forces, and ad hoc triads are used as part of the shared decision-making process. In administrative meetings, cooperative procedures dominate to model what the school district should be like. If administrators compete to see who is the best administrator in the district, they are unlikely to be able to promote cooperation among staff members of each school. The more the district and school personnel work in cooperative teams, the easier it will be for teachers to use cooperative learning, and vice versa.

Contributing to team efforts is becoming paramount at every rung of the ladder in modern organizations. Schools are no exception. Students and faculty have to want to belong to teams, they have to contribute their share of the work,

and they must take positions and know how to advocate their views in ways that spark creative problem solving. Lone wolves who do not pull with their peers will increasingly find themselves the odd person out.

QUALITY EDUCATION IN THE COOPERATIVE SCHOOL

In the mass-production school, teachers are primarily organized on a horizontal basis (grade-level or departmental teams). Students are sent from workstation to workstation to be partially educated (e.g., from math class to science class to social studies class, or from first grade to second grade to third grade). Each teacher is responsible for a small part of the student's education. Barriers exist to separate teachers from each other so that each teacher can focus his or her full attention on the small piece of the overall program he or she is responsible for.

In the cooperative school all important work is done by teams. Teams are not an option; they are a given. The primary faculty team focuses on instruction and teaching. Teachers can be formed into *vertical (cross-disciplinary) teams* so that a number of teachers are responsible for the same students for a number of years. An elementary team may be made up of two primary and two secondary teachers who are given responsibility for educating about 120 students for six years. A secondary team may be made up of an English, math, science, social studies, and foreign language teacher. The team is given responsibility for educating 120 students for three years (for example, from seventh through ninth grades). An integrated curriculum is constructed. Thematic teaching is emphasized. Vertical teams break down the barriers that separate teachers, grade levels, and academic departments and ensure that all teachers see the overall process toward which their efforts are contributing. Each team is genuinely accountable since it has the students for a full six (or three) years. No one can blame a student's deficiencies in reading or math on last year's teacher or just mark time with a problem student until he or she is passed on to next year's teacher. Teachers have to confront difficulties and live with the consequences of their decisions. On the other hand, because they are part of a team, teachers need never face these challenges alone.

Once teachers are organized into vertical teaching teams, a setting has been created to focus on the quality of education in the school. Quality education is loosely based on W. Edwards Deming's fourteen points (Walton, 1986). From Deming's recommendations, a set of guidelines can be established for achieving quality education in the cooperative school. First, a constancy of purpose must be established within the school through clarifying and highlighting the overall positive goal interdependence. Faculty and staff must believe that they "sink or swim together." They must perceive that they are responsible not only for improving their own expertise, but for improving the expertise of every other employee in the school. A set of overall goals must be agreed upon by the faculty and staff that highlights their interdependence and the need for a joint effort. The goals reflect a new definition of the school that focuses attention, not on standardized test scores, but rather on the continuous improvement of the quality of education and instruction.

Second, the school must adopt the philosophy that faculty teams must successfully educate and socialize every student placed in their care. No failures to educate and graduate are accepted. Instead of a tolerance of mistakes and failures, every student must be educated and socialized. When teachers work with the same students for a number of years, faculty can provide the support and problem solving that results in every student learning, graduating, and going on to postsecondary education.

Third, instead of relying on mass standardized testing to achieve quality, educators must focus on improving the instructional process. Inspection is unnecessary if every faculty member is committed to quality instruction. Fourth, if faculty are going to take risks to increase their competence, fear must be driven out of the school. Anything that causes humiliation, self-defense, or fear in a school is a force for destruction. The major source of fear within schools is competition and the extrinsic motivation it promotes. Grading on a curve, ranking students or teachers from highest to lowest, and giving merit pay on a normative basis all create anxiety, evaluation apprehension, and fear. This takes more than simply saying, "Do not compete." Students and educators generally tend to impose competition on a situation unless cooperation is clearly structured. The social support and positive relationships in cooperative teams reduce fear and provide the security teachers and students need to change and grow.

Fifth, faculty must develop strong personal relationships with students. Faculty must stay "close to the customer" for at least two reasons—to attain the information needed to provide quality education and to motivate students to do their best. Schools have a number of clients, including students, parents, the community, society, and the employment and postsecondary educational institutions to which the school's graduates go. The most direct client of schools, however, is students. Things get done through relationships. To influence students to commit energy to learning, faculty have to build a caring relationship with students in which students are convinced that the faculty are committed to the students' well-being and success. Long-term, hard, persistent efforts to succeed come from the heart, not the head, and relationships are the fastest way to the heart (Johnson & Johnson, 1989b).

Sixth, faculty should persistently strive to reduce waste in the instructional system and school. Reducing waste is an essential aspect of increasing quality within an organization. Integrating the curriculum and thematic teaching, for example, may reduce the redundancy among subject areas. Lengthening the school year may reduce the amount of time spent in review each fall.

Seventh, careful attention must be paid to structuring the five basic elements of cooperation at each level of the cooperative school. The five basic elements must be explicitly structured in each lesson, in each learning group, in each classroom, in each family of classes, and in the school as a whole. Cooperation does not magically happen with proximity. Cooperative efforts reach their potential only when positive interdependence, face-to-face promotive interaction, individual ac-

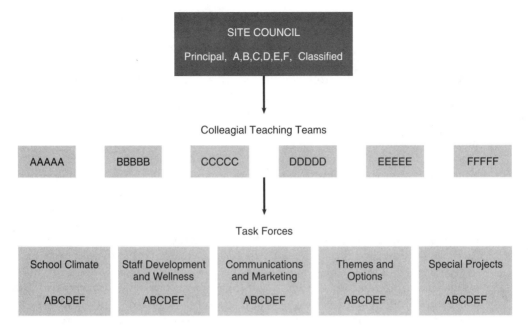

FIGURE 11.2 The cooperative school II

countability, the appropriate use of social skills, and group processing are carefully structured within the situation.

The overall purpose of a school is to provide students with high-quality learning experiences that maximize their learning and socialization into society. Good instruction is the school's bottom line. In order to provide good instruction, schools require the use of colleagial teams focused on continuous improvement of expertise in using cooperative learning. In the next three sections of this chapter these topics (colleagial teams, continuous improvement, and expertise) will be discussed.

COLLEAGIAL TEACHING TEAMS

In mass-production schools, teachers are isolated from each other and may feel alienated, overloaded, harried, and overwhelmed. The isolation and alienation are reduced when teachers form colleagial teaching teams aimed at increasing the quality of instruction in the school. Teachers generally teach better when they work in colleagial teaching teams to jointly support each other's efforts to increase their instructional expertise. The purposes of colleagial teaching teams include giving teachers ownership of the professional agenda, breaking down the barriers to colleagial interaction, and reducing program fragmentation. There are three key activities of a colleagial teaching team (Johnson & Johnson, 1989b).

1. Frequent professional discussions of cooperative learning in which a common vocabulary is developed, information is shared, successes are celebrated, and problems connected with implementation are solved. Colleagial interaction is essential for building collaborative cultures in schools (Hargreaves, 1991; Little, 1990). Colleagial social support is critical for the ongoing professional development of teachers (Nias, 1984). Expertise in using cooperative learning begins with conceptual understanding of (a) the nature of cooperative learning, (b) how to implement cooperative learning, and (c) what results can be expected from using cooperative learning. Teachers must also think critically about the strategy and adapt it to their specific students and subject areas. In team discussions teachers consolidate and strengthen their knowledge about cooperative learning and provide each other with relevant feedback about the degree to which mastery and understanding have been achieved. It is within colleagial teams that faculty exchange understandings of what cooperative learning is and how it may be used within their classes.

2. Co-planning, co-designing, co-preparing, and co-evaluating cooperative learning lessons and instructional units. Once cooperative learning is understood conceptually, it must be implemented. Members of professional support groups should frequently plan, design, prepare, and evaluate lesson plans together. Doing so shares the work of developing the materials and machinery for implementing cooperative learning. Integrated curriculum and thematic teaching depend on co-planning and co-designing. The process of planning a lesson together, each conducting it, and then processing it afterwards fuels continuous improvement of teaching expertise. This cycle of *co-planning, parallel teaching, and co-processing* may be followed by one of *co-planning, co-teaching, and co-processing* .

3. Co-teaching cooperative lessons and jointly processing those observations. If faculty are to progress through the initial awkward and mechanical stages to a routine-use, automatic level of mastery, they must (a) receive continual feedback as to the accuracy of their implementation and (b) be encouraged to persevere in their implementation attempts long enough to integrate cooperative learning into their ongoing instructional practice. The more colleagues are involved in your teaching, the more valuable the help and assistance they can provide. Frequently co-teaching cooperative lessons and then providing each other with useful feedback provides members with shared experiences to discuss and refer to.

Colleagial teams ideally meet daily. At a minimum, teams should meet weekly. During a typical meeting team members review how they have used cooperative learning since the previous meeting, share a success in doing so, complete a quality chart on their implementation of cooperative learning, set three to five goals to accomplish before the next meeting, establish how each will help the others achieve their goals, learn something new about cooperative learning, and celebrate how hard all members are working (Johnson & Johnson, 1989b). Following this agenda ensures that (a) teachers have the learning environment that they are creating for students (i.e., they meet with supportive peers who encourage them to learn and grow), (b) teachers have a procedure for continuously improving their use of cooperative learning, (c) continuous training of teachers in how to use cooperative learning is provided, (d) pride of workmanship can be encouraged and self-improvement are recognized and celebrated (any time a faculty member makes an effort to improve and increase his or her competence, the effort can be recognized and celebrated by teammates), and (e) poor workmanship and negativism are discouraged.

CONTINUOUS IMPROVEMENT OF COOPERATIVE LEARNING EXPERTISE

To have joy one must share it. Happiness was born a twin.

Indian proverb

For schools to be successful, everyone in the school must be dedicated to continuous improvement. In Japan, this mutual dedication is called *kaizen,* a society-wide covenant of mutual help in the process of getting better and better, day by day. In order for continuous improvement to occur, a school must commit the resources required for it to occur. These resources include eliminating all competition among teachers (and among students), structuring cooperation at all levels of the school, focusing faculty's attention on daily improvement of cooperative learning and other aspects of instruction, and providing the time for faculty colleagial teaching teams to meet.

Colleagial teaching groups are aimed at increasing faculty expertise in using cooperative learning. The professional discussions, co-planning, and co-teaching are aimed at progressive refinement of expertise in cooperative learning. Faculty progressively refine their competence in using cooperative learning by (Johnson & Johnson, 1989b):

1. **Understanding conceptually what cooperative learning is and how it may be implemented in their classrooms.** Teachers must understand the five basic elements of effective cooperation and the teacher's role in using formal and informal cooperative learning and cooperative base groups. Approaches to using cooperative learning may be ordered on a continuum from *conceptual–adaptive approaches* (using general conceptual models to plan and tailor cooperative learning specifically for a teacher's circumstances, students, and needs) to *direct–prescriptive approaches* (prepackaged lessons, curricula, strategies, and activities that are used in a lock-step prescribed manner). Conceptual approaches are aimed at training teachers to be engineers in their use of cooperative learning; direct approaches are aimed at training teachers to be technicians. Engineers conceptually understand cooperative learning and, therefore, can (a) adapt it to their specific teaching circumstances, students, and curriculums and (b) repair it when it does not work. Technicians are trained to teach packaged lessons, curricula, and strategies in a lock-step (step 1, step 2, step 3) prescribed manner, without really understanding what cooperation is or what makes it work. The conceptual approach is used in all technological arts and crafts. An engineer designing a bridge,

for example, applies validated theory to the unique problems imposed by the need for a bridge of a certain length, to carry specific loads, from a bank of one unique geological character to a bank of another unique geological character, in an area with specific winds, temperatures, and susceptibility to earthquakes. Our conceptual approach to cooperative learning requires teachers to engage in the same process by (a) learning a conceptualization of essential components of cooperative learning and the teacher's role in using formal and informal cooperative learning and cooperative base groups and (b) applying that conceptual model to their unique teaching situation, circumstances, students, and instructional needs. Each teacher has to adapt and refine cooperative learning to fit an idiosyncratic situation. Each class may require a different adaptation in order to maximize the effectiveness of cooperative learning. Understanding the essential elements allows teachers to (a) think metacognitively about cooperative learning, (b) create any number of lessons, strategies, and activities, and (c) achieve the goals of developing enough expertise to take any lesson in any subject area and structure it cooperatively, to practice and practice the use of cooperative learning until they are at a routine/integrated level of use and to implement cooperative learning at least 60 percent of the time in their classrooms. Teachers need to be able to describe precisely what they are doing and why they are doing it in order to communicate to others the nature of cooperative learning, teach colleagues how to implement cooperative learning, and apply the principles of cooperation to other settings, such as colleagial relationships and faculty meetings.

2. Trying cooperative learning out in their classrooms with their students. Faculty must be willing to take risks by experimenting with new instructional and managing strategies and procedures. Faculty risk short-term failure to gain long-term success in increasing their expertise by experimenting with new strategies and procedures. It is assumed that one's efforts will fail to match an ideal of what one wishes to accomplish for a considerable length of time until the new strategy is overlearned to a routine-use, automated level.

3. Assessing how well cooperative learning lessons went and obtaining feedback on one's teaching from others. Although the lesson may have not gone well, from the progressive refinement point of view failure never occurs. There are simply approximations of what one wants and with refining and fine-tuning of procedures and more practice the approximations to get successively closer and closer to the ideal.

4. Reflecting on what one did and how it may be improved. The discrepancy between the real and the ideal is considered and plans are made about altering one's behavior in order to get a better match in the future. Quality charts help this reflection process.

5. Trying out cooperative learning again in a modified and improved way. Perseverance in using cooperative learning again and again is required until the teacher can teach a cooperative lesson routinely and without conscious planning or thought. As Aristotle said, "For things we have to learn before we can do them, we learn by doing them." With every lesson taught (until the teacher retires), teachers should seek feedback, reflect on how to improve their implementation of cooperation, and modify the next lesson. It is through this progressive refinement process that a teacher's expertise in using cooperative learning is fine-tuned.

Expertise is reflected in a person's proficiency, adroitness, competence, and skill in structuring cooperative efforts. Cooperation takes more expertise than do competitive or individualistic efforts, because it involves dealing with other people as well as dealing with the demands of the task (i.e., simultaneously engaging in taskwork and teamwork). Expertise is usually gained in an incremental step-by-step manner, using the progressive refinement process over a period of years in a team.

Gaining expertise in using cooperative learning in the classroom and cooperative teams in the school and district does not happen overnight—it takes at least one lifetime. With only a moderately difficult teaching strategy, for example, teachers may require from twenty to thirty hours of instruction in its theory, fifteen to twenty demonstrations using it with different students and subjects, and an additional ten to fifteen coaching sessions to attain higher-level skills. For a more difficult teaching strategy such as cooperative learning, several years of training and support may be needed to ensure that teachers master it. We prefer three years to train a teacher fully in the fundamentals of cooperative learning, the advanced use of cooperative learning, the use of academic controversies to encourage students within cooperative groups to challenge each other intellectually, and the use of a peer-mediation system to ensure that students can negotiate constructive solutions to their conflicts with classmates and help their groupmates do likewise. There is a similar sequence for administrators with the added training on leading the cooperative school. Interested "cooperative learning superstars" are then trained to provide the three-year training program within their district.

During the training sessions teachers learn about cooperative learning and the essential elements that make it work. Teachers then have to transfer this knowledge to their own classrooms and maintain their use of cooperative learning for years to come. The success of training depends on transfer (teachers trying out cooperative learning in their classrooms) and maintenance (long-term use of cooperative learning). Transfer and maintenance, therefore, depend largely on teachers themselves being organized into teaching teams that focus on helping each member progressively improve his or her competence in using cooperative learning.

To build a long-term "on-the-job" training program on cooperative learning, teachers need to be organized into teams for two reasons. The first is that supportive colleagues are necessary for a teacher to progressively refine his or her expertise in using cooperative learning. The second reason is that there is no better way to learn how to use cooperative learning than to teach a colleague how to use cooperative learning. Harvey Firestone (of Firestone Tires) stated, "It is only when we develop others that we permanently succeed." To gain expertise in using cooperative learning, teachers have to help their colleagues gain expertise.

QUALITY OF IMPLEMENTATION

In order for teachers' expertise in implementing cooperative learning to improve continuously, teachers must assess the quality of their efforts. The procedure for such assessment is to establish a set of criteria and rate the extent to which each member of the colleagial support group is meeting the criteria. The results are then charted each week to help the group (a) determine the frequency and fidelity with which each group member is implementing cooperative learning and (b) set goals for implementation efforts for the coming week. An example of a quality chart is as follows. First, in the faculty teaching team meeting each member shows his or her implementation log and reports the degree to which he or she (a) taught at least one cooperative learning lesson per day, (b) planned a classroom routine to be done cooperatively, (c) taught at least one social skill, (d) assisted a colleague in using cooperative learning, (e) co-taught a lesson with a colleague, and (f) visited the classrooms of all other group members and noted something positive that was taking place. These criteria may be changed to make them more challenging according to the experience and competence level of group members. More advanced criteria include using four types of positive interdependence in each lesson, conducting sequences of cooperative strategies within one lesson, and reading an article or chapter on cooperative learning.

Second, team members receive points according to the extent to which they reached each criterion (0 = Did not do, 1 = Half did, 2 = Did). Thus, a group member could earn between 0 and 12 points for the week. Third, the points earned by team members are added together and divided by the number of members. The result is the team score. The score is plotted on the group's quality chart. Fourth, the team discusses the results and the long-term trend and plans either how to improve their implementation efforts during the coming week or how to maintain their high level of implementation.

BENCHMARKING

Benchmarking is establishing operating targets based on best-known practices. First, teachers identify the "best of the best" in instructional procedures in the world. Two of the criteria for identifying are (a) surveying the research to see what is proven to be effective and (b) locating the schools where it is most successfully implemented. If possible, teachers visit the schools identified. Second, teachers set a goal to achieve that level of performance in their classes as a minimum. Third, the teachers plan the methods they will use to achieve the goals without mimicking the past. Fourth, performance measures are developed to evaluate every procedure's contribution toward reaching goals. Finally, the benchmark is moved higher as the initial goals are reached.

PROVIDING LEADERSHIP

Knowing is not enough; we must apply. Willing is not enough; we must do.

Goethe

For the cooperative school to flourish, the school has to have leadership. In general, leadership is provided by five sets of actions (Johnson & Johnson, 1989b).

1. *Challenging the Status Quo.* The status quo is the competitive–individualistic mass-production structure that dominates schools and classrooms. In the classroom it is represented by lecturing, whole-class discussion, individual worksheets, and a test on Friday. In the school it is one teacher to one classroom with one set of students, as well as separating teachers and students into grade levels and academic departments. Leaders challenge the efficacy of the status quo.

2. *Inspiring a Mutual Vision of What the School Could Be.* Leaders enthusiastically and frequently communicate the dreams of establishing the cooperative school. The leader is the keeper of the dream who inspires commitment to joint goals of creating a team-based, cooperative school.

3. *Empowering Through Cooperative Teams.* This is the most important of all leadership activities. When faculty or students feel helpless and discouraged, providing them with a team creates hope and opportunity. It is social support from and accountability to valued peers that motivates committed efforts to achieve and succeed. Students are empowered by cooperative learning groups. Faculty members are empowered through support groups and involvement in site-based decision making.

4. *Leading by Example.* Leaders model the use of cooperative strategies and procedures and take risks to increase their professional competence. Actions must be congruent with words. What is advocated must be demonstrated publicly.

5. *Encouraging the Heart to Persist.* Long-term, committed efforts to continuously improve one's competencies come from the heart, not the head. It takes courage and hope to continue to strive for increased knowledge and expertise. It is the social support and concrete assistance from teammates that provide the strength to persist and excel.

To implement the cooperative school, leadership that helps faculty do a better job must be provided (Johnson & Johnson, 1989b). Leaders do not spend their time in an office talking on the phone, writing memos, and "putting out fires." Leaders spend their time "where the action is." (In Japan this is called *genba*.)

In schools, the action is in classrooms. Thus, leaders have to challenge the status quo of the mass-production organization, inspire a mutual vision of the cooperative school, empower faculty through organizing them in teams, lead by example by using cooperative procedures continually, and encourage faculty's heart to persist by being in the classroom recognizing and celebrating their efforts to teach a perfect lesson every time.

SUMMARY

Schools are not buildings, curricula, and machines. Schools are relationships and interaction among people. How the interpersonal interaction is structured determines how effective schools are. When teachers are seen as interchangeable parts in a machine created to mass-produce educated students, they tend to become isolated and alienated from each other and from their work. The benefits of cooperative are as great for faculty as they are for students. A cooperative, team-based, high-performance school begins with the use of cooperative learning the majority of the time. The next level of the cooperative school is colleagial teaching teams in which teachers meet regularly to improve continuously members' expertise in implementing cooperative learning and other instructional procedures. The third level is a school-based decision-making procedure involving (a) task forces that research and document schoolwide issues and make a proposal to the entire faculty, (b) small ad hoc decision groups that consider the proposal, and (c) decisions made by the entire faculty. Faculty meetings, when dominated by cooperative procedures, become a microcosm of what school leaders wish the school to be. Through the use of teams a congruent organizational structure is created that promotes quality education by creating a constancy of purpose, being committed to educating every student, focusing on improving the quality of instruction, eliminating competition at all levels, building strong personal relationships, reducing waste, and paying careful attention to implementing the five basic elements on a school as well as a learning group level. Colleagial teaching teams provide the setting in which a process of continuous improvement in expertise can take place. Teachers and administrators progressively refine their expertise through a procedure involving action, feedback, reflection, and modified action. Teachers help each other learn an expert system of how to implement cooperative learning that they use to create a unique adaptation to their specific circumstances, students, and needs.

12

Reflections

INTRODUCTION

I'm just a cowhand from Arkansas, but I have learned how to hold a team together. How to lift some men up, how to calm down others, until finally they've got one heartbeat together, a team. There's just three things I'd ever say:

If anything goes bad, I did it.
If anything goes semi-good, then we did it.
If anything goes real good, then you did it.

That's all it takes to get people to win football games for you.

Bear Bryant, former football coach, University of Alabama

The school is an organization and, similar to all organizations, it has to achieve its goals, maintain effective working relationships among members, and adapt to changes in its community, society, and the world. Like all organizations, schools must adapt to changes in their environment or risk fading away like the dinosaurs. The dinosaur presumably made good day-to-day adaptations to its environment. It probably made a pretty good choice of what leaves to eat from what trees, and selected the most desirable swamps in which to slosh. At a tactical level of decision, we have no reason to believe that these giant beasts were not reasonably competent. But when faced with major changes in the earth's climate and the resulting changes in plant and other animal life, the dinosaur was unable to make the fundamental changes required to adapt to the new environmental conditions. Schools may now be faced with new environmental conditions that require them to do what the dinosaur could not. Schools need to make fundamental changes in the ways students are instructed.

This book has two purposes. The first is to present a framework in which cooperative, competitive, and individualistic learning can be used as an integrated whole. The second is to present a framework that integrates the conceptual and direct approaches to cooperative learning.

INTEGRATED USE OF ALL THREE GOAL STRUCTURES

Lessons may be structured competitively (so students engage in a win–lose struggle to see who is best), individualistically (so that each student works on his or her own to achieve his or her own learning goals), or cooperatively (so that students work in small groups to ensure that all members master the assigned material). For each lesson taught, teachers must decide which goal structure or combination of goal structures to use. In order to make the decision, teachers must understand what each goal structure is, know the conditions under which each can be used appropriately, master the teacher's role in using each goal structure, and understand how to use all three in an integrated way.

Competition is based on perceived scarcity; it requires social comparisons. Competitions vary as to how many winners will result, the criteria used to select a winner, and the way contestants interact. Individualistic efforts are based on independence and isolation from others. Cooperation is based on joint action to achieve mutual goals. It is the heart of human biology, family life, economic systems, legal systems, evolution, and community life. Cooperation is also the heart of education.

For nearly all of American history, with the possible exception of the 1970s and early 1980s, cooperative learning has been an essential aspect of classroom learning. Although there have been consistent advocates of cooperative learning throughout history, there have also been critics, such as Michaels (1977) who favored competitive learning over cooperative learning and Slavin (1977b) who favored individualistic learning over cooperative learning. These critics were silenced, however, when in the early 1980s the question was asked, "What instructional procedures has research proved increase achievement?" The amount and consistency of research supporting the use of cooperative learning makes it unique in education. It is time for the discrepancy to be reduced between what research indicates is effective in teaching and what teachers actually do.

The use of competitive and individualistic efforts, on the other hand, have been even more controversial. In the late 1930s, the 1940s and 1950s, and even during most of the 1960s, competitive learning was seen as the answer to education's problems. Lessons were supposed to pit students against each other with the intensity of a 100-yard dash; each class was supposed to be normatively evaluated on a normal curve, and class rank was the total summary of a student's performance. In addition to its advocates, however, competition has had its critics. Many of the critics, such as John Holt, disagreed on philosophical grounds. Alfie Kohn

(1986) did an extensive review of the research and concluded that all competition is destructive and should never be used in instructional situations. W. Edwards Demming sees competition as a "force for destruction" that must be eliminated in all of its forms from schools.

In the 1960s, 1970s, and early 1980s, individualistic learning had numerous advocates, including B. F. Skinner. Individualistic learning was seen as a way to correct the faults of competition and to apply behavioral psychology to learning situations. There were also critics (such as Urie Brofrenbrenner). Today more than ever there are educators and psychologists who are disturbed by the isolating aspects of individualistic learning and have recommended it never be used. They see individualistic learning as a "force for alienation" creating psychological pathology that must be eliminated in all its forms.

The current research efforts seem to support the critics of competitive and individualistic learning. Over the past ninety-five years there have been more than 600 research studies comparing the relative effectiveness of cooperative, competitive, and individualistic efforts. Cooperation has consistently been found to promote higher achievement, more positive interpersonal relationships, and greater psychological health than do competitive or individualistic efforts. The number of outcomes simultaneously promoted by cooperative efforts makes cooperative learning highly "cost-effective." The research promise, however, does not extend to seating arrangements and aggregates. The elimination of all competitive and individualistic efforts in schools leaves cooperative learning as the only viable way to structure students' learning goals.

There is, however, a middle ground. Although competitive and individualistic efforts may be destructive when they dominate classrooms, there may be conditions under which they may have constructive effects when they are occasionally used to supplement cooperative learning. Competitive learning may be most constructive when it is intergroup (rather than interpersonal), when it involves simple

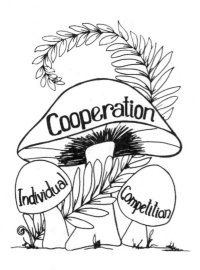

skills and knowledge that previously have been overlearned in cooperative learning groups, when the goal is not perceived to be important, when every student perceives that he or she has a chance to win, and when the number of winners is maximized. Individualistic learning may be most constructive when it involves the acquisition of simple skills or knowledge; when students can work on their own, at their own pace, undisturbed by classmates; when they have a complete set of materials; when instructions and rules are simple and clear; and when what has been learned subsequently contributes to a cooperative effort with classmates.

The conditions under which competitive and individualistic learning may be constructive are best met when they are used as supplements to cooperative learning. What is learned cooperatively can be reviewed in a fun and energetic competition. When students need simple skills and knowledge to contribute to a cooperative effort, individualistic learning may be helpful. The format for integrating the three goal structures is as follows. Students meet in cooperative learning groups and begin working on a task. The simple skills and knowledge needed to complete the assignment are identified and are assigned to different group members. Each member works individualistically to learn his or her part of the material. The group then continues the cooperative work with members contributing their resources to the joint effort. As a fun change of pace, an intergroup competition is conducted where students compete with members of other groups in a game-like, tournament format. Winning or losing does not affect their grades. Finally, the cooperative group completes the assignment and hands it in, and the overall learning of members is assessed and evaluated. Lessons always begin and end with cooperative efforts.

THE INTEGRATION OF CONCEPTUAL AND DIRECT APPROACHES TO COOPERATIVE LEARNING

There are two approaches to implementing cooperative learning—*conceptual* approaches that train teachers to engineer unique adaptations of cooperative learning tailored specifically to their circumstances, students, and needs, and *direct* approaches that train teachers to implement packaged lessons, curricula, and strategies in a lock-step prescribed manner. Conceptual approaches are largely based on theoretically oriented research, and direct approaches are largely based on demonstration research. There has been disagreement as to which approach is most valid and little effort to integrate them.

This book presents an integration of the two approaches. A conceptual framework of cooperative learning is presented in which the direct curricula, scripts and strategies, lessons, and activities can be used. From this combined approach, the steps to gaining expertise in using cooperative learning are as follows. First, teachers must understand the five basic elements that make cooperative work. These five elements differentiate cooperative learning from traditional classroom grouping, and differentiate well-structured cooperative lessons from poorly structured cooperative lessons. In order to be truly cooperative, teachers have to ensure that students (a) perceive that they are positively interdependent with each other, (b) promote each other's success through help, assistance, and encouragement, (c) are individually accountable to do their share of the work, (d) have the interpersonal and small-group skills needed to work effectively with others, and (e) process how well they are working together. If any of these elements is absent, cooperative learning groups will not reach their full potential.

Second, teachers must know their role in using all three types of cooperative learning—formal cooperative learning, informal cooperative learning, and cooperative base groups—and have the skills to implement each type effectively in their classrooms. Informal cooperative learning creates active cognitive processing when direct teaching must be used. Cooperative base groups provide more permanent supportive relationships in which students can ensure that members are making long-term academic progress. In addition, teachers may structure repetitive lessons and classroom routines with cooperative scripts or structures.

Teachers first need to master formal cooperative learning by being able to (a) set objectives, (b) make appropriate preinstructional decisions, (c) communicate the task and the cooperative structure, (d) conduct the lesson while monitoring the learning groups and intervening to help the groups complete the assignment and work together effectively, and (e) evaluate students' learning and ensure that the groups process how effectively they are functioning. The lesson can be a unique lesson planned by the teacher or a cooperative learning script or structure that students have been taught to follow, or a combination of the two. Direct applications (curricula, scripts and structures, lessons, and activities) are more effective and versatile when they are placed within a formal cooperative learning framework. In addition, the teacher's role in using informal cooperative learning and cooperative base groups needs to be mastered.

In cooperative learning groups, students are required to learn (a) academic subject matter (taskwork) and (b) the interpersonal and small-group skills required to function as part of a team (teamwork). If teamwork skills are not learned, then the taskwork cannot be completed. Teamwork skills need to be taught just as systematically as academic skills. Teamwork skills include forming the group into an effective team, ensuring that the group functions effectively in completing assigned learning tasks and maintaining effective working relationships among members, formulating new understandings and conceptual structures as the team members work together, and fermenting each other's thinking through intellectual challenges and disagreements.

Third, teachers must be able to teach students the procedures and skills they need to resolve conflicts constructively. Cooperation and conflict are intertwined. It is hard to find one without the other. The more members care about achieving the group's goals and about each other, the more likely they are to have conflicts with each other. On the other hand, in order to resolve conflicts constructively, a cooperative context must be established that highlights the importance of ongoing working relationships as well as the personal needs and wants involved. To ensure productive teamwork, members must learn the procedures and skills involved in academic controversy (so they can challenge each other's reasoning and conclusions) and in negotiating and mediating constructive resolutions to their conflicts of interests. There are two types of conflict procedures that teachers must teach students. The first is *academic controversy* in which intellectual conflict among group members is created. Students have to be able to prepare an intellectual position, advocate it, attack the positions of others while defending their own from attack, reverse perspectives, and create a synthesis that incorporates the best reasoning from all sides. The second is the *peer-mediation* (peacemaker) procedure of helping classmates negotiate constructive resolutions to conflicts among their wants, needs, and goals (interests). Learning to be peacemakers establishes a discipline program in the classroom and school that focuses on giving students the procedures and skills they need to be self-regulating, rather than on imposing adult authority on their actions.

Fourth, teachers must use all three types of cooperative learning frequently enough to gain a routine level of use. The cooperative learning procedures must become automatic habit patterns. Like all skills, expertise in using cooperative learning is gained through practice, practice, practice, and more practice.

Fifth, teachers must work for creating a team-based organizational structure in their schools just as hard as they work to master cooperative learning. Cooperation is needed among teachers just as much as it is needed among students. When educators set out to mass-produce educated students, they can lose sight of the fact that the enemies to learning are isolation, loneliness, anxiety, fear, and failure. The goals of education are not achieved when schools are mass-production factories in which each student is passed from workstation to workstation (English, math, science, foreign language) to have academic content poured into his or her head and eventually turned out as a finished product. Education proceeds when a learning community is created by (a) involving students in cooperative efforts with each other and the faculty, (b) involving faculty in collegial teaching teams and school-based decision making, and (c) emphasizing positive relationships and social support as essential ingredients to learning and teaching situations. Creating a team-based, high-performance cooperative school provides the structure in which quality education can take place through continuous improvement of teachers' expertise in using cooperative learning and other instructional procedures.

When these five steps are followed, expertise in using cooperative learning is enhanced and the conceptual and direct approaches to cooperative learning have been integrated.

CHANGING PARADIGM OF TEACHING

Cooperative learning is part of a broader paradigm shift that is occurring in teaching. Essential elements of this paradigm shift are presented in Table 12.1 (Johnson, Johnson, & Holubec, 1992; Johnson, Johnson, & Smith, 1991).

The old paradigm of teaching is based on John Locke's assumption that the untrained student mind is like a blank sheet of paper waiting for the instructor to write on it. Student minds are viewed as empty vessels into which teachers pour

TABLE 12.1 Comparison of Old and New Paradigms of Teaching

	OLD PARADIGM	NEW PARADIGM
Knowledge	Transferred from Faculty to Students	Jointly Constructed by Students and Faculty
Students	Passive Vessel to Be Filled by Faculty's Knowledge	Active Constructor, Discoverer, Transformer of Own Knowledge
Faculty Purpose	Classify and Sort Students	Develop Students' Competencies and Talents
Relationships	Impersonal Relationships Among Students and Between Faculty and Students	Personal Transaction Among Students and Between Faculty and Students
Context	Competitive/Individualistic	Cooperative Learning in Classroom and Cooperative Teams Among Faculty
Assumption	Any Expert Can Teach	Teaching Is Complex and Requires Considerable Training

their wisdom. Because of these and other assumptions, teachers think of teaching in terms of these principal activities:

1. *Transferring knowledge from teacher to students.* The teacher's job is to give it; the student's job to is get it. Teachers transmit information that students are expected to memorize and then recall.

2. *Filling passive empty vessels with knowledge.* Students are passive recipients of knowledge. Teachers own the knowledge that students memorize and recall.

3. *Classifying students* by deciding who gets which grade and *sorting students into categories* by deciding who does and does not meet the requirements to be graduated, go on to college, and get a good job. There is constant inspection to "weed out" any defective students. Teachers classify and sort students into categories under the assumption that ability is fixed and is unaffected by effort and education.

4. *Conducting education within a context of impersonal relationships among students and between teachers and students.* Based on the Taylor model of industrial organizations, students and teachers are perceived to be interchangeable and replaceable parts in the "education machine."

5. *Maintaining a competitive organizational structure* in which students work to outperform their classmates and teachers work to outperform their colleagues.

6. *Assuming that anyone with expertise in the field can teach without training to do so.* This is sometimes known as the content premise—if you have a Ph.D. in the field, you can teach.

The old paradigm is to transfer the teacher's knowledge to a passive student so that teachers can classify and sort students in a norm-referenced, competitive way. The assumption was that if you have content expertise, you can teach. Many teachers consider the old paradigm the only alternative. Lecturing while requiring students to be passive, silent, isolated, and in competition with each other seems the only way to teach. The tradition of the old paradigm is carried forward by sheer momentum, while almost everyone persists in the hollow pretense that all is well. All is not well.

Teaching is changing. The old paradigm of teaching is being dropped for a new paradigm based on theory and research that have clear applications to instruction. Educators perhaps should think of teaching in terms of several principal activities.

First, *knowledge is constructed, discovered, transformed, and extended by students.* Teachers create the conditions within which students can construct meaning from the material studied by processing it through existing cognitive structures and then retaining it in long-term memory where it remains open to further processing and possible reconstruction.

Second, *students actively construct their own knowledge.* Learning is conceived of as something a learner does, not something that is done to a learner. Students do not passively accept knowledge from the teacher or curriculum. Students activate their existing cognitive structures or construct new ones to subsume the new input.

Third, *teacher effort is aimed at developing students' competencies and talents.* Student effort should be inspired and secondary schools must "add value" by cultivating talent. A "cultivate and develop" philosophy must replace a "select and weed out" philosophy. Students' competencies and talents are developed under the assumption that with effort and education, any student can improve.

Fourth, *education is a personal transaction among students and between the teachers and students as they work together.* All education is a social process that cannot occur except through interpersonal interaction (real or implied). Learning is a personal but social process that results when individuals cooperate to construct shared understandings and knowledge. Teachers must be able to build positive relationships with students and to create the conditions within which students build caring and committed relationships with each other. The school then becomes a learning community of committed scholars in the truest sense. The more difficult and complex the learning, the harder students have to struggle to achieve, the more important the social support students need. There is a general rule of instruction: The more pressure placed on students to achieve and the more difficult the material to be learned, the more important it is to provide social support within the learning situation. Challenge and social support must be balanced if students are to cope successfully with the stress inherent in learning situations.

Fifth, *all of the above can take place within a cooperative context only.* When students interact within a competitive context, communication is minimized, misleading and false information often is communicated, helping is minimized and viewed as cheating, and classmates and faculty tend to be disliked and distrusted. Competitive and individualistic learning situations, therefore, discourage active construction of knowledge and the development of talent by isolating students and creating negative relationships among classmates and with teachers. Classmates and teachers need to be viewed as collaborators rather than as obstacles to students' own academic and personal success. Teachers therefore structure learning situations so that students work together cooperatively to maximize each other's achievement. Ideally, administrators would in turn create a cooperative, team-based organizational structure within which faculty work together to ensure each other's success (Johnson & Johnson, 1989b).

Sixth, *teaching is assumed to be a complex application of theory and research that requires considerable teacher training and continuous refinement of skills and procedures.* Becoming a good teacher takes at least one lifetime of continuous effort to improve.

The primary means of achieving the new paradigm of teaching is to use cooperative learning. Cooperative learning provides the means of operationalizing the new paradigm of teaching and provides the context within which the development of student talent is encouraged. Carefully structured cooperative learning ensures that students are cognitively, physically, emotionally, and psychologically actively involved in constructing their own knowledge and is an important step in changing the passive and impersonal character of many classrooms.

CREATING A LEARNING COMMUNITY

Frances Hodgson Burnett, in her book *The Secret Garden,* stated, "Where you tend a rose, a thistle cannot grow." Schools should tend roses. They do so by creating a learning community characterized by cooperative efforts to achieve meaningful goals. In a recent review of the research (*Within Our Reach: Breaking the Cycle of Disadvantage*) Lisbeth Schorr concludes that the most important attribute of effective schools is caring. Educational historians David Tyack and Elizabeth Hansot (1982) concluded that the theme that runs through all successful schools is that students, teachers, administrators, and parents share a sense of community and a "socially integrating sense of purpose."

A *community* is a limited number of people who share common goals and a common culture. The smaller the size of the community, the more personal the relationships, and the greater the personal accountability. Everyone knows everyone else. Relationships are long-term and have a future rather than being tempo-

rary brief encounters. Instruction becomes personalized. The students are thought of as citizens, and the teachers are thought of as the community leaders. A sense of belonging tends to boost the desire to learn. The learning community becomes an extended family where mutual achievement and caring for one another are important. With citizenship in the community comes an ethical code that includes such rules as (a) be prepared for classes each day, (b) pay attention in class, (c) be your personal best, and (d) respect other people and their property. In order to create a learning community, students (and teachers) need to be organized into cooperative teams.

At the end of this book you are at a new beginning. Years of experience in using cooperative learning in your classroom are needed to gain expertise in its use. Such expertise is difficult to attain without the help of a faculty teaching team. Long-term, persistent efforts to improve continuously come from the heart, not the head. A teaching team will provide you with the support and joint commitment essential to maintaining a love affair with teaching. Through implementing cooperative learning in your classes and being a contributing member of a colleagial teaching team, a true learning community of scholars may be created for both your students and yourself.

IN RETROSPECT

Cooperation is the "air" of society that we constantly breathe—it is completely necessary but relatively unnoticed. We notice changes in the air—a whiff of perfume or a blanket of smog—but these are the rare instances. Like the perfume, the time we are locked (or licked) in competition and the things we achieve "on our own" stand out and are remembered because they are different from the majority of our efforts, which are cooperative. Just as the parochial myth that "smog is what most air is like, and we need to learn to live with it" can grow in the minds of those who live in a large city, so egocentric myths like "it's a survival-of-the-fittest society" have grown and have nourished by those who ignore the many cooperative aspects of their lives while concentrating on those aspects that are competitive. In American society (and schools) we share a common language, we drive on the appropriate side of the street, we take turns going through doors, we raise families, we seek friendship, we share the maintenance of life through an intricate division of labor. This is not to say that the skills of competitive and individualistic efforts are unimportant. They are important, but only within the larger context of cooperation with others. A person needs to know when it is appropriate to compete or work individualistically and when to cooperate. Unfortunately, instruction in schools at present stresses competitive and individualistic efforts without much attention to the skills needed to facilitate effective cooperation. To encourage a positive learning environment and to promote the outcomes of schools, we must realize that cooperation is the forest—competitive and individualistic efforts are but trees.

As the authors look back on the aspects of our growing up together, we realize that we may have misled you. The competition between us was a rather small part of the time we spent together. What made the instances of competition bearable was our partnership and the constant supportive cooperation within our family, and later with our friends and our families.

Without cooperation and the skills that it requires, life in a society or a school would not be possible.

References

ARMENTO, B. (1977). Teacher behaviors related to student achievement on a social science concept test. *Journal of Teacher Education, 28,* 46–52.

ARONSON, E., BLANEY, N., STEPHAN, C., SIKES, J., & SNAPP, M. (1978). *The jigsaw classroom.* Beverly Hills, CA: Sage.

ASHMORE, R. (1970). Solving the problems of prejudice. In B. E. Collins (Ed.), *Social psychology.* Reading, MA: Addison-Wesley Publishing Co.

ASTIN, A. (1985). *Achieving educational excellence.* San Francisco: Jossey-Bass.

ASTIN, A., GREEN, K., KORN, W. (1987). *The American freshman: Twenty year trends.* Los Angeles: University of California, Higher Education Research Institute.

ASTIN, A., GREEN, K., KORN, W., SHALIT, M. (1986). *The American freshman: National norms for fall 1986.* Los Angeles: University of California, Higher Education Research Institute.

ASTIN, H., ASTIN, A., BISCONTI, A., & FRANKEL, H. (1972). *Higher education and the disadvantaged student.* Washington, DC: Human Science Press.

ATKINSON, J. (1965). The mainsprings of achievement-oriented activity. In J. D. Krumholtz (Ed.), *Learning and the educational process* (pp. 25–66). Chicago: Rand McNally & Co.

BANDURA, A., ROSS, D., & ROSS, S. (1963). Imitation of film-mediated aggressive models. *Journal of Abnormal and Social Psychology, 66,* 3–11.

BIGELOW, R. (1972). The evolution of cooperation, aggression, and self-control. In J. Cole and D. Jenson (Eds.), *Nebraska symposium on motivation* (pp. 1–110). Lincoln: University of Nebraska Press.

BLANCHARD, F., ADELMAN, L., & COOK, S. (1975). The effect of group success and failure upon interpersonal attraction in cooperating interracial groups. *Journal of Personality and Social Psychology, 32,* 519–530.

BLIGH, D. (1972). *What's the use of lectures.* Harmondsworth, Eng.: Penguin.

BONOMA, T., TEDESCHI, J., & HELM, B. (1974). Some effects of target cooperation and reciprocated promises on conflict resolution. *Sociometry, 37,* 251–261.

BOVARD, E. (1951a). Group structure and perception. *Journal of Abnormal and Social Psychology, 46,* 398–405.

BOVARD, E. (1951b). The experimental production of interpersonal affect. *Journal of Abnormal Psychology, 46,* 521–528.

BOWERS, J. (1986). Classroom communication apprehension: A survey. *Communication Education, 35*(4), 372–378.

BRONFRENBRENNER, U. (1970). *Two worlds of childhood.* New York: Russell Sage.

BROWN, J., COLLINS, A., & DUGUID, P. (1989). Situated cognition and the culture of learning. *Educational Researcher, 18*(1), 32–42.

BURNS, M. (1981, September). Groups of four: Solving the management problem. *Learning,* 46–51.

CAMPBELL, J. (1965). *The children's crusader: Colonel Francis W. Parker.* Ph.D. dissertation, Teachers College, Columbia University.

COHEN, E. (1986). *Designing groupwork.* New York: Teachers College Press.

COLEMAN, J. (1959). Academic achievement and the structure of competition. *Harvard Educational Review, 29,* 339–351.

COLEMAN, J. (1961). *The adolescent society.* New York: Macmillan.

COLLINS, B. (1970). *Social psychology.* Reading, MA: Addison-Wesley.

CONGER, J. (1988). Hostages to fortune: Youth, values and the public interest. *American Psychologist, 43,* 291–300.

COOK, S. (1969). Motives in a conceptual analysis of attitude-related behavior. In W. Arnold and D. Levine (Eds.), *Nebraska symposium on motivation* (Vol. 17). Lincoln: University of Nebraska Press.

COSTIN, F. (January 1972). Lecturing versus other methods of teaching: A review of research. *British Journal of Educational Technology, 3*(1), 4–30.

COTTRELL, N., WACK, D., SEKERAK, G., & RITTLE, R. (1968). Social facilitation of dominant responses by the presence of an audience and the mere presence of other. *Journal of Personality and Social Psychology, 9,* 245–250.

CROCKENBERG, S., BRYANT, B., & WILCE, L. (1976). The effects of cooperatively and competitively structured learning environments on inter- and intrapersonal behavior. *Child Development, 47,* 386–396.

CRONBAG, H. (1966). Cooperation and competition in means-interdependent triads: A replication. *Journal of Personality and Social Psychology, 4*(6), 692–695.

DANSEREAU, D. (1985). Learning strategy research. In J. Segal, S. Chipman, and R. Glaser (Eds.). *Thinking and learning skills* (Vol. 1, *Relating instruction to research.*) Hillsdale, NJ: Lawrence Erlbaum Associates, Inc.

DEUTSCH, M. (1949a). A theory of cooperation and competition. *Human Relations, 2,* 129–152.

DEUTSCH, M. (1949b). An experimental study of the effects of cooperation and competition upon group processes. *Human Relations, 2,* 199–232.

DEUTSCH, M. (1958). Trust and suspicion. *Journal of Conflict Resolution, 2,* 25–279.

DEUTSCH, M. (1960). The effects of motivational orientation upon trust and suspicion. *Human Relations, 13,* 123–139.

DEUTSCH, M. (1962). Cooperation and trust: Some theoretical notes. In M. R. Jones (Ed.), *Nebraska symposium on motivation* (pp. 275–319). Lincoln: University of Nebraska Press.

DEUTSCH, M. (1973). *The resolution of conflict.* New Haven, CT: Yale University Press.

DEUTSCH, M., & KRAUSS, R. (1962). Studies of interpersonal bargaining. *Journal of Conflict Resolutions, 6,* 52–76.

DEVRIES, D., & EDWARDS, K. (1973). Learning games and student teams: Their effects on classroom process. *American Educational Research Journal, 10,* 307–318.

DEVRIES, D., & EDWARDS, K. (1974). Student teams and learning games: Their effects on cross-race and cross-sex interaction. *Journal of Educational Psychology, 66*(5), 741–749.

DEVRIES, D., MUSE, D., & WELLS, E. (1971). *The effects of working in cooperative groups: An exploratory study.* (Report #120.) Baltimore: Johns Hopkins University, Center for Social Organization of Schools.

DEWEY, J. (1924). *The school and society.* Chicago: University of Chicago Press.

DIAMOND, J. (1989, May). The great leap forward. *Discover, 10,* 50–60.

DIPARDO, A., & FREEDMAN, S. (1988). Peer response groups in the writing classroom: Theoretic foundations and new directions. *Review of Educational Research, 58,* 119–150.

DREEBEN, R. (1968). *On what is learned in school.* Reading, MA: Addison-Wesley.

EBLE, K. (1983). *The aims of college teaching.* San Francisco: Jossey-Bass.

FARB, P. (1963). Ecology. New York: Time, Inc.

FAY, A. (1970). The effects of cooperation and competition on learning and recall. Unpublished master's thesis, George Peabody College.

FRANK, M. (1984). A comparison between an individual and group goal structure contingency that differed in the behavioral contingency and performance-outcome components. Unpublished Ph.D. dissertation, University of Minnesota.

FRENCH, J. (1951). Group productivity. In H. Guetzkow (Ed.), *Groups, leadership and men* (pp. 44–55). Pittsburgh: Carnegie Press.

GABBERT, B., JOHNSON, D. W., & JOHNSON, R. (1986). Cooperative learning, group-to-individual transfer, process gain and the acquisition of cognitive reasoning strategies. *Journal of Psychology, 120(3),* 265–278.

GLASSER, W. (1969). *Schools without failure.* New York: Harper & Row.

GOOD, T., & GROUWS, D. (1977). Teaching effects: A process-product study in fourth grade mathematics classrooms. *Journal of Teacher Education, 28,* 49–54.

GREEN, D. (1977). The immediate processing of sentences. *Quarterly Journal of Experimental Psychology, 29,* 135–146.

GROSSACK, M. (1953). Some effects of cooperation and competition upon small group behavior. *Journal of Abnormal and Social Psychology, 49,* 341–348.

GUETZKOW, H., KELLY, E., & MCKEACHIE, W. (1954). An experimental comparison of recitation, discussion, and tutorial methods in college teaching. *Journal of Educational Psychology, 45,* 193–209.

HALISCH, F., & HECKHAUSEN, H. (1977). Search for feedback information and effort regulation during task performance. *Journal of Personality and Social Psychology, 35,* 724–733.

HARKINS, S., & PETTY, R. (1982). The effects of task difficulty and task uniqueness on social loafing. *Journal of Personality and Social Psychology, 43,* 1214–1229.

HELMREICH, R. (1982, August). *Pilot selection and training.* Paper presented at the annual meeting of the American Psychological Association, Washington, DC.

HELMREICH, R., BEANE, W., LUCKER, W., & SPENCE, J. (1978). Achievement motivation and scientific attainment. *Personality and Social Psychology Bulletin, 4,* 222–226.

HELMREICH, R., SAWIN, L., & CARSUD, A. (1986). The honeymoon effect in job performance: Temporal increases in the predictive power of achievement motivation. *Journal of Applied Psychology, 71,* 185–188.

HELMREICH, R., SPENSE, J., BEANE, W., & MATTHEWS, K. (1980). Making it in academic psychology: Demographic and personality correlates of attainment. *Journal of Personality and Social Psychology, 39,* 896–908.

HENRY, J. (1963). *Culture against man.* New York: Random House.

HILL, G. (1982). Group versus individual performance: Are N+1 heads better than one? *Psychological Bulletin, 91,* 517–539.

HOLT, J. (1964). *How children fail.* New York: Dell Publishing Co.

HUNT, P., & HILLERY, J. (1973). Social facilitation in a coaction setting: An examination of the effects over learning trials. *Journal of Experimental Social Psychology, 9,* 563–571.

HURLOCK, E. (1927). Use of group rivalry as an incentive. *Journal of Abnormal and Social Psychology, 22,* 278–290.

HWONG, N., CASWELL, A., JOHNSON, D. W., & JOHNSON, R. (1993). Effects of cooperative and individualistic learning on prospective elementary teachers' music achievement and attitudes. *Journal of Social Psychology, 133*(1), 53–64.

ILLICH, I. (1971). *Deschooling society.* New York: Harrow Books.

INGHAM, A., LEVINGER, G., GRAVES, J., & PECKHAM, V. (1974). The Ringelmann effect: Studies of group size and group performance. *Journal of Personality and Social Psychology, 10,* 371–384.

JACKSON, P. (1968). *Life in classrooms.* New York: Holt, Rinehart & Winston.

JANKE, R. (1980). Computational errors of mentally-retarded students. *Psychology in the schools, 17,* 30–32.

JOHNSON, D. W. (1970). *The social psychology of education.* New York: Holt, Rinehart & Winston.

JOHNSON, D. W. (1971). Role reversal: A summary and review of the research. *International Journal of Group Tensions, 111,* 318–334.

JOHNSON, D. W. (1973). Communication in conflict situations: A critical review of the research. *International Journal of Group Tensions, 3,* 46–47.

JOHNSON, D. W. (1974). Communication and the inducement of cooperative behavior in conflicts: A critical review. *Speech Monographs, 41,* 64–78.

JOHNSON, D. W. (1979). *Educational psychology.* Englewood Cliffs, NJ: Prentice Hall.

JOHNSON, D. W. (1980). Constructive peer relationships, social development, and cooperative learning experiences: Implications for the prevention of drug abuse. *Journal of Drug Education, 10,* 7–24.

JOHNSON, D. W. (1991). *Human relations and your career* (3rd ed.). Englewood Cliffs, NJ: Prentice Hall.

JOHNSON, D. W. (1993). *Reaching out: Interpersonal effectiveness and self-actualization* (5th ed.). Needham Heights, MA: Allyn & Bacon.

JOHNSON, D. W., & JOHNSON, F. (1991). *Joining together: Group theory and group skills* (4th ed.). Englewood Cliffs, NJ: Prentice Hall.

JOHNSON, D. W., & JOHNSON, R. (1974). Instructional goal structure: Cooperative, competitve, or individualistic. *Review of Educational Research, 44,* 213–240.

JOHNSON, D. W., & JOHNSON, R. (1975). *Learning together and alone:* Cooperation, competition, and individualization (1st ed.). Englewood Cliffs, NJ: Prentice Hall.

JOHNSON, D. W., & JOHNSON, R. (1977). *Controversy in the classroom* (Videotape). Edina, MN: Interaction Book Company.

JOHNSON, D. W., & JOHNSON, R. (1978). Cooperative, competitive, and individualistic learning. *Journal of Research and Development in Education, 12,* 3–15.

JOHNSON, D. W., & JOHNSON, R. (1979). Conflict in the classroom: Controversy and learning. *Review of Educational Research, 49,* 51–70.

JOHNSON, D. W., & JOHNSON, R. (1981). Effects of cooperative and individualistic learning experiences on interethnic interaction. *Journal of Educational Psychology, 23*(3), 454–459.

JOHNSON, D. W., & JOHNSON, R. (1983a). The socialization and achievement crisis: Are cooperative learning experiences the solution? In L. Bickman (Ed.), *Applied Social Psychology Annual 4* (pp. 119–164). Beverly Hills, CA: Sage.

JOHNSON, D. W., & JOHNSON, R. (1983b). Social interdependence and perceived academic and personal support in the classroom. *Journal of Social Psychology, 120,* 77–82.

JOHNSON, D. W., & JOHNSON, R. (1985). Classroom conflict: Controversy vs. debate in learning groups. *American Educational Research Journal, 22,* 237–256.

JOHNSON, D. W., & JOHNSON, R. (1987). *Creative conflict.* Edina, MN: Interaction Book Company.

JOHNSON, D. W., & JOHNSON, R. (1989a). *Cooperation and competition: Theory and research.* Edina, MN: Interaction Book Company.

JOHNSON, D. W., & JOHNSON, R. (1989b). *Leading the cooperative school.* Edina, MN: Interaction Book Company.

JOHNSON, D. W., & JOHNSON, R. (1991a). *Teaching students to be peacemakers.* Edina, MN: Interaction Book Company.

JOHNSON, D. W., & JOHNSON, R. (1991b). *Teaching students to be peacemakers* (Videotape). Edina, MN: Interaction Book Company.

JOHNSON, D. W., & JOHNSON, R. (1991c). *My mediation notebook.* Edina, MN: Interaction Book Company.

JOHNSON, D. W., & JOHNSON, R. (1991d). Cooperative learning and classroom and school climate. In B. Fraser and H. Walberg (Eds.), *Educational environments: Evaluation, antecedents and consequences* (pp. 55–74). New York: Pergamon Press.

JOHNSON, D. W., & JOHNSON, R. (1992a). *Creative controversy: Intellectual challenge in the classroom.* Edina, MN: Interaction Book Company.

JOHNSON, D. W., & JOHNSON, R. (1992b). *Positive interdependence: The heart of cooperative learning.* Edina, MN: Interaction Book Company.

JOHNSON, D. W., & JOHNSON, R. (1992c). *Positive interdependence: The heart of cooperative learning* (Videotape). Edina, MN: Interaction Book Company.

JOHNSON, D. W., JOHNSON, R., & ANDERSON, D. (1983). Social interdependence and classroom climate. *Journal of Psychology, 114,* 135–142.

JOHNSON, D. W., JOHNSON, R., BUCKMAN, L., & RICHARDS, P. (1986). The effect of prolonged implementation of cooperative learning on social support within the classroom. *Journal of Psychology, 119,* 405–411.

JOHNSON, D. W., JOHNSON, R., & HOLUBEC, E. (1984/1993). *Circles of learning: Cooperation in the classroom.* Edina, MN: Interaction Book Company.

JOHNSON, D. W., JOHNSON, R., & HOLUBEC, E. (1991). *Cooperation in the classroom* (5th ed.). Edina, MN: Interaction Book Company.

JOHNSON, D. W., JOHNSON, R., & HOLUBEC, E. (1992). *Advanced cooperative learning.* Edina, MN: Interaction Book Company.

JOHNSON, D. W., JOHNSON, R., & HOLUBEC, E. (1993). *Cooperation in the classroom* (6th ed.). Edina, MN: Interaction Book Company.

JOHNSON, D. W., JOHNSON, R., & MARUYAMA, G. (1983). Interdependence and interpersonal attraction among heterogeneous and homogeneous individuals: A threoretical formulation and a meta-analysis of the research. *Review of Educational Research, 53,* 5–54.

JOHNSON, D. W., JOHNSON, R., ORTIZ, A., & STANNE, M. (1991). Impact of positive goal and resource interdependence on achievement, interaction and attitudes. *Journal of General Psychology, 118,* 341–347.

JOHNSON, D. W., JOHNSON, R., & SMITH, K. (1986). Academic conflict among students: Controversy and learning. In R. Feldman (Ed.), *Social psychological applications to education.* Cambridge, MA: Cambridge University Press.

JOHNSON, D. W., JOHNSON, R., & SMITH, K. (1991). *Active learning: Cooperative in the college classroom.* Edina, MN: Interaction Book Company.

JOHNSON, D. W., JOHNSON, R., STANNE, M., & GARIBALDI, A. (1990). The impact of leader and member group processing on achievement in cooperative groups. *The Journal of Social Psychology, 130,* 507–516.

JOHNSON, D. W., & MATROSS, R. (1977). The interpersonal influence of the psychotherapist. In A. Gurman & A. Razin (Eds.), *The effective therapist: A handbook.* Elmsford, NY: Pergamon Press.

JOHNSON, D. W., & NOONAN, P. (1972). Effects of acceptance and reciprocation of self-disclosures on the development of trust. *Journal of Counselling Psychology, 19(5),* 411–416.

JOHNSON, D. W., & NOREM-HEBEISEN, A. (1981). Relationships between cooperative, competitive, and individualistic attitudes and differentiated aspects of self-esteem. *Journal of Personality, 49,* 415–426.

JOHNSON, D. W., SKON, L., & JOHNSON, R. (1980). Effects of cooperative, competitive, and individualistic conditions on children's problem-solving performance. *American Educational Research Journal, 17(1),* 83–94.

KAGAN, J. (1965, Summer). Personality and the learning process. *Daedalus,* 553–563.

KAGAN, S. (1985). *Cooperative learning*. Mission Viejo, CA: Resources for Teachers.

KAGAN, S. (1988). *Cooperative learning*. San Juan Capistrano, CA: Resources for Teachers.

KAGAN, S. (1989). *Cooperative learning: Resources for teachers*. Laguna Naguel, CA: Resources for Teachers.

KAGAN, S., & MADSEN, M. (1972). Experimental analyses of cooperation and competition of Anglo-American and Mexican children. *Developmental Psychology, 6(1)*, 49–59.

KERR, N. (1983). The dispensability of member effort and group motivation losses: Free-rider effects. *Journal of Personality and Social Psychology, 44*, 78–94.

KERR, N., & BRUUN, S. (1981). Ringelmann revisited: Alternative explanations for the social loafing effect. *Personality and Social Psychology Bulletin, 7*, 224–231.

KLEIBER, D., & ROBERTS, G. (1981). The effects of experience in the development of social character: An exploratory investigation. *Journal of Sport Psychology, 3*, 114–122.

KOHL, H. (1969). *The open classroom*. New York: Vintage Books.

KOHN, A. (1986). *No contest: The case against competition*. Boston: Houghton-Mifflin Company.

KOHN, A. (1990). *The brighter side of human nature*. New York: Basic Books.

KOUZES, J., & POSNER, B. (1987). *The leadership challenge*. San Francisco: Jossey-Bass.

KRAUSS, R., & DEUTSCH, M. (1966). Communication in interpersonal bargaining. *Journal of Personality and Social Psychology, 4*, 572–577.

KROLL, W., & PETERSON, K. (1965). Study of values test and collegiate football teams. *Research Quarterly, 36*, 441–447.

KULIK, J., & KULIK, C. L. (1979). College teaching. In P. L. Peterson & H. J. Walberg (Eds.), *Research on teaching: Concepts, findings, and implications*. Berkeley, CA: McCutcheon.

LAMM, H., & TROMMSDORFF, G. (1973). Group versus individual performance on tasks requiring ideational proficiency (Brainstorming): A review. *European Journal of Social Psychology, 3*, 361–388.

LANGER, E., & BENEVENTO, A. (1978). Self-induced dependence. *Journal of Personality and Social Psychology, 36*, 886–893.

LARSON, C., DANSEREAU, D., O'DONNELL, A., HYTHECKER, V., LAMBIOTTE, J., & ROCKLIN, T. (1984). Verbal ability and cooperative learning: Transfer of effects. *Journal of Reading Behavior, 16(4)*, 289–296.

LATANE, B., WILLIAMS, K., & HARKINS, S. (1979). Many hands make light the work: The causes and consequences of social loafing. *Journal of Personality and Social Psychology, 37*, 822–832.

LAUGHLIN, P. (1965). Selection strategies in concept attainment as a function of number of persons and stimulus display. *Journal of Experimental Psychology, 70(3)*, 323–327.

LAUGHLIN, P. (1973). Selection strategies in concept attainment. In R. L. Solso (Ed.), *Contemporary issues in cognitive psychology: The Loyola symposium*. Washington, DC: V. H. Winston.

LAUGHLIN, P., & JACCARD, J. (1975). Social facilitation and observational learning of individuals and cooperative pairs. *Journal of Personality and Social Psychology, 32(5)*, 873–879.

LAUGHLIN, P., McGLYNN, R., ANDERSON, J., & JACOBSEN, E. (1968). Concept attainment by individuals versus cooperative pairs as a function of memory, sex, and concept rule. *Journal of Personality and Social Psychology, 8(4)*, 410–417.

LAVE, J. (1988). *Cognition in practice: Mind, mathematics and culture in everyday life*. Cambridge, MA: Cambridge University Press.

LEPLEY, W. (1937). Competitive behavior in the albino rat. *Journal of Experimental Psychology, 21*, 194–201.

LEVIN, H., GLASS, G., & MEISTER, G. (1984). *Cost-effectiveness of educational interventions*. Stanford, CA: Institute for Research on Educational Finance and Governance.

LEVINE, J. (1983). Social comparison and education. In J. Levine & M. Wang (Eds.), *Teacher and student perceptions: Implications for learning*. New York: Erlbaum.

LEW, M., MESCH, D., JOHNSON, D. W., & JOHNSON, R. (1986a). Positive interdependence, academic and collaborative-skills group contingencies and isolated students. *American Educational Research Journal, 23*, 476–488.

LEW, M., MESCH, D., JOHNSON, D. W., & JOHNSON, R. (1986b). Components of cooperative learning: Effects of collaborative skills and academic group contingencies on achievement and mainstreaming. *Contemporary Educational Psychology, 11*, 229–239.

LEWIN, K. (1935). *A dynamic theory of personality*. New York: McGraw-Hill.

LEWIN, K. (1948). *Resolving social conflicts*. New York: Harper.

LIGHT, R. (1990). *The Harvard assessment seminars*. Cambridge, MA: Harvard University.

LITTLE, J. (1990). The persistence of privacy: Autonomy and initiative in teachers' professional relations. *Teacher's College Record, 9*, 509–536.

LOY, J., BIRRELL, S., & ROSE, P. (1976). Attitudes held toward agnostic activities as a function of selected social identities. *Quest, 26*, 81–95.

McGLYNN, R. (1972). Four-person group concept attainment as function of interaction format. *Journal of Social Psychology, 86*, 89–94.

McKeachie, W. (1951). Anxiety in the college classroom. *Journal of Educational Research, 45,* 153–160.

McKeachie, W. (1954). Individual conformity to attitudes of classroom groups. *Journal of Abnormal and Social Psychology, 49,* 282–289.

McKeachie, W. (1967). Research in training: The gap between theory and practice. In C. Lee (Ed.), *Improving college teaching* (pp. 211–239). Washington, DC: American Council of Education.

McKeachie, W. (1986). *Teaching tips: A guidebook for the beginning college teacher* (8th ed.). Boston: D. C. Heath.

McKeachie, W. (1988). Teaching thinking. *Update, 2*(1), 1.

McKeachie, W., & Kulik, J. (1975). Effective college training. In F. Kerlinger (Ed.), *Review of research in education.* Itasca, IL: Peacock.

Mackworth, J. (1970). *Vigilance and habituation.* Harmondsworth, Eng.: Penguin.

Madsen, M. (1967). Cooperative and competitive motivation of children in three Mexican subcultures. *Psychological Reports, 20,* 1307–1320.

Maller, J. (1929). *Cooperation and competition: An experimental study in motivation.* New York: Teachers College, Columbia University.

Markus, H. (1978). The effect of mere presence on social facilitation: An unobtrusive test. *Journal of Experimental Social Psychology, 14,* 389–397.

Masters, J. (1972). Effects of social comparisons upon the imitation of neutral and altruistic behaviors by young children. *Child Development, 43,* 131–142.

Matthews, B. (1979). Effects of fixed and alternated payoff inequity on dyadic competition. *The Psychological Record, 29,* 329–339.

May, M., & Doob, L. (1937). Competition and cooperation. *Social Science Research Council Bulletin* (No. 25). New York: Social Science Research Council.

Mayer, A. (1903). Uber einzel und gesamtleistung des schul kindes. *Archiv fur die Gesamte Psychologie, 1,* 276–416.

Mead, M. (Ed.) (1936). *Cooperation and competition among primitive peoples.* New York: McGraw-Hill.

Mesch, D., Johnson, D. W., & Johnson, R. (1988). Impact of positive interdependence and academic group contingencies on achievement. *Journal of Social Psychology, 128,* 345–352.

Mesch, D., Lew, M., Johnson, D. W., & Johnson, R. (1986). Isolated teenagers, cooperative learning and the training of social skills. *Journal of Psychology, 120,* 323–334.

Michaels, J. (1977). Classroom reward structures and academic performance. *Review of Educational Research, 47,* 87–99.

Miller, L., & Hamblin, R. (1963). Interdependence, differential rewarding, and productivity. *American Sociological Review, 28,* 768–778.

von Mises, L. (1949). *Human action: A treatise on economics.* New Haven, CT: Yale University Press.

Moede, W. (1927). Die richtlinien der leistungs-psychologie. *Industrielle Psychotechnik, 4,* 193–207.

Montagu, A. (1965). *The human revolution.* New York: World.

Montagu, A. (1966). *On being human.* New York: Hawthorn.

Motley, M. (1988, January). Taking the terror out of talk. *Psychology Today, 22*(1), 46–49.

National Association of Secondary School Principals (1984). *The mood of American youth.* Reston, VA: Author.

Neer, M. (1987). The development of an instrument to measure classroom apprehension. *Communication Education, 36,* 154–166.

Nelson, L., & Kagan, S. (1972). Competition: The star-spangled scramble. *Psychology Today, 6,* 53.

Nesbitt, M. (1967). *A public school for tomorrow.* New York: A Delta Book.

Nias, J. (1984). Learing and acting the role: Inschool support for primary teachers. *Educational Review, 33,* 181–190.

Noel, L. (1985). Increasing student retention: New challenges and potential. In L. Noel, R. F. Levitz, & D. Saluri (Eds.), *Increasing student retention: Effective programs and practices for reducing the dropout rate* (pp. 1–27). San Francisco: Jossey-Bass.

Norem-Hebeisen, A. (1974). Differentiated aspects of the self-esteeming process among suburban adolescents and dysfunctional youth. Unpublished dissertation, University of Minnesota–Minneapolis.

Norem-Hebeisen, A. (1976). A multi-dimensional construct of self-esteem. *Journal of Educational Psychology, 68,* 559–565.

Norem-Hebeisen, A., & Johnson, D. W. (1981). Relationships between cooperative, competitive, and individualistic attitudes and differentiated aspects of self-esteem. *Journal of Personality, 49,* 415–425.

Ogilvie, B., & Tutko, T. (1971). Sport: If you want to build character, try something else. *Psychology Today, 5,* 60–63.

PELZ, D., & ANDREWS, F. (1976). *Scientists in organizations: Productive climates for research and development.* Ann Arbor: Institute for Social Research, University of Michigan.

PENNER, J. (1984). *Why many college teachers cannot lecture.* Springfield, IL: Charles C Thomas.

PEPITONE, E. (1980). *Children in cooperation and competition.* Lexington, MA: Lexington Books.

PETTY, R., HARKINS, S., WILLIAMS, K., & LATANE, B. (1977). The effects of group size on cognitive effort and evaluation. *Personality and Social Psychology Bulletin, 3,* 575–578.

POSTMAN, N., & WEINGARTNER, C. (1969). *Teaching as a subversive activity.* New York: Delacorte Press.

RATHBONE, C. (1970). Open education and the teacher. Unpublished Ph.D. dissertation, Harvard University.

ROGERS, V. (1970). *Teaching in the British primary schools.* London: MacMillan and Co.

ROSENBERGER, B. (1984, April). What made humans human? *New York Times Magazine,* 80–81, 89–95.

ROSENSHINE, B. (1968, December). To explain: A review of research. *Educational Leadership, 26,* 303–309.

ROSENSHINE, B., & STEVENS, R. (1986). Teaching functions. In M. C. Wittrock (Ed.), *Handbook of research on teaching* (3rd ed.) (pp. 376–391). New York: Macmillan.

RUGGIERO, V. R. (1988). *Teaching thinking across the curriculum.* New York: Harper & Row.

SALOMON, G. (1981). Communication and education: Social and psychological interactions. *People & Communication, 13,* 9–271.

SANDERS, G., & BARON, R. (1975). The motivating effects of distraction on task performance. *Journal of Personality and Social Psychology, 32,* 956–963.

SCHOENFELD, A. (1985). *Mathematical problem solving.* Orlando, FL: Academic Press.

SCHOENFELD, A. (1989). Ideas in the air: Speculations on small group learning, peer interactions, cognitive apprenticeship, quasi-Vygotskean notions of internalization, creativity, problem solving, and mathematical practice. *International Journal of Education Research, 73.*

SELIGMAN, M. (1988, October). Boomer blues. *Psychology Today, 22,* 50–55.

SHARAN, S., & HERTZ-LAZAROWITZ, R. (1980). *A group-investigation method of cooperative learning in the classroom.* Tel-Aviv, Israel: University of Tel-Aviv. (Technical report.)

SHARAN, S., & SHARAN, Y. (1976). *Small group teaching.* Englewood Cliffs, NJ: Educational Technology Publications.

SHEINGOLD, K., HAWKINS, J., & CHAR, C. (1984). I'm the thinkist, you're the typist: The interaction of technology and the social life of classrooms. *Journal of Social Issues, 40*(3), 49–61.

SHERIF, M., & HOVLAND, C. (1961). *Social judgment: Assimilation and contrast effects in communication and attitude change.* New Haven, CT: Yale University Press.

SILBERMAN, C. (1971). *Crisis in the classroom.* New York: Vintage Books.

SKON, L., JOHNSON, D. W., & JOHNSON, R. (1981). Cooperative peer interaction versus individual competition and individualistic efforts: Effects on the acquisition of cognitive reasoning strategies. *Journal of Educational Psychology, 73*(1), 83–92.

SLAVIN, R. (1974). *The effects of teams in Teams-Games-Tournament on the normative climates of classrooms.* Baltimore: Johns Hopkins University, Center for Social Organization of Schools, unpublished report.

SLAVIN, R. (1977a). *A student team approach to teaching adolescents with special emotional and behavioral needs.* (Report No. 227.) Baltimore: Johns Hopkins University, Center for Social Organization of Schools.

SLAVIN, R. (1977b). Classroom reward structure: An analytical and practical review. *Review of Educational Research, 47,* 633–650.

SLAVIN, R. (1980). Cooperative learning. *Review of Educational Research, 50,* 315–342.

SLAVIN, R. (1983). *Cooperative learning.* New York: Longman.

SLAVIN, R. (1985). An introduction to cooperative learning research. In R. Slavin et al. (Eds.), *Learning to cooperate, cooperating to learn.* New York: Plenum Press.

SLAVIN, R. (1991). Group rewards make groupwork work. *Educational Leadership, 5,* 89–91.

SLAVIN, R., LEAVEY, M., & MADDEN, N. (1982). *Team-assisted individualization: Mathematics teacher's manual.* Johns Hopkins University, Center for Social Organization of Schools.

SMITH, L., & LAND, M. (1981). Low-inference verbal behaviors related to teach clarity. *Journal of Classroom Interaction, 17,* 37–42.

SPILERMAN, S. (1971). Raising academic motivation in lowerclass adolescents: A convergence of two research traditions. *Sociology of Education, 44,* 101–108.

SPURLIN, J., DANSEREAU, D., LARSON, C., & BROOKS, L. (1984). Cooperative learning strategies in processing descriptive text: Effects of role and activity level of the learner. *Cognition and Instruction, 1*(4), 451–463.

STAUB, E. (1971). Helping a person in distress: The influence of implicit and explicit "rules" of conduct on children and adults. *Journal of Personality and Social Psychology, 17,* 137–144.

STEVENS, R., MADDEN, N., SLAVIN, R., & FARNISH, A. (1987). Cooperative integrated reading and composition: Two field experiments. *Reading Research Quarterly, 22*(4), 433–454.

STEVENSON, H., & STIGLER, J. (1992). *The learning group.* New York: Simon & Schuster.

STONES, E. (1970). Students' attitudes to the size of teaching groups. *Educational Review, 21*(2), 98–108.

STUART, J., & RUTHERFORD, R. (1978, September). Medical student concentration during lectures. *The Lancet, 2,* 514–516.

THOMAS, D. (1957). Effects of facilitative role interdependence on group functioning. *Human Relations, 10,* 347–366.

TINTO, V. (1975). Dropout from higher education: A theoretical synthesis of recent research. *Review of Educational Research, 45*(1), 89–125.

TINTO, V. (1987). *Leaving college: Rethinking the causes and cures for student attrition.* Chicago: University of Chicago Press.

TREISMAN, P. (1985). A study of the mathematics performance of black students at the University of California, Berkeley. (Ph.D. dissertation, University of California–Berkeley). *Dissertation Abstracts International, 47,* 1641-A.

TRIPLETT, N. (1898). The dynamogenic factors in pacemaking and competition. *American Journal on Psychology, 9,* 507–533.

TSENG, S. (1969). An experimental study of the effect of three types of distribution of reward upon work efficiency and group dynamics. Unpublished Ph.D. dissertation, Columbia University, New York.

VERNER, C., & DICKINSON, G. (1967). The lecture, an analysis and review of research. *Adult Education, 17,* 85–100.

WALBERG, H., & THOMAS, S. (1971). *Characteristics of open education: Toward an operational definition.* Newton, MA: TDR Associates.

WALES, C., & SAGER, R. (1978). *The guided design approach.* Englewood Cliffs, NJ: Educational Technology Publications.

WALTON, M. (1986). *The Deming management method.* New York: Dodd Mead & Co.

WATSON, G., & JOHNSON, D. W. (1972). *Social psychology: Issues and insights.* Philadelphia: Lippincott.

WEBB, H. (1969). Professionalization of attitudes toward play among adolescents. In D. Kenyon (Ed.), *Aspects of contemporary sport sociology.* Chicago: The Athletic Institute.

WEBB, N., ENDER, P., & LEWIS, S. (1986). Problem-solving strategies and group processes in small group learning computer programming. *American Educational Research Journal, 23,* 243–261.

WILHELMS, F. (1970). Educational conditions essential to growth in individuality. In V. Howes (Ed.), *Individualization of instruction: A teaching strategy.* New York: Macmillan.

WILLIAMS, K. (1981). *The effects of group cohesiveness on social loafing.* Paper presented at the annual meeting of the Midwestern Psychological Association, Detroit.

WILLIAMS, K., HARKINS, S., & LATANE, B. (1981). Identifiability as a deterrent to social loafing: Two cheering experiments. *Journal of Personality and Social Psychology, 40,* 303–311.

WILSON, R. (1987). Toward excellence in teaching. In L. M. Aleamoni (Ed.), *Techniques for evaluating and improving instruction* (pp. 9–24). San Francisco: Jossey-Bass.

WITTROCK, M. (1990). Generative processes of comprehension. *Educational Psychologist, 24,* 345–376.

WULFF, D., NYQUIST, J., & ABBOTT, R. (1987). Students' perception of large classes. In M. E. Weimer (Ed.), *Teaching large classes well* (pp. 17–30). San Francisco: Jossey-Bass.

YAGER, S., JOHNSON, D. W., & JOHNSON, R. (1985). Oral discussion, group-to-individual transfer, and achievement in cooperative learning groups. *Journal of Educational Psychology, 77*(1), 60–66.

ZAJONC, R. (1965). Social facilitation. *Science, 149,* 269–272.

Glossary

Acceptance: Communication of high regard for another person, for his or her contributions, and for his or her actions.

Additive tasks: Tasks for which group productivity represents the sum of individual member efforts.

Ad hoc decision-making groups: Faculty members listen to a recommendation, are assigned to small groups, meet to consider the recommendation, report their decision to the entire faculty, and then participate in a whole-faculty decision as to what the course of action should be.

Arbitration: The submission of a dispute to a disinterested third person who makes a final judgment as to how the conflict will be resolved. A form of third-party intervention in negotiations in which recommendations of the intervening person are binding on the parties involved.

Base group: A long-term, heterogeneous cooperative learning group with stable membership.

Benchmarking: Establishing operating targets based on best-known practices.

Bumping: A procedure used to ensure that competitors are evenly matched. It involves (a) ranking the competitive triads from the highest (the three highest achievers are members) to the lowest (the three lowest achievers are members), (b) moving the winner in each triad up to the next higher triad, and (c) moving the loser down to the next lower triad.

Cohesiveness: All of the forces (both positive and negative) that cause individuals to maintain their membership in specific groups. These include attraction to other group members and a close match between individuals' needs and the goals and activities of the group. The attractiveness that a group has for its members and that the members have for one another.

Colleagial teaching teams: Small cooperative groups (from two to five faculty members) whose purpose is to increase teachers' instructional expertise and success.

Communication: A message sent by a person to a receiver(s) with the conscious intent of affecting the receiver's behavior. The exchange of thoughts and feelings through symbols that represent approximately the same conceptual experience for everyone involved.

Communication networks: Representations of the acceptable paths of communication between persons in a group or organization.

Competition: A social situation in which the goals of the separate participants are so linked that there is a negative correlation among their goal attainments; when one student achieves his or her goal, all others with whom he or she is competitively linked fail to achieve their goals.

Compliance: Behavior in accordance with a direct request. Behavioral change without internal acceptance.

Conceptual/adaptive approaches to cooperative learning: Teachers are trained in how to use a general conceptual framework to plan and tailor cooperative learning lessons specifically for their students, circumstances, curricula, and needs.

Conceptual conflict: When incompatible ideas exist simultaneously in a person's mind.

Conflict of interests: When the actions of one person who is attempting to maximize his or her needs and benefits prevent, block, interfere with, injure, or in some way make less effective the actions of another person who is attempting to maximize his or her needs and benefits.

Conformity: Changes in behavior that result from group influences. Yielding to group pressures when no direct request to comply is made.

Conjunctive tasks: Tasks for which group productivity is determined by the effort or ability of the weakest member.

Consensus: A collective opinion arrived at by a group of individuals working together under conditions that permit communication to be sufficiently open and the group climate to be sufficiently supportive for everyone in the group to feel that he or she has had a fair chance to influence the decision.

Controversy: When one person's ideas, information, conclusions, theories, and opinions are incompatible with those of another, and the two seek to reach an agreement.

Co-op co-op: A complex cooperative learning script in which each group is assigned one part of a class learning unit, each group member is assigned part of the work and then presents it to the group, the group synthesizes the work of its members, and the group presents the completed project to the class.

Cooperation: Working together to accomplish shared goals and to maximize one's own and others' success. Individuals perceiving that they can reach their goals if and only if the other group members also do so.

Cooperation imperative: We desire and seek out opportunities to operate jointly with others to achieve mutual goals.

Cooperative curriculum package: Set of curriculum materials specifically designed to contain cooperative learning as well as academic content.

Cooperative Integrated Reading and Composition (CIRC): A set of curriculum materials to supplement basal readers; students read, write, spell, and learn language mechanics in pairs and fours but are evaluated individualistically.

Cooperative learning: Students working together to accomplish shared learning goals and to maximize their own and their groupmates' achievements.

Cooperative learning scripts: Standard content-free cooperative procedures for either conducting generic, repetitive lessons or managing classroom routines that prescribe student actions step by step.

Cooperative learning structures: See cooperative learning scripts.

Cooperative school: Team-based, high-performance organizational structure specifically applied to schools, characterized by cooperative learning in the classroom, collegial teaching teams and school-based decision making in the building, and colleagial administration teams and shared decision making at the district level.

Decision making: Obtaining some agreement among group members as to which of several courses of action is most desirable for achieving the group's goals. The process through which groups identify problems in achieving the group's goals and attain solutions to them.

Delusion of individualism: Believing that (a) one is separate and apart from all other individuals and, therefore, (b) others' frustration, unhappiness, hunger, despair, and misery have no significant bearing on one's own well-being.

Deutsch, Morton: Social psychologist who theorized about cooperative, competitive, and individualistic goal structures.

Developmental conflict: When a recurrent conflict cycles in and out of peak intensity as a child develops socially.

Direct/prescriptive approach to cooperative learning: Teachers are trained to use prepackaged lessons, curricula, strategies, and activities in a lock-step prescribed manner (step 1, step 2, step 3).

Disjunctive tasks: Tasks for which group performance is determined by the most competent or skilled member.

Distributed-actions theory of leadership: The performance of acts that help the group to complete its task and to maintain effective working relationships among its members.

Divisible task: Can be divided into subtasks that can be assigned to different people.

Effective communication: When the receiver interprets the sender's message in the same way the sender intended it.

Egocentrism: Embeddedness in one's own viewpoint to the extent that one is unaware of other points of view and of the limitations of one's perspectives.

Expertise: A person's proficiency, adroitness, competence, and skill.

Expert system: An understanding of a conceptual system that is used to engineer effective applications in the real world.

Feedback: Information that allows individuals to compare their actual performance with standards of performance.

Fermenting skills: Skills needed to engage in academic controversies to stimulate reconceptualization of the material being studied, cognitive conflict, the search for more information, and the communication of the rationale behind one's conclusions.

Formal cooperative group: A learning group that may last from several minutes to several class sessions to complete a specific task or assignment (such as solving a set of problems, completing a unit, writing a theme or report, conducting an experiment, or reading and comprehending a story, play, poem, chapter, or book).

Forming skills: Management skills directed toward organizing the group and establishing minimum norms for appropriate behavior.

Formulating skills: Skills directed toward providing the mental processes needed to build deeper-level understanding of the material being studied, to stimulate the use of higher-quality reasoning strategies, and to maximize mastery and retention of the assigned material.

Functioning skills: Skills directed toward managing the group's efforts to complete its tasks and maintain effective working relationships among members.

Genba: Where the action is.

Goal: A desired place toward which people are working; a state of affairs that people value.

Goal structure: The type of social interdependence structured among students as they strive to accomplish their learning goals.

Group: Two or more individuals in face-to-face interaction, each aware of his or her membership in the group, each aware of the others who belong to the group, and each aware of their positive interdependence as they both strive to achieve mutual goals.

Group investigation: A complex learning script in which students form cooperative learning groups according to common interests in a topic, develop a division of labor in researching the topic, synthesize the work of group members, and present the finished product to the class.

Group processing: Reflecting on a group session to (a) describe what member actions were helpful or unhelpful and (b) make decisions about what actions to continue or change.

Horizontal teams: A number of teachers from the same grade level or subject area are given responsibility for a number of students for one year or one semester.

Individual accountability: The measurement of whether or not each group member has achieved the group's goal. Assessing the quality and quantity of each member's contributions and giving the results to all group members.

Individualistic goal structure: No correlation among group members' goal attainments; when group members perceive that obtaining their goal is unrelated to the goal achievement of other members. Individuals working by themselves to accomplish goals unrelated to and independent from the goals of others.

Informal cooperative learning: The use of temporary, ad hoc discussion groups that last for only one discussion or one class period, whose purposes are to (a) focus student attention on the material to be learned, (b) create an expectation set and mood conductive to learning, (c) help organize in advance the material to be covered in a class session, (d) ensure that students cognitively process the material being taught, and (e) provide closure to an instructional session.

Jigsaw: The work of a group is divided into separate parts that are completed by different members and taught to their groupmates.

Leadership: The process through which leaders exert their impact on other group members.

Learning goal: A desired future state of demonstrating competence or mastery in the subject area being studied, such as conceptual understanding of math processes, facility in the proper use of a language, or mastering the procedures of inquiry.

Lewin, Kurt: Father of group dynamics; social psychologist who originated field theory, experimental group dynamics, and applied group dynamics.

Maintenance of use: Continual, long-term use of cooperative learning over a period of years.

Maximizing task: Success is determined by quantity of performance.

Means interdependence: The actions required on the part of group members to achieve their mutual goals and rewards. There are three types of means interdependence: resource, task, and role.

Mediation: When a third person intervenes to help resolve a conflict between two or more people. A form of third-party intervention in which a neutral person recommends a nonbinding agreement.

Motivation: A combination of the perceived likelihood of success and the perceived incentive for success. The greater the likelihood of success and the more important it is to succeed, the higher the motivation.

Negotiation: A process by which persons with shared or opposing interests who want to come to an agreement try to work out a settlement by exchanging proposals and counterproposals.

Norms: The rules or expectations that specify appropriate behavior in the group; the standards by which group members regulate their actions.

Optimizing task: Success is determined by quality of performance; a good performance is one that most closely approximates the optimum performance.

Outcome interdependence: When the goals and rewards directing individuals' actions are positively correlated; that is, if one person accomplishes his or her goal or receives a reward, all others with whom the person is cooperatively linked also achieve their goals or receive a reward. Learning goals may be actual, based on involvement in a fantasy situation, or based on overcoming an outside threat.

Paraphrasing: Restating the sender's message in one's own words.

Perspective taking: Ability to understand how a situation appears to another person and how that person is reacting cognitively and emotionally to the situation.

Positive environmental interdependence: When group members are bound together by the physical environment in some way.

Positive fantasy interdependence: When students imagine that they are in an emergency situation (such as surviving a shipwreck) or must deal with problems (such as ending air pollution in the world) that are compelling but unreal.

Positive goal interdependence: When students perceive that they can achieve their learning goals if, and only if, all other members of their group also attain their goals.

Positive identity interdependence: When the group establishes a mutual identity through a name, flag, motto, or song.

Positive interdependence: The perception that you are linked with others in a way so that you cannot succeed unless they do (and vice versa); that is, their work benefits you and your work benefits them.

Positive outside enemy interdependence: When groups are placed in competition with each other; group members then feel interdependent as they strive to beat the other groups.

Positive resource interdependence: When each member has only a portion of the information, resources, or materials necessary for the task to be completed and members' resources have to be combined for the group to achieve its goal. Thus, the resources of each group member are needed if the task is to be completed.

Positive reward interdependence: When each group member receives the same reward for achieving the goal.

Positive rule interdependence: When each member is assigned complementary and interconnected roles that specify responsibilities that the group needs in order to complete a joint task.

Positive task interdependence: When a division of labor is created so that the actions of one group member have to be completed if the next team member is to complete his or her responsibilities. Dividing an overall task into subunits that must be performed in a set order is an example of task interdependence.

Procedural learning: Learning conceptually what the skill is, when it should be used, how to engage in the skill; practicing the skill while eliminating errors, until an automatic level of mastery is attained.

Promotive interaction: Actions that assist, help, encourage, and support the achievement of each other's goals.

Roadblock: Hurdle that causes temporary difficulties in reaching a goal.

Routine-use level: Automatic use of a skill as a natural part of one's behavioral repertoire.

School-based decision making: Task force considers a school problem and proposes a solution to the faculty as a whole, small ad hoc decision-making groups consider the proposal, the entire faculty decides what to do, the decision is implemented by the faculty, and the task force assesses whether or not the problem is solved.

Self-efficacy: The expectation of successfully obtaining valued outcomes through personal effort; expectation that if one exerts sufficient effort, one will be successful.

Self-regulation: Ability to act in socially approved ways in the absence of external monitors.

Social dependence: When the outcomes of Person A are affected by Person B's actions; but the reverse is not true.

Social facilitation: The enhancement of well-learned responses in the presence of others. Effects on performance resulting from the presence of others.

Social independence: When individuals' outcomes are unaffected by each other's actions.

Social interaction: Patterns of mutual influence linking two or more persons.

Social interdependence: When each individual's outcomes are affected by the actions of others.

Social loafing: A reduction of individual effort when working with others on an additive group task.

Social skills: The interpersonal and small-group skills needed to interact effectively with other people.

Social skills training: A structured intervention designed to help participants improve their interpersonal skills.

Student Teams-Achievement Divisions (STAD):   A modification of TGT that is basically identical except that instead of playing an academic game, students take a weekly quiz. Teams receive recognition for the sum of the improvement scores of team members.

Socioemotional activity: Behavior that focuses on interpersonal relations in the group.

Sunburst Integrated Co-Op Learning Geometry Course: A combination of a geometry curriculum, an interactive computer program, discovery learning, and cooperative learning.

Superordinate goals: Goals that cannot easily be ignored by members of two antagonistic groups, but whose attainment is beyond the resources and efforts of either group alone; the two groups, therefore, must join in a cooperative effort in order to attain the goals.

Support: Communicating to another person that you recognize his or her strengths and believe he or she has the capabilities needed to productively manage the situation.

Synthesizing: Integrating a number of different positions containing diverse information and conclusions into a new, single, inclusive position that all group members can agree on and commit themselves to.

T-chart: Procedure to teach social skills by specifying the nonverbal actions and verbal phrases that operationalize the skill.

Team: A set of interpersonal relationships structured to achieve established goals.

Team-Assisted-Individualization (TAI): A highly individualized math curriculum for grades 3 to 6 in which students work individualistically to complete math assignments using self-instructional (programmed learning) curriculum materials and have their answers checked, and help given, by groupmates.

Teams-Games-Tournaments (TGT): An instructional procedure in which cooperative groups learn specified content and then compete with each other in a tournament/game format to see which group learned the most.

Transfer: Teachers take what they learn about cooperative learning in training sessions and use it in their classrooms.

Trust: Perception that a choice can lead to gains or losses, that whether you will gain or lose depends on the behavior of the other person, that the loss will be greater than the gain, and that the person will likely behave so that you will gain rather than lose.

Trusting behavior: Openness (sharing of information, ideas, thoughts, feelings, and reactions) and sharing (offering of one's resources to others in order to help them achieve their goals).

Trustworthy behavior: Expressing acceptance (communication of high regard for another person and his or her actions), support (communicating to another person that you recognize his or her strengths and believe he or she has the capabilities needed to productively manage the situation), and cooperative intentions (expectations that you are going to behave cooperatively and that everyone else will do likewise).

Unitary task: Cannot be divided into subtasks; one person has to complete the entire task.

Vertical teams: A team of teachers representing several different subject areas are given responsibility for the same students for a number of years.

Index

References to figures and tables are represented by f and t respectively

2503